Burma's Mass
Lay Meditation Movement

This series of publications on Africa, Latin America, Southeast Asia, and Global and Comparative Studies is designed to present significant research, translation, and opinion to area specialists and to a wide community of persons interested in world affairs. The editor seeks manuscripts of quality on any subject and can usually make a decision regarding publication within three months of receipt of the original work. Production methods generally permit a work to appear within one year of acceptance. The editor works closely with authors to produce a high-quality book. The series appears in a paperback format and is distributed worldwide. For more information, contact the executive editor at Ohio University Press, 19 Circle Drive, The Ridges, Athens, Ohio 45701.

Executive editor: Gillian Berchowitz
AREA CONSULTANTS
Africa: Diane M. Ciekawy
Latin America: Brad Jokisch, Patrick Barr-Melej, and Rafael Obregon
Southeast Asia: William H. Frederick

The Ohio University Research in International Studies series is published for the Center for International Studies by Ohio University Press. The views expressed in individual volumes are those of the authors and should not be considered to represent the policies or beliefs of the Center for International Studies, Ohio University Press, or Ohio University.

Burma's Mass Lay Meditation Movement

Buddhism and the Cultural Construction of Power

Ingrid Jordt

OHIO UNIVERSITY RESEARCH IN INTERNATIONAL STUDIES
SOUTHEAST ASIA SERIES NO. 115
OHIO UNIVERSITY PRESS
ATHENS

16 15 14 13 12 11 10 09   5 4 3

The books in the Ohio University Research in International Studies Series
are printed on acid-free paper ⊗ ™

Library of Congress Cataloging-in-Publication Data

Jordt, Ingrid.
  Burma's mass lay meditation movement : Buddhism and the cultural construction of power / Ingrid Jordt.
       p. cm. — (Ohio University research in international studies. Southeast Asia
series ; no. 115)
  Includes bibliographical references and index.
  ISBN-13: 978-0-89680-255-1 (pbk. : alk. paper)
  ISBN-10: 0-89680-255-8 (pbk. : alk. paper)
  1. Buddhism—Social aspects—Burma. 2. Buddhist laymen—Burma. 3. Buddhism
and politics—Burma. 4. Human rights movements—Burma. I. Title.
  BQ438.J67 2007
  294.309591—dc22
                                                          2007031090

For Rita and David Jordt

Who have been with me every step of the way

Contents

Illustrations

Monks take their midday meal at U Pandita's meditation center
Department of Religious Affairs book distribution storeroom
Office at the Department of Propagation, Kaba Aye, Yangon
Mosquito nets protect yogis at an upscale meditation center

Preface

In my first contact with Burma, I was pursuing answers to a set of questions markedly different from those I address in this volume. While majoring in anthropology in college, I took a job at the Gorilla Foundation, teaching sign language to the gorilla Michael (Koko's counterpart) in Francine Patterson's laboratory in Woodside, California. I was interested in cognitive science and linguistics, and research with the gorilla seemed a good place to begin. My questions were broad and open, suitable to a young person's curiosity. A conversation with a friend about some of the issues raised in my work at the Gorilla Foundation (how dependent coherent thought is on language, for instance) led him to recommend me to a meditation course.

The practice of vipassanā meditation, which has by now reached millions of people's awareness around the world, was at that time an exotic import, principally from Burma (I will discuss its contemporary sources later). I completed a ten-day, intensive course and then went on several longer retreats. As I reflected on my experiences in meditation, I became impressed by how the technique draws on universal cognitive principles for its effect, even though its framing is culturally specific to the situation of its application— be that a hospital in Massachusetts, a monastery in Yangon (formerly Rangoon), or a prison in New Delhi. The neurocognitive dimension of meditation is now no longer a matter for amateur speculation but has become the subject of much medical, psychological, and neuroscientific research. Interested in the cultural-cognitive interface and curious about vipassanā as a discipline that seemed to focus on separating percept from concept—ordinarily taken by anthropologists, especially at that time, to be impossible—I went to study under the guidance of a renowned meditation teacher in Burma. This same monk later taught meditation to Aung San Suu Kyi of the National League for Democracy.

The monastery where I was subsequently ordained as a Buddhist nun and where I continued to study meditation and Buddhist (Pāli) texts—the Mahasi Thathana Yeiktha (MTY, also called Mahasi Sāsana Yeiktha)—turned out to be more than just another religious sanctuary. The MTY center had played a key role in the plan advanced by Burma's first prime minister, U Nu, for building a nation-state along Buddhist lines. Moreover, MTY's founding monk, Mahasi Sayadaw (1904–82), had been the scholar-meditator who systematized and revitalized the practice of vipassanā meditation in keeping with a twentieth-century Burmese Buddhist idea about the possibility and rectitude of laity pursuing enlightenment. MTY's lay guardian committee's executive members were former governors and diplomats, military leaders, and wealthy businessmen. Their wives were jewelers and socialites but also meditators, donors, and volunteers at the center. The monks were among the most prestigious in the country (it is estimated that 3 percent of Burmese males at any given time are in the monkhood), and they continued to receive visits from key military personnel and ministers, some of whom were themselves ordained as temporary monks or went to MTY to practice meditation and participate in collective donations to the monastery. There was also a substantial contingent of visitors from other Buddhist countries and from the West. Vipassanā meditation was a diplomatic link between Burma and these other places—and is recognized as such by the Foreign Ministry—and at one point, it was hailed as the country's leading export. Keeping a roster of over a million meditators reputed to have made attainments toward enlightenment in centers around the country, MTY is also the hub of the mass lay meditation movement.

The relative paucity of scholarly investigation into the phenomenon of a mass religious revitalization involving millions of followers and all of the resources and influence that such a movement inevitably entails seems an immense oversight. There is evidence that this mass revitalization has generated an enormous economy in its wake, and it has also reformed the conceptual—fair to say, epistemological—context in which power may be expressed and supported. An extremely telling (but not the most spectacular) fact about the mass lay meditation movement is that several of the postindependence rulers of Burma have been sincere participants in meditation and in raising to prominence those monks most revered in the movement. It is my intention to explain this relationship between the movement as a moral/political and economic force, on the one hand, and as a catalyst for epistemological reconstruction, on the other, with the very dynamic of the regime's efforts to legitimize its political position since 1947.

I open my methodological introduction from this personal angle because I wish to relate how I initially had not the slightest inkling of a relationship between religion and politics in Burma. After some months at MTY, it became impossible for me to ignore that the religious and cosmological domain tracked unmistakably into the seats of political power—the military, the ministries, even the everyday devotional trails of the junta secretariat. The standard scholarly reduction of the religious sphere, in which it is held that the military is just using religion for its own ends, seemed untenable to me. Between the influence of political scientific presuppositions about state and civil society, which I will discuss later, and fashionable trends in postcolonial studies, there somehow came to reign an assumption among Burma scholars that Burmese history stretched only back to colonialism or independence and that cosmological, political cultural, and institutional elements dating from before that time could safely be disregarded.

The scholarly confirmation that a deep analysis of the relationship between Burmese Buddhist cosmology and contemporary politics was apposite came from the work of my graduate school adviser, S. J. Tambiah, a leading authority on the relationship of Buddhism and society in neighboring Thailand. Under Tambiah's mentorship, I returned to Burma for another extended visit, from 1994 to

1995. Most recently, I was in Burma in 2001. There, I was situated at MTY and at Kaba Aye, the grounds of the World Peace Pagoda, where I was a regular visitor to the Department of Home and Religious Affairs. My connections to this government bureaucracy provided an excellent location from which to observe the ways in which Buddhism was officially engaged at the state level. Interviews but also incidental observations at the ministry illuminated the ways in which the politics of the state accommodate and take advantage of Buddhist institutions and public practice.

The association with high-level monks led me naturally to government ministries, where I questioned ranking officials on religious activities within their purview. The overlap and crosscutting of function and personnel, the official and unofficial, and the political and personal spheres (similar to what X. L. Ding [1994] means by his term *institutional amphibiousness,* applied to communist China) were, I discovered, exemplified if not represented by the fact that at one point in my fieldwork, I found myself in the office of the man whose two job titles were director of home and religious affairs and director of military intelligence.

It is, in fact, common for religious affairs directors to be brigadier generals and for these personnel to be more than superficially involved in Buddhist goings-on around Yangon. The sheer frequency of such events, to which top military commanders and ministers devote so much of their time, suggests that Buddhist ceremonies are a vital component of Burmese statecraft. I do not propose to settle the question of the sincerity of members of the regime in this pageantry. However, since that question is a preoccupation of many Burmese and since it is both embedded in Buddhist phenomenological logics and often discussed in terms of the regime's legitimacy, I address the subject at some length in the text. For now, it suffices to say that not just the fact but also the way in which members of the junta participate in Buddhism is worthy of analysis.

My unique access to sources of high-level information in Burma has been predicated on my first contact with the country as a meditator. My repeat visas were issued directly from the Ministry of

Home and Religious Affairs as person-to-country visas, and I was permitted to stay for long periods when most visitors were restricted to a week or two. My status as an "old yogi" at the monastery, as well as my status as a foreigner studying at a prestigious American university, brought me the opportunity to interview leading ministers and religious figures. On my visits, I often stayed at the house of the president of the monastery's lay committee, a former high-ranking official (under U Nu). Although he was always circumspect in voicing his political discontent, I nevertheless learned a great deal about the more subtle communications that took place between the influential religious establishment of which he was president and the acting members of the junta.

One of my closest and most fortuitous contacts was with U Nu, Burma's first prime minister (1947–62), who took an interest in me as an aspiring scholar and former Buddhist nun. He recounted to me the history of the postindependence period from his point of view. My close association with U Nu also got me into trouble in the final days before the demonstrations and government-orchestrated violence that took place on August 8, 1988. He had insisted on seeing me when many of my other friends advised against it. I could not easily refuse. We met at the monastery and exchanged harmless pleasantries. On his way out, he announced that he was next going to visit Brigadier General U Aung Gyi, who had recently "taken up residence" at Insein Prison, where political prisoners are held, following the publication of his critical open letter to Ne Win—a letter that sparked events leading to the fall of his Burmese Socialist Program Party government. A listening device in the room where we spoke apparently picked up this indiscreet statement, and I was inadvertently implicated in the suspicion that some kind of political information had passed between us. I was blacklisted from reentering the country for four years. In the interim, I planned to divert my research to Laos. I studied Lao and spent several months in Laos before I received notification from my sponsors in Burma that they had arranged for me to be readmitted to their country.

A final comment on my position in the field is in order. The situation and timing of my research were such that the main individuals who informed this study were from the generation that had witnessed and participated in the nationalist period and the first parliamentary democratic government. After 1962, many of the individuals who had been connected to the U Nu government "retired" to the meditation center at MTY. Although I certainly circulated among different age-groups and strata, my main source of data was a kind of passing elite—elderly monks, statesmen, civil servants, wealthy businesspersons, and educated professionals. Both the strengths and weaknesses of my analysis draw from the "studying up" perspective that has characterized my experience as a fieldworker and my personal connections to Burma.

The generation I knew is passing away, along, perhaps, with their distinctive point of view and approach to Buddhist living and institution making. Ne Win reportedly said that once this generation was gone, members of the next generation would know only what the military told them: then the regime would be secure. Today, Ne Win is dead (d. 2002), U Nu is dead (d. 1995), and U Kyi Maung from the National League for Democracy is dead (d. 2004). The next generation of military strongmen has now stepped in to rule. Aung San Suu Kyi (b. 1945) at least symbolically ties the country to its past generation through reclaiming her father's legacy for the people, after the military regime (noting that Aung San was the founder of the Burma army) had sought to connect its legitimacy to the martyred "father of the nation."

In chapter 1, I provide background on how the mass lay meditation movement emerged as a revitalization effort with several objectives: a reassertion of Burmese identity in Buddhist terms; a fulfillment of the lost functions of kingship vis-à-vis *sāsana* (dispensation and teachings of the Buddha) following colonialism; an effort at purification of the *sangha* (the monastic order) by the laity in terms reminiscent of the ternary order that obtained between sangha, state, and laity in precolonial sociopolitical arrangements;

and most important, the systematizing, routinizing, and universal-izing of the penultimate practices of vipassanā meditation that would affirm on an individual experiential level the truth of the Buddha's teachings and the identity of the practitioner-citizen in Burmese sāsana society and in the world. In a context in which other totalizing epistemic orientations to experience and the world (sci-ence, modernity, or Marxism, for example) competed for supremacy in the task of nation-state building, the verification of "sāsana re-ality" by ordinary laypersons served to verify the truths found in the Pāli Tipiṭaka texts. From the government's point of view, these recursive validations of an indigenous system of knowledge and experience would be the foundations from which national identity would be constructed and the goals of society articulated. The glue that would hold the nation-state together and unify it in a common purpose would come from the moral rearmament of the citizenry through an epistemic transformation of the individual via vipas-sanā meditation.

Chapter 2 is an analysis of the experience of vipassanā medita-tion from the yogi practitioner's perspective, with an emphasis on pedagogy. Narrative accounts of the vipassanā experience (with their emphasis on nonconceptualizing) tend to conform to ortho-dox and vernacular styles in which the speakers are required to ex-plain the meaning or interpretations of their experiences. By focus-ing on pedagogy, I show how the yogi is encouraged to move away from conceptualization during the period of practice. The emphasis brings us to an understanding of how the inculcation of vipassanā techniques has resulted in a kind of epistemic reconstruction of lay consciousness in which the universal constitution of reality is given empirical proof, with implications for political realities. Vipassanā as a movement to create an "enlightened citizenry" has meant that the laity have assumed responsibility for the welfare of society. It is their *sīla* (moral precepts of restraint) on which the cosmic condi-tions depend, just as, during the time of kings, it was the king's sīla on which the natural and social conditions depended. The laity have undertaken moral purification through "purification of view." In part, this is the gist of the project of verifying empirically the epistemology of the Abhidhamma texts through vipassanā.

In chapter 3, I begin to shift attention outward and away from the site of vipassanā meditation—its institutional form and individual yogi practitioners—to consider what the economic underpinnings of the phenomenon are. The regime's demonstrable participation in sacred giving (*dāna*) illustrates the intertwined character of its sāsana activities and its exercise of secular authority. I consider dāna in four ways: (1) as cause for the materialization of sāsana institutions (meditation centers, monasteries, schools, and the like); (2) as a process creating economic and political cliques, as well as moral communities established around monks; (3) as a cognitive practice, a "system of intention" directed toward progressive mental purification that delineates the intersection between transcendent and worldly realities; and (4) as a way for the state military to legitimize its role of foremost donor and head of patron-client chains and therefore as a source for moral validation of its rule.

Chapter 4 opens with the question of how Burmese people, under conditions of extreme repression in the public sphere, debate and/or present counterpositions or resistant positions to the government. One location for critique of the state, I argue, is in the popular articulation, through participation in the mass lay meditation movement, of Buddhist-specific notions of morality, power, and authority that present a decipherable criticism of the regime that cannot simply be suppressed. The principles of conversion from moral community to political power are intricate. Regime leaders are forced into demonstrating their sincerity and "right intentions" about building a just society in Buddhist terms by giving dāna (chapter 3) and by "capturing the potency" of key monks. These monks and the moral communities that surround them pose a threat to the regime because they can claim a higher moral ground; they adjudicate on the questions of potency and sincerity. The regime fears being widely deemed insincere in its efforts to support and protect the sāsana, which is the will of the religious masses. This is true in regard to the regime both on a collective level and on an individual level, as many members of the regime are themselves observant Buddhists who do not wish to alienate themselves from their sources of merit: leading monks. Because the New Laity is prominently represented in meditation and other religious activities by women, in chapter 4 I also consider the question of gender and the embodiment of power and the impact of this on the moral debate over (un)just government and everyday life.

In chapter 5, I apply the paradigm of political claims to (symbolic and performative) legitimacy, as developed in the text, to a sequence of rulers throughout the postindependence period. Each of the governments became entangled, in different ways, with sāsana projects. The point at which the military regime abandoned its secularist policies and became Buddhist in practice—starting in the 1980s with the Ne Win government—is especially revealing of the simultaneous process of co-optation and control of the sangha, on the one hand, and the submission to Buddhist populism, on the other. This analysis both situates the exercise of power within the cosmological framework of Burmese Buddhism and illustrates the competing frameworks for legitimacy under which the regime must and does operate.

Acknowledgments

Most books, but ethnographic ones in particular, are collaborative projects. I am privileged to have received intellectual mentorship from Stanley Jeyarajah Tambiah, F. K. Lehman, and Nur Yalman in the United States and Sayadaw U Pandita in Burma, beginning nearly two decades ago.

Ongoing discussion with and encouragement from my colleagues in Burma studies, most notably Gustaaf Houtman, Juliane Schober, Robert Taylor, and Michael Aung Thwin, have helped shape my conceptions and have brought focus and motivation to the project. Juliane Schober's and Robert Taylor's gracious and thorough readings of the book in manuscript form improved its clarity and accuracy considerably, as have suggestions from anonymous reviewers along the way.

I have ruminated aloud with and have received in return insightful evaluations of my ideas from Nurit Bird-David, John Farrell, Thomas Malaby. The myriad contributions of my partner in life and intellect, Kalman Applbaum, could be adequately enumerated only in a separate appendix to the text. The quite tangible sacrifices he and my daughter Nurit made for the sake of this project over many years are more equal to the constancy of family devotion than to mere scholarship. In what miraculous currency could an acknowledgment suffice?

On the ground in Southeast Asia, Goh Poay Hoon has for many years placed no limit on the effort she is willing to expend on my behalf, in friendship and in devotion to the advancement of my work. Her indefatigable devotion to the sāsana is inspirational. Sadhu, Hoon!

Gillian Berchowitz at Ohio University Press inspires me to add the role of editor to those of neighbor, friend, and teacher on the list of people invaluable to a successful life.

Finally, to my many friends and supporters in Burma—I dare not name you. I can only offer silent gratitude to your many, many gestures of kindness, attention, and noble friendship.

INTRODUCTION

The Question of Legitimacy

State-society relations and the question of nation-state formation in Burma's postindependence period have been the central preoccupations of Burma scholars and commentators outside the country. Burma has known more than forty years of brutal and repressive military rule. The regime has quashed every attempt to establish civilian rule, despite the fact that this was the junta's stated intention when it took control of the country in 1962. This false promise has been reiterated over the years by the governments of the State Law and Order Restoration Council (SLORC), renamed for cosmetic reasons as the State Peace and Development Council (SPDC). The most striking refusal about which foreign scholars and activists in particular have been concerned occurred following the 1990 elections, when Aung San Suu Kyi's National League for Democracy (NLD) party won by a landslide but then was not permitted to assume power.

Under the current circumstances, therefore, it would be easy to assume that for Burma, all authority is an exercise in force and that submission to the iron rule of the regime is entirely coerced. But rather than exploring the dimensions of the regime's illegitimacy, as has so often been done, this book instead takes as its starting point Max Weber's assertion that legitimacy, even in a minimal form, is a necessity for rule. In other words, political legitimacy can never be accomplished solely by means of violence.[1] As a result, as I will demonstrate, the regime in Burma has been constrained to accommodate the framework for legitimate state action in terms of moral action in general and Buddhism in particular. It is clear that the regime performs a kind of continual legitimating dance in its participation in

Buddhist ritual and economy, not as just another contributor but as the chief donor. Many of the military brass have mentor monks, and they participate quite earnestly in meditation, donation, and other Buddhist venues.

All this will be documented in the pages that follow. At present, I wish to emphasize that for my analysis, what is at stake is not whether the people *confer* legitimacy on the military regime as an act of election, as may be based on performance criteria. Rather, legitimacy is verified so long as it has been demonstrated as a self-evident fact of nature, consistent with moral-epistemological principles grounded in Buddhist cosmological practice.

The persistence of the regime's ability to retain authority by such domestic criteria should also alert us to the fact that inside Burma itself, the idiom of legitimation is scarcely related to international criteria of "regime performance"—human rights, economic development, democracy, peaceful succession of leadership, and so forth—as may be true in many countries in this age of internationalism. Burma is unmitigatedly repressive, and it would be difficult to find a basis for its leaders' sometimes legitimate authority in regime performance terms, at any rate. If one is looking for performance criteria, then one can only be drawn to Burma's failures and to attempted resistances based on these failures.[2] What I have observed is that the internal language employed and the symbols leveraged for legitimating authority are relevant principally in the realm of Buddhist understandings and in overt reference to "traditional" Burmese kingship.

The questions that will lead to an understanding of the political process in Burma are not those relating to the forcefulness of regime measures or the assertion (or lack) of choice by citizens. Instead, I begin with questions along the following lines: What is the dynamic by which society and the military regime engage in defining the limits of authority over the individual, private life and public society? How are abuses of power met by the populace? To what extent are the powers of the regime constrained? How does the regime work to describe its actions as legitimate? With these questions, I seek to examine how the state has sought to shore up its authority through appeals to principally native criteria for legitimacy, what these criteria are, and how they act as constraints on the regime. What is "granted" by the people is a moral right—or, at least, the moral terms by which regime performance will be evaluated.

Substantively, my concern lies with identifying practices through which moral preoccupations shape social and political realities. I identify a "mass lay meditation movement" as serving as the primary location for these considerations. I do so for three reasons. First, because lay meditation has become a mass movement, it has fulfilled, on an institutional level, several functions of kingship that had previously been considered essential to the state's role vis-à-vis society. Conversely, the king's performance of this role toward the citizens of the state was also determinate in legitimizing his right to rule.

Second, the mass lay meditation movement is not restricted to only one group of practitioners within Burmese Buddhist society. Meditators—the New Laity[3]—come from all walks of social life: they are rural, urban, educated, peasants, traders, professionals, government workers, military personnel, men, women, and children. As such, the mass lay meditation movement is a location from which we may observe how primary individual experiences come to be codified and collectively shared.

Third, meditation is seen not only as the technique leading the individual to true experiences and ultimate reality but also as a core, reliable source of knowledge verifying what the goals of society are, what the obligations and rights of the state are, and how the individual is situated in relation to state, society, and soteriology. Monks, laity, and the state draw on these epistemological and concrete resources (sometimes cynically, sometimes sincerely) in order to make claims and assert limits in terms that are highly moralized and in reference to a variety of phenomena that together reflect and validate normative and emergent social practices.

In short, I examine how political legitimacy is formulated in processual terms. I accomplish this by looking at how Buddhist laity and lay institutions influence politics through moral and religious appeals. This approach permits a reconsideration of the dynamics of power and authority in Burma, as both depend on morally argued justifications as well as verifications of the moral worldview. This is a dynamic process in the generation of emergent social forms and political realities.

I am not the first scholar to have noticed the close relationship between religious symbolism and the exercise of political authority in Burma.[4] The theories of other writers, partly reviewed in the pages ahead, may be subtly rendered but nevertheless reduce to a scheme of the regime's manipulation of religious symbols to further its political aims. In this case, religion functions as mere expediency to rule.

The cornerstone work in this area is E. Michael Mendelson's *Sangha and State in Burma* (1975). Mendelson describes the Buddhist Revival efforts of Burma's first postindependence government and has this to say about the state's promotion of meditation in 1954: "Another well-known but perhaps not as successful aspect of the Buddhist Revival was the meditation center program. As usual, one has to wonder if the government really initiated and developed it or merely joined and then attempted to control an already popular movement. The actual practice of Buddhism for the sophisticated urbanites involved in the revival meant mainly the practice of meditation" (314). He also observes, "While the majority of the sangha may well have been on the fence waiting, an active few eventually became involved in a new Burmese phenomenon born of the nationalist fervor of the first decades in this [the twentieth] century. I refer to the birth of lay Buddhist associations that may have started with religious motives as paramount but which eventually became deeply involved in the politics of seeking freedom from colonial rule" (196).

What Mendelson could not have seen from his historical position was just how significant meditation would become as a mass *lay* phenomenon and how it would implicate the arrangements between the laity, the sangha (the monastic order), and the state. Indeed, it was really not until the Ne Win regime had come into power and purged the government's Buddhist elements that the lay meditation movement's popularity surged. A central question addressed in chapter 1 is: Why did the mass lay meditation movement gather speed once the state removed its patronage? Before turning to this question, I wish to say something of the circumstances of data collection, which led to the formulation of the problem.

It is a segue to my own approach to the subject to point out that much of the sparse but competent and engaged foreign scholarship on Burma since the mid-1980s has been concerned with the question of what social mechanisms and processes are used by the military regime to retain power. This question is a preoccupation both because of the strong commitment scholars of Burma share in envisioning a more just political environment than prevails at present and because the success of the regime in retaining its hold despite overwhelming objection to it within and without the country demands explanation.

Scholarly Engagement with Burmese Politics

Since 1962, when the country was closed to foreigners, the military government has permitted only limited access to researchers. In those rare instances when a researcher is allowed in, the government imposes strict controls on his or her movements inside the country and on the topics that may be investigated. This limitation is reflected in the partial, sometimes distorted picture of political processes depicted in the work of these researchers, who are forced to rely on piecemeal accounts from outside or on surface appearances inside the country. Joseph Silverstein (1981) has reflected on this difficulty in a review article: "[S]cholars and journalists alike have provided mixed assessments of events and developments in Burma which do not give a clear and uniform picture of politics and life in that nation. Since most writers and official agencies rely primarily upon the economic and social data provided by the Burma government, the reports reflect the government's view of itself; however, a few writers and observers manage to make short visits to the country and travel its borders from neighbor states and make different assessments of conditions inside Burma."[5] As a result of this situation, I believe that scholarship about Burma has been more greatly influenced by academic models than are studies about other ethnographic sites, where research on the ground permits a questioning, revision, or reformulation of those models.

An anthropological—and increasingly a culturally sophisticated political science—reading of the situation would assert that as long as we continue, if only passively, to treat the social forces that support the regime as a black box of tradition, we will not improve our understanding of what continues to animate and generate the political landscape of Burma. The studies that result from such an approach conform to the old modernization theory that conceives of tradition as an obstacle to progress.[6] To wit, one often hears in association with these studies the call for an education to democracy, an education to modernity, and even a "revolution of the spirit."[7]

In *Mental Culture in Burmese Crisis Politics* (1999), Gustaaf Houtman has come closest to engaging the question of the social basis for the construction of political realities. Accounting for the armature of Buddhist practices that are of apparent relevance to all cultural life in Burma, including politics, Houtman examines how the "terminology and practices of mental culture inform, indeed constitute coherent internal cultural debates surrounding the politics of the military régimes since 1962, and in particular since 1988" (9). Houtman focuses on "the role of Buddhist discourse surrounding Buddhist techniques of meditation and contemplation in providing a structure for coping with the political crisis [and an] idiom for political opposition" (10). His emphasis is on what he calls "mental culture" ("the techniques of mind purification and mind control," as he describes it elsewhere [2005, 136]), particularly as they structure political discourse. This work provides us with a sorely needed corrective to the old saws of development and modernization theories. Houtman looks to indigenous concepts and understandings as they affect the political processes of nation-state building, national identity construction, and the legitimation of state power and authority. His examination of Burmese Buddhist notions of power and authority draws attention to the ways in which power is itself culturally constituted.[8]

The present study dovetails with Houtman's work, for like him, I have also been drawn to examining the significance of mental practices as personal and social dispositional stances that motivate individual action and articulate shared social goals. Enumerating the cultural particularities of power is likewise a goal we hold in common. My fundamental dispute with Houtman begins with what I think is also one of the strengths in his work: the identification of the Burmese political conceptions of *awza* (influence) and *ana* (authority) with mental practices of meditation. Ably though he details these native conceptions, in aiming to demonstrate the influence of mental culture on social and political realities, Houtman forces an overdetermined dichotomy between the NLD and Aung San Suu Kyi, on the one hand, and the military regimes of the Burmese Socialist Program Party (BSPP), SLORC, and SPDC, on the other. He therein inadvertently reifies conventional political scientific analytical categories that would juxtapose democracy against authoritarianism, equality against hierarchy, freedom and autonomy against control, justice against arbitrary power, and internationalism against the local (1999, 12). This simplification, I believe, conforms less with the facts on the ground than with a conventional scholarly distinction that is often made between civil society and the state and between democracy and authoritarianism. Houtman's conclusion conveniently places *vipassanā* (insight) meditation, the ethnographic focus of both our researches, on the morally good side of the issue while simultaneously making democracy a native Burmese concept and value.

Houtman's discussion of mental culture is echoed in Stefan Collignon's work. Collignon (2001, 80) poses the question "as to how the culturally determined cognitive model, which the SLORC generals share with many other people in Burma, can be transformed." He also works from a Western-inspired binarism that describes an opposition of individualism to social, collective identity. Taking inspiration from the great Indianist anthropologist Louis Dumont, Collignon finds the opposite of individualism in Burma in totalitarian rule. Under totalitarian rule, it is the human rights of *individuals* that are principally distorted. He says, "Dumont explains totalitarianism as the attempt to subordinate individualism to the primacy of society-as-totality in a society where individualism is already profoundly rooted and predominant" (77). Totalitarianism, we are to understand, emerges in an environment in which Western-style individualism is already part and parcel of local conceptions of selfhood and identity. Having asserted this, it is only a short step for Collignon to advocate revolutionary change through capitalist development, since "capitalist development transforms the class structure enlarging the working and middle classes," which leads to more "individualistic values . . . booming market economies . . . [and] ultimately cause[s] the downfall of repressive régimes" (79).

Collignon considers what is necessary for Burmese society to acquire a "cognitive model that allows human rights to be claimed" (79). He recapitulates Robert Taylor's argument that colonialism did not develop a modern civil society capable of sustaining democracy in Burma (77). He hopes to sever the logical possibility for the assertion that "traditionalist" political forms (that is, authoritarianism) are legitimate. Whereas Houtman seeks to legitimize democracy for Burma by demonstrating its traditional moorings and compatibility in history and cognitive-cultural dispositions, Collignon advocates the introduction of changes that would transform those cognitive dispositions "which reproduce . . . concrete violations of human rights on a daily basis." He says: "The long and sometimes painful experience of 200 years of democracy in the West could teach us one lesson: the institutions of democracy only work correctly and are only sustainable if they are supported by a democratic culture, i.e., a shared set of values, fundamental interests and concerns that form meaning in society, and that help to structure people's behaviour, knowledge and attitudes towards democratic practices and institutions" (72). Any political system that bases its legitimacy on "customs and traditions," Collignon observes (79), can never be legitimate because of its natural tendency to revert to authoritarianism; the cognitive underpinnings for human rights claims are not present.

Collignon assumes individualism to be part of a universal construction of selfhood, and thus follows his individual-based notion of ethics and human rights, currently suppressed in Burma. One can perhaps debate the ideal normativeness of a rights-based ethics. Descriptively, where ethics are conceived first in terms of their conformity to prior collective models, as is the case explicitly where religious and cosmological representations of ethical norms are predominant, then it makes less sense to describe norms in terms of rights-based selfhood but to see instead the impact of local consensus about how individuals ought to act and relate in the social world, as well as how selfhood is constructed.

At last, unable to reconcile what seems to him a lack of drive or initiative to rights claiming among the Burmese, Collignon concludes, "[I]n Burma there exists no consensus about the mode of exercising power, nor about its purpose" (72). Power and the authority to exercise it are certainly contested in contemporary Burma, but the terms by which power may be legitimately employed hardly constitutes a field of chaotic misapprehension. Collignon should first be asking if power is truly universal or if it is culturally determined. The "transhistorical appearance [of relations of force] is an analogical illusion," Paul Veyne says. "Their sociology is set within the limits of an arbitrary and historical program."[9]

In a related framework (without the specifically cognitive orientation), Juliane Schober (2005) argues that a "modern Buddhism" (113) has emerged since 1988 and has polarized religious communities around Aung San Suu Kyi and the State Peace and Development Council. Assertions of moral authority depend on competing approaches for acquiring power, and they find their authority in the "Theravada textual tradition" (114). Schober juxtaposes "nationalist, centralized, and ritualistic patronage of Buddhism by the State Peace and Development Council (SPDC) . . . [with] the socially engaged Buddhism advocated by Aung San Suu Kyi that emphasizes personal, social engagement, ethics, and meditation. The former employs large-scale rituals to legitimate a political hierarchy of the state, while the latter advocates meditation, individual empowerment, and social ethics to resist spiritual and material exploitations by the state" (114).

Schober's analysis is compelling for the way in which it brings to our attention how Buddhist practices by the military government use pageantry and rituals to affirm the holism of the state, whereas resistance to the state (for example, as offered by Aung San Suu Kyi) invokes a superior personal morality on the part of its political actors.[10] This is, as we will see, consistent with a historical pattern in which pretenders to the throne legitimized their right to revolt against a king.

Schober concludes her paper on "Buddhist Visions of Moral Authority and Civil Society" (2005) with the following: "[L]acking secular means of legitimation the politics of the state depends on the moral authority of Buddhist communities . . . [and] on Buddhist sources of authority. . . . One can readily imagine numerous developments in Burma that will foster a modern civil society and sustain political, economic, social, and religious pluralism. It will be the work of future generations to conceptualize, establish, and institutionalize this kind of postcolonial project in Burma" (129). Will Aung San Suu Kyi's political use of Buddhist moral conceptions and practices lead necessarily from resistance to the state to the denial and utter abandonment of Buddhist theories of the sources of power and political legitimacy?

Mary Callahan (2003) offers a refreshing and thought-provoking break with earlier debates. She seeks to explain, first, why Burma did not modernize as other new nation-states had in the post–World War II period and, second, how the military has succeeded in maintaining power for over forty years. She rightly criticizes the naive culture and personality studies of the 1950s and 1960s, which sought, among other things, to explain these failings in terms of an alleged "paranoid and dysfunctional national character" (6) that could be traced to child-rearing practices.[11] Callahan's thesis is that it is the structure of organized violence itself that "created institutions with staying power" (2). Her book concludes that "the relationship between state building and warfare is a recursive one that has tangled up Burmese state and society in such a way as to produce the most durable incarnation of military rule in history" (3).

However, Callahan jettisons the culturally determinative model only to adopt an implicit framework that takes as natural the dichotomy between rights-based politics and political repression. She attempts to explain only the coercive and repressive practices of the regime. The abundant and obvious ways in which the regime seeks legitimacy for its authority—and what this engagement looks like and means as a two-sided communication, even if manipulated (per Schober 1997, for example)—finds no place in her analysis. Her model of state-society relations is that of a simple command relationship. In my view, even if we accept the notion of command states, we must nevertheless explore how these states assert the grounds for their authority and also what their weaknesses and limitations are.

It is in these discussions, it seems to me, that other scholars come closest to the recognition that Buddhism and politics in Burma constitute a shared social field and not, in the words of one uninformed outsider, a "bizarre state-sponsored realism" (Appadurai 1991, 208). My objection to the focus held in common by many of the writers I have mentioned thus far pertains to the way in which democracy and its variously interpreted opposites are taken as an analytical basis for representing Burma. By this, I do not mean to dispute the existence of a Burmese aspiration for democracy following the 1988 protests and killings and the 1990 elections resulting in the landslide victory of Aung San Suu Kyi's party. Nor do I dispute the desirability of such an outcome in whatever form it might take. My argument is that the mainstream political analyst's notion of democracy—in which an idealized version of Western-style freedoms becomes the basis for applying criteria as to what is and is not a consensual form of governance—brings with it an assumed framework for accounting for both the nature of the political system *tout court* (rule by force, manipulativeness, disregard for human rights, and so on) and the psychological or psychological-cultural characteristics that make this possible (apathy, tradition-boundedness, and the like). Among other failings I seek to repair in my analysis is what Michael Aung

Thwin describes as a flattening and simplification of political realities in terms of good and evil—a notion around which a kernel of interpretive scholarship on Burma has hardened. As Aung Thwin observes

[T]he struggle today is not an issue of "democracy versus authoritarianism," or military versus civilian rule," a framework that has been simplified by various news and political groups for our consumption. Rather, it is much more complex and has several other, in my opinion more important, dimensions to it: historical, personal cum generational, and institutional. In fact, I would argue that the ideological factor (democracy) is probably the least important to those living in Burma, although Western media and the antigovernment groups have made it the *only* issue. (1998, 157–58)[12]

In this view, the particulars of Burmese political society are betrayed by the application of familiar Western standards in the attempt to make sense of Burma's confusing array of political realities—realities that have not as yet taken shape in the familiar arrangements of statehood that we have come to expect among the legitimate nations of the world.

Finally, in defense of what some readers might mistake for a sympathetic approach to the political status quo but what in actuality seeks to be a culturally *empathetic* approach to understanding processes of political legitimation, I would direct the reader to the introduction of James Scott's *Seeing Like a State* (1998). There, Scott offers a defense in advance of charges he feared might be leveled against him:

The first charge is that my argument is uncritically admiring of the local, the traditional, and the customary. I understand that the practical knowledge I describe is often inseparable from the practices of domination, monopoly, and exclusion that offend the modern liberal sensibility. My point is not that practical knowledge is the product of some mythical, egalitarian state of nature. Rather, my point is that formal schemes of order are untenable without some elements of the practical knowledge that they tend to dismiss. (7)

Scott's observation that "a certain understanding of science, modernity, and development has so successfully structured the dominant discourse that all other kinds of knowledge are regarded as backward, static traditions" (331) is relevant here as well. Unexpected forms of "practical knowledge," as in the case I have elaborated here regarding insight knowledge (through vipassanā meditation) and its role in economic and political practices, may be criticized as irrelevant to the conventional political-moral debate. "The clarity of the high-modernist optic," Scott notes, "is due to its resolute singularity. Its simplifying fiction is that, for any activity or process that comes under its scrutiny, there is only one thing going on" (347). The view from outside Burma, then, is often just such a simplifying fiction— reducing all the surfaces of knowledge to a single plane in order to erase complexity and ambiguity.

It is often commented that Burma's political forms (authoritarian, military, royalist) draw from earlier models of the Buddhist state or from colonialism. The military is seen as the only viable institution because it has been careful to disallow the rise of any other institutions that might make claims to power sharing.[13] In *The State in Burma,* a thematic political and historical analysis of the Burmese state over nearly a millennium, Robert Taylor, for instance, concludes that the state had found stability and legitimacy in Ne Win's military regime. "[F]or better or worse the state is accepted as inevitable and dominates other institutions" (1987, 372). In the vein of other famous last words, less than a year later this assertion would be undermined by the grassroots antigovernment demonstrations and uprisings that culminated in Ne Win relinquishing power. Invisible to this view—the unacknowledged sacred white elephant in the room—is the very significant role monks and laity play in shaping the terms of political legitimation through apolitical actions.

In a country in which staying out of politics is mandated in every aspect of social engagement and all forms of administration are under the sole purview of the military, it should not be surprising to see that alternative solutions to social problems are addressed in apolitical ways. I do not mean "misrecognized" political approaches masquerading as apolitical approaches. This is not a "hidden transcript" for political action.[14] Rather, in Burma's politically repressed environment, other causal frameworks, social networks, and behavioral practices are employed by individuals to navigate the world with full intentionality, agency, and power. What that world looks like to these individuals—its limitations, potentiality, and freedoms—are explored here. How that world engages with the brute power of the military and the state is also considered, with an eye to showing how it shapes in critical ways the very framework in which political legitimacy can be claimed by regimes in power.

Chapter 1

RISE OF THE NEW LAITY
AND THE RESTITUTION OF
THE TERNARY ORDER

A New Institutional Form

Burma's largest lay meditation center, the Mahasi Thathana Yeiktha
(MTY), is different from any Buddhist institution that has ever existed in Burma or, indeed, in historical Buddhism. Its uniqueness is
immediately apparent to both the Burmese Buddhist and the Western observer entering the Yeiktha grounds. For the Burmese, who is
implicitly matching his or her impressions of the center against the
traditional *pongyi kyaung* (monk's monastery) prototype, the center
presents a variety of contradictions. Principally, the presence of so
many laypersons taking their rounds side by side with monks is most
irregular. And for the Burmese, as for the Western observer, the industrious preoccupation of hundreds of monks and laypersons (men,
women, and, at certain times of the year, scores of children as well),
sitting or walking slowly in parallel and intensely undertaking practices of meditation, arrests the attention.

The center is constantly busy and organized around the solemn
activity of meditation. For more than half a century, a twenty-four-
hour meditation schedule—alternating one hour of sitting meditation
and one hour of walking meditation, with only short breaks set aside
for sleep and meals—has been in continuous effect. Bells strike out the

hour and half hour. The deep, resonant thud of a log striker summons monks, nuns, and laypeople to the two meals offered, at daybreak and at 10 a.m., by a devoted laity.

By contrast, the ordinary pongyi kyaung has a less purposeful rhythm marking the activities of its day. Monks teach the scriptures to the young koyin (novitiates), they take pindabat (alms rounds) and recite prayers and chants, and they receive lay devotees who have come to pay their respects and offer donations. According to his aptitude, a monk may study the scriptures or he may meditate. Sir J. G. Scott provides a charming description that perhaps best captures the easygoing rhythms of a typical kyaung.[1] "Most of the older members of the kyaung do, however, what an Englishman would call nothing, all the afternoon. They talk with whatever idlers—and there are always an abundance of them—come about the place, and then sink into meditation and many of the weaker of them into sleep" (Shway Yoe 1963, 35).[2]

At the Yeiktha, frivolous speech (in Pāli, samphappalapa) is not permitted. Monk and lay wardens are quick to chastise the yogi (meditator), visitor, or monk who is not mindful of the code of silence that is everywhere in effect. The injunction against speaking while undertaking a course of meditation is required so that the yogi may cultivate greater concentration. Speech acts engage one in conventional conceptualization that can interrupt the practice of giving continuous attention to the six sense doors of perception. When it is necessary for a yogi to break the silence, it should be with mindfulness (in Burmese, thati; in Pāli, sati). This means that the yogi takes up a relationship toward speech acts that is consistent with the method applied to all other activities and cogitations while at the Yeiktha. Thus, the yogi first notes the intention to speak. Then, the physical procedures of opening the mouth and resonating the voice box are observed as separate acts. Finally, the yogi is to observe the formation of the words and the intention embedded in their specific meanings. When speech is mindfully enacted in this manner, satipaṭṭhāna vipassanā (mindfulness meditation)[3] has not ceased.[4]

To anticipate much of the discussion that follows, I will point out here that MTY emerged as a contradiction between two conventional cultural ideas. The first is that the specific vocation of the sangha, or monastic order, is to strive for *nibbāna* (enlightenment), whereas it is the laity's role to provide for the sangha the material requisites for the monks' practice. The second idea is that the traditional location for enlightenment is the forest, where striving can be undertaken by virtuosi monks trained in ascetic practices and meditation.[5] Even at first blush, it is evident that the Yeiktha contravenes both these conventions. At the Yeiktha, the modal inhabitant is a layperson who is engaged full-time in vipassanā meditation, which is to say in the pursuit of enlightenment. And MTY is not nestled deep in a remote forest away from other human settlements; it is situated in a well-to-do neighborhood close to Yangon's city center.

In the folk ideal, a monk spent the first part of his career studying the texts and transmitting them to the next generation of monks. In the final third of his life, he pursued nibbāna, ideally in the forest and away from the goings-on of worldly society. There, he meditated and attended to his individual salvation. Laity were not expected to conform to this pattern, although in the last third of one's life, it was considered prudent to visit the monastery on full-moon and dark-moon days to meditate and keep precepts to prepare the way for an auspicious next life.[6] The *pāramī* (purification leading to enlightenment) of laypersons was held to be inferior to that of monks, and thus, they would be incapable of renouncing worldly life for an arduous spiritual exercise in the forest. Instead, after performing acts of *dāna* (charity) and observing *sīla* (moral precepts of restraint), lay individuals might pursue *bhāvanā* (mental development) through the practice of *samatha* (tranquility) meditations, such as bead telling, recitation of a mantra, and the like.[7] (Later, I will explain the significant distinction between *samatha-bhāvanā* and *vipassanā-bhāvanā* [insight meditation], which is what is mainly practiced at MTY.) Dāna, sīla, and bhāvanā constitute the three dimensions of Buddhist practice, and each is related to the others in a causal and developmental progression. Together, these practices form the whole of the Noble Eightfold Path of purification.[8]

The blatant contradiction in the characteristic activities of the Yeiktha is therefore that laypersons are undertaking the penultimate pursuit of enlightenment without also taking up the vocation of the world renouncer. This contradiction is magnified by the breadth of the phenomenon. Under the auspices of many centers such as MTY, vipassanā meditation has been pursued on a mass scale *primarily* by laypersons, often educated but untrained in the scriptures. These meditation courses take place in bureaucratically routinized lay institutions located in urban centers, usually (but not necessarily) under the guidance of a monk who trains yogi practitioners in the procedures for first-person observation of the psychophysical process. This practice forms the basis for a series of cognitive insights building one on the other, culminating in a metamorphosis in perception that is interpreted as the experience of enlightenment. At MTY and its branch organizations alone, more than a million people are said to have attained one or more of the insights (*nyanzin*) in the progression that leads to enlightenment (*nibbāna*) or one of the stages of enlightenment (*sotāpanna, sakadāgāmī, anāgāmī, arahat*).

On completion of short, intensive meditation courses, these individuals return to their worldly lives. The laity's pursuit of enlightenment has meant, among other things, the development of new expectations and roles between the sangha and laity. As the official embodiment and resource of the Buddha *dhamma* (the truth proclaimed by the Buddha), monks are the appropriate teachers of meditation, and this has become one of their principal responsibilities.[9] In this sense, the laity has, to a large degree, domesticated the institution of the sangha by asserting that the penultimate goals of the Buddha's teachings are not for virtuosi monks alone but for all people from all walks of life. What can be called the mass lay meditation movement (a term that incorporates the movement's political and sociological dimensions) or the vipassanā movement (in recognition of its practical and phenomenological distinction from other forms of meditation practice) has reconfigured Buddhist practice in Burma.

The Emergence of the Lay Institutions

The emergence of the new Buddhist institutional form of the lay-dominated meditation center was gradual. As a concept, the Yeiktha developed from the seed of an idea about how to revitalize *sāsana* (the dispensation of the Buddha's teachings; in Burmese, *thathana*), society, and the state. Institutionally, this unusual undertaking was the creative synthesis of a vision held by three men: the wealthy donor Sir U Thwin; Burma's first prime minister, U Nu; and a monk renowned for his learning and experience in satipaṭṭhāna vipassanā meditation practice, Mahasi Sayadaw. However, the real interest in observing this institutional fusion of resources, visions, and abilities is in how the procedure conformed and borrowed from classical arrangements and patterns drawn from cosmology, myth, metahistory, canonical texts, and classical commentaries.

To appreciate this, one must learn something of the backdrop of classical structure in the arrangements between sangha and laity. A *nayaka sayadaw* (senior monk teacher) at the Yeiktha described this relationship simply: the laymen's obligation is and always has been to be *pyisey nuggaha,* meaning "supporters of the materials"—the material sustenance of the sangha and the monasteries—and monks, by contrast, are *dhamma nuggaha,* meaning "supporters of the teachings." The sangha conveys the teachings to the laity, and the laity supports the sangha materially. Historically, this symbiosis of functions implied distinct roles and emphases. The sangha was to teach the laity by means of conducting discourses, training new adepts, shepherding temporary monks, and encouraging the laity to keep their precepts and develop their sīla through donations, in which the monks were vehicle-recipients. The mutually supportive activities together perpetuated the Buddha sāsana. In the late nineteenth and early twentieth centuries, the strict division between these roles began to change in response to events triggered by colonialism, as follows.

In the classical kingship pattern that lasted approximately eight hundred years until the British dismantled the monarchy, periodic revitalization of religion and society was carried out under the idiom and logic of purification movements. A minority of the sangha's members purified themselves "outside" of society (physically in the forest) by means of ascetic practices and meditation. They then returned to the center and purified the rest of the sangha by reforming the *vinaya* (behavioral code of monks) and by expelling nonorthodox elements through sectarian pressures and rivalries.[10] These internally driven sangha purification movements often involved the king, who participated in them in two ways. First, to bolster his own political legitimacy, he might identify with the supposedly purified sects and monks; second, because purification of the sangha was itself a potent source of protection, strength, and power radiating outward toward the polity and society, he often initiated purification movements in the sangha. New kings in particular typically began their reigns with some form of sangha purification and the identification and participation of their rule with the "purest" elements of the sangha and therefore also the dhamma (truth or law) that was the source for their own potency and power. These were not simply symbolic acts of political legitimation but instrumental acts for the production of power. Kings also took purification rituals on themselves, retreating into private meditation and emerging potently charged and radiating these powers toward the kingdom.[11] To guide them in these activities, the kings had personal specialists—monks who would meditate and transfer the merits to them.[12] Laity also participated in purification rituals through meditation or, perhaps more commonly, through undertaking five or ten precepts as a form of purification by sīla. As I will explain at greater length, the sources of potency and power in the social world, in former as in contemporary purifications, are found in renunciation, ascetic practice, and meditation. The common, unifying principle underwriting all of these is their relationship to purity.[13]

Lay interest in meditation in itself became a new mode for perpetuating the sāsana while purifying the monkhood at the same time. The classic pattern by which a rich monk donor (*daga*) identified and supported an exemplary monk became elaborated. Rather than merely functioning as a field for the laity's merit accumulation (the sangha is considered the incomparable object of donation and devotion), monks were now being asked to teach meditation. Simultaneously, they were spurring the laity on to practice and encouraging other monks to enter the forest for years at a stretch in order to attain enlightenment so that they could spread the sāsana to the laity on completing their courses.

In the context of the present discussion, the relevant arc of contemporary history began in the 1930s. Mingun Sayadaw (Bearer of the Three Pitikas and Keeper of the Dhamma Treasure)[14] sent Mahasi Sayadaw and Taung Pulu Sayadaw into the forest for practice, after which they became two of the most renowned meditation monks of their generation. This created a purification effort in two directions. The sangha became more attentive to its code of conduct, scholarship, and realization of the teachings through vipassanā meditation. And the laity asserted influence over the sangha's purity by addressing more seriously their own purity through meditation and by forming religious societies with lay-owned and lay-controlled religious resources.

The Mahasi Thathana Yeiktha reflects the new variation in the classical arrangement between sangha and laity. First, it is an institutional given that the monks are obliged to teach *paṭipatti* (practical meditation) to the laity so that the latter may realize (*paṭivedha*) the Buddha's teachings.[15] This represents, as I have said, a shift away from conventional or classical expectations that lay practices should be confined to merit-making activities and the keeping of morality (dāna, sīla), while monks should be focused on scriptural study (*pariyatti*), adhering to their code of conduct (*wini* in Burmese; in Pāli, *vinaya*), acting as merit fields for the laity's generous charity, and attending to their personal liberation from the cycle of rebirths through meditation. It is worth citing at length the historical instruction I received on this matter from U Ko Lay, the former rector of Mandalay University and a Burmese Buddhist historian:

Monks have two duties. One is to teach pariyatti [scriptures]. The other is to practice bhāvanā [mental development], that is, paṭipatti [pursuance of the teachings through practice]. . . . [In the nineteenth century, the renowned monk] Ledi Sayadaw reasoned that Buddha did not spend eons and eons accumulating his pāramī [perfection leading to enlightenment] to get this ñāṇa [wisdom] just for the sake of a handful of monks only. It is meant for all the sentient beings. So why shouldn't these teachings be made available to laypeople?

Ledi Sayadaw was the first . . . who thought along that line. Likewise he thought about Abhidhamma. Abhidhamma studies are so difficult that it is not the concern of laypeople. Laypeople just listen to instructions of the monks about dāna and sīla, and that's all they have to do. But Ledi Sayadaw reasoned that Abhidhamma was quintessential among the Buddha's teachings and that it should be available to laypeople. That's why he formed societies in nearly every town, where laypeople were taught Abhidhamma. And then the natural consequence was to follow by paṭipatti. That was how he started making people realize that Buddha's teachings, actually paṭipatti itself, should be available to everyone. . . .

Ledi Sayadaw instructed one of his brilliant students, Monyin Sayadaw, to go into the forest and practice vipassanā for twelve years and afterward come out and teach meditation. . . . Monyin Sayadaw started teaching . . . in 1934.

When we became independent, U Nu became prime minister and he picked up the trail. . . . During the war years, especially during the Japanese occupation, the urban nationalist intelligentsia turned their attentions more seriously to sāsana practice in the realization that a national identity based on race, language and religion required familiari[ty] . . . with their traditions, while simultaneously connecting with the urban and rural populations in a single national vision. That was how Mahasi Sayadaw's practice became known.[16]

Several key orientations emerge from this account. First, new possibilities for lay practice were concomitant with what would become a mandate for monks to instruct the laity. As the laity became more learned in the esoterica of meditation, they could exert more articulate pressure on monks to be competent and pure in respect to the new domain (that is, bhāvanā). The lineage from Ledi Sayadaw (1846–1923) to Monyin Sayadaw to his protégé Mahasi Sayadaw mirrors the institutionalization of the new arrangement, as all three— but in particular Mahasi Sayadaw—supervised the formation of innumerable lay centers that are now governed by lay committees.

The integration of paṭipatti, or practice-oriented Buddhism, directly into the plans of nation-state building following independence completed what I have been referring to as the new arrangement for the ternary order of sangha, state, and laity. Also implicit in U Ko Lay's instruction is the historical context for the rise of the mass lay meditation movement as a millenarian revitalization of Buddhism. When one reads accounts of how, in the face of British colonialism, Ledi Sayadaw exhorted his lay students to "practice [that is, meditate] as though your heads are on fire," then the suggestion that the meditation movement had its origins as a culturally particular reaction to British colonialism and the dismantling of Buddhist kingship becomes sensible.[17]

What had changed for Burma was the organization of the state in terms of its classical arrangements relative to Buddhist practice. The colonial administration first dismantled the kingship. The British reorganized the state into a bureaucracy suitable for the pursuit of efficiencies in extracting resources and reordering civil society toward progressive social goals. In the prior ternary order, sangha, state, and laity mutually participated in the reproduction of what might be termed—following Ernst Troeltsch's description of pre-Reformation Europe as church-directed civilization—sāsana-directed civilization. These mutually supportive and sustaining roles of the sangha, state, and laity were organized along the lines of cosmic and worldly divisions: monks renounced the world and served as repositories for righteous action; lay householders supported the sangha materially, thus building their pāramī; and rulers had the obligation to uphold the purity and propagation of the sāsana. This arrangement was the very foundation of a king's claim to legitimacy.[18]

Colonial rule sought to impose alien ideas for restructuring the prior relations away from the Burmese Buddhist monarchical state, with its ternary arrangements and directive to perpetuate sāsana, and toward a modern, progressive state oriented toward productivity and rational bureaucratic administration. As Robert Taylor observes: "The leaders of the nationalist groups were pulled between these two ideals, one learned from Burma's 1,000 year old culture and the other from the institutions of British science and imperialism."[19] Early nationalist groups, such as the Young Men's Buddhist Association (YMBA) and subsequently the General Council of Burmese Associations (GCBA), gained the support of wide sections of Burmese rural society. The Burmese Buddhist response to this subjugation took various forms, three of which were particularly significant. The first was the millenarian movement of the *weiksa* (wizard) cults that sought to bring back kingship and hasten the arrival of the next Buddha, the Meitreya Buddha. The second was the independence struggle of the Thakins, whose Dobama movement culminated in the 1300 Ayaydawbone (Revolution of 1938). The Thakins looked to Buddhism as a rallying point for shared national identity.[20] They did so with the aid of a nativist confrontation with Western ideas and political ideologies. Buddhist scripture and practice served as tools for exploring the incipient dimensions for a Burmese national identity—one they hoped would unify the educated urban center and the rural periphery at the same time that it contested Western political and philosophical doctrines and scientific verification procedures on their own grounds.[21] The Thakin movement, supported by an urban intelligentsia, attempted to construct a uniquely Burmese road to national unity and identity;[22] The third was the vipassanā movement, which flowered slightly later then the others and was neither politically engaged initially nor self-consciously directed at restoring the monarchy. Vipassanā revitalization, like the weiksa millenarian movement, was drawn from prophecy in Buddhist scriptures. Both these movements represented attempts to secure a moral cosmic order in the face of overwhelming sociopolitical transformations.

Both movements also depended on meditation—samatha in the case of the weiksa cults and vipassanā in the case of the lay meditation movement—as the foundation for the production of sources of potency and political power. Both attempted to extend the broadest universalizing cosmological canopy under which the multiple forms of devotion, practice, and beliefs about the nature of conventional truth (*sammuti-sacca*) might be situated vis-à-vis the ultimate truth (*paramattha-sacca*) of the Buddha dhamma. However, the two movements emerged as distinct types. In the weiksa tradition, the prophecy of the end of the World Age simultaneous with the end of Buddhist kingship motivated people to practice in such a way—through alchemy, wizard practices, astrological divination, and samatha meditation—so as to hasten the end and bring about the Meitreya Buddha.[23] The vipassanā movement also focused on the end of the World Age, but the aim was to stem the decline itself by means of purifying the laity's own actions and mental intentions. This manner of revitalization drew from existing ideas (and ideals) concerning the "original society"—most notably as represented in the Mahasammatha myth expounded in the Aganna Sutta—in which the first king was elected on the basis of being the most moral member of society.[24]

The difference between these two millenarian impulses would become important in the postindependence period in defining two separate mythicohistorical directions in which state and Buddhism could be reunited. The weiksa tradition, which, as will be shown, remains relevant to an understanding of how contemporary military rulers are trying to retain power, draws from the Ashokan (*cakkavatti,* or world-conquering king) paradigm, in which the kings' legitimacy was premised on their role as protectors of the faith.[25] Vipassanā, by contrast, was based on the early apostolic period, in which the Buddha went out into the world to enlighten all he encountered. In the first cultural model, the state takes care of religion through paternalistic, authoritarian action. In the second, the teachings transform individuals and collectivities, including the state, and beyond that the rest of the world. The second, apostolic model undertakes revitalization as a kind of grassroots process (and very much a proselytizing one) in which the purification of the state occurs by means of the purification of the citizenry and the improvement of its morality. In this model's contemporary manifestation, it falls to the laity and their self-purification efforts to reverse the moral decline that has been hastening the end of the World Age. To underscore this point by way of reiteration, moral sāsana society, in the logic of the vipassanā movement, would not be triggered into a purification cycle from the top down (that is, from the king downward). Instead, purification would proceed from the ground up through an enlightened citizenry, which would eventually purify the sangha *and the state*.

The Kopaka Apwe, *U Nu, and the Founding of the Mahasi Thathana Yeiktha*

The formation of a lay-owned and lay-sponsored institution on the scale of MTY was made possible by the existence of an institutional template, in the form of *kopaka apwe*—lay voluntary institutions composed of like-minded members dedicated to performing sāsana work. The devoted support that Burma's first prime minister, U Nu, gave to the task was also instrumental to its realization.

The direct translation of kopaka apwe—guardian associations—conveys the purpose of these organizations. Kopaka apwe are widespread in Burma. They are patterned on an arrangement between the lay donor and the monk recipient. At different times in Burmese history, the kopaka apwe have functioned differently, according to the needs of the times. During the British colonial period, for example, lay societies were apparently a convenient setting for the formation of incipient political associations.[26] As I have argued earlier, sectarian rivalries abounded in the colonial period, and monks were perceived to be degenerating in their morality and their adherence to the vinaya. Decay in the sangha's morality in turn threatened the laity's merit fields, as a person's merit is partly dependent on his or her monk's moral purity. The proliferation of kopaka apwe at that time probably reflected the self-conscious efforts laypeople made to reverse the decay. This deduction proceeds from the outcome. Lay institutions formed by kopaka apwe became centers where monks resided in a new arrangement. In these centers, the monks were (and continue to be) regulated by the lay societies. Then as now, lay societies invited and disinvited monks according to their discretion.

This kind of lay control over the sangha was virtually impossible in the formerly dominant pattern, in which laity offered monasteries, agricultural lands, and buildings outright to the sangha. On donation, these became sangha property and frequently that of an individual monk. Although there were customary laws concerning the rights of donors in stewarding their donations to the sangha, these were, for the most part, difficult arrangements to manipulate, especially on the death of a monk. Rarely could the lay steward decide to which monk or sect the property should devolve. In this light, one can appreciate the uniqueness of a bureaucratically rationalized center such as MTY, in which the lay association exercises far greater control over the sangha presence and activity than has been the case in other monkly institutions. Within the confines of their own centers, the laity act as kings, performing the role of chief patrons and protectors of the sangha. It is my intention, however, to render this assertion not so much in metaphorical terms but as a structural feature of the landscape. The ternary order of sangha, state, and laity is reproduced behind the walls of these expansive yet enclosed institutions; the kopaka apwe act as kings would do. It was, therefore, no coincidence that "the pietistic Thakin Nu" ("Lord" Nu) spearheaded the establishment of MTY as the seat of his Buddhist state program.

The first step taken toward the Yeiktha's establishment was the formation of a lay voluntary association headed by U Nu himself. The affluent Sir U Thwin (knighted by the British for his sundry donations and good works in the time of the colonial administration), along with several other patrons, some of whom were U Nu's ministers, acted as chief donors. The Union of Burma's Buddha Sāsana Nuggaha Apwe (BSNA) was established on November 13, 1947, with Sir U Thwin as president.

In the Yeiktha's official history and charter, U Nu himself pens the mythicohistorical account of the founding of the center. This account is highly instructive both as history and as a prospectus for the organization; it also serves as a "real-life myth,"[27] situating the Nuggaha (the specific name of the MTY kopaka apwe, as ordinarily referred to by its members) in a Buddhist cosmological framework. All the familiar sensibilities of an origin myth are in evidence—auspicious signs, symbolic associations, and the evoking of Buddhist scripture and cosmology. The most glorified themes, however, concern the symbolic connections between the Nuggaha (most specifically U Nu) and the Buddhist kings in their role as propagators and protectors of the Buddha sāsana. The strongly Burmese nationalist flavor of the history is also apparent. We see this in the emphasis placed on the continuity of kingship and Buddhism in Burma. Under the British, U Nu bemoans, sāsana had been neglected and had almost died out. Thanks to the dedication of those laypeople who took an interest in dhamma and to those monks who continued their practice, the sāsana came once more into view "like the moon comes forth from behind a cloud" (BSNA 1954, 15).

A lengthy metahistorical review of the history of Buddhism in Burma follows, starting with an account of the 334,569 kings said to have ruled in Burma prior to the enlightenment of the Buddha. Some key Jataka stories (tales of the lives of the Buddha before he attained his penultimate form as the Buddha) and a description of the Buddha's enlightenment are provided. We read of how Buddhism arrived in Burma via two flying *arahat*s (fully enlightened saints) named Sona and Uttara from Ceylon. From that point forward, we are told, Buddhist polities were continuously in existence until the British annexation. A short history of Burmese Buddhist kings (221 up to King Thibaw) is given, and the British annexation, the British period, the Dobama (independence) movement, Japanese occupation, independence, and the assassination of Aung San are all described. The review culminates in the rise of U Nu to the position of Burma's first prime minister—legitimizing his place in the history of kings and reiterating the role of kings in the history of the Buddha sāsana.

U Nu recounts the circumstances in which he met Mahasi Saya-daw, whom he took to be an arahat. He would later invite Mahasi to Rangoon to become the head monk at the Buddha Sāsana Nuggaha Apwe's new lay meditation center, and the center would come to be known as the Mahasi Thathana Yeiktha. All rulers were said to be associated with particular monks. In the months prior to indepen-dence, U Nu went to Thaton, the place where, according to legend, the first kings ruled; where Sona and Uttara are said to have estab-lished sāsana in Burma; where a pagoda houses the hair relic of Thagyamin, the king of *devās* (gods); and where many arahats have gone to renounce the world. In this auspicious place, U Nu met Ma-hasi, and following a nine-day reflection of the nine qualities of the Buddha and a cultivation of *mettā* (loving-kindness), he formed his particular vision for the Buddha Sāsana Nuggaha Apwe.[28] On his return to Rangoon, U Nu effected renovations and repairs to the old buildings leading to the Mya th'baik Zedi Pagoda.

As told in the unique genre of the charter, U Nu's actions re-peated, represented, and created history. The details of the history not only re-present its main features but also leave open the possi-bility for variation and improvisation. U Nu's participation in the historical and/or metahistorical motif of famous meetings between arahats and kings situates the founding of the new nation-state. Such a cosmogenic historical recapitulation is not just classificatory and representative, it is also efficacious and predictive. It establishes the "history of the future" just as it establishes the self-evident condition of reality and power in the present.

The founding of the Yeiktha was the crown of U Nu's propaga-tion of the paṭipatti (meditation) project.[29] The land and the original *dhammayone* (meditation and discourse hall) were donated by Sir U Thwin; other buildings were funded in conjunction with other donors. The prime minister invited monks from each township in Burma, together with their *kappia* (lay attendants), to meditate for one month at the center. For every yogi-month spent in meditation, U Nu's government donated money. Thus began what people at the Yeiktha recollect as the "age of paṭipatti," vipassanā's golden age. A government worker who later became a monk described for me the environment in 1953: "Under U Nu's pressure, *all* heads of departments came and meditated."

U Nu had, in fact, made it a requirement for his cabinet members to meditate long enough to achieve either first-stage enlightenment or the final stage leading up to this (*saṅkāruppekhāñāṇa*). I will explain what is meant by stages of enlightenment more fully in chapter 2, but what is immediately implied by attaining first-stage enlightenment is that the person can no longer break the Buddhist five precepts: not to kill, steal, lie, commit adultery, or take intoxicants. The seriousness of the belief (generally held among practitioners) that individuals became incorruptible through achieving enlightenment was reflected by the fact U Nu introduced vipassanā into the prisons. Those who "passed the course" were given their permanent freedom. They were now considered trustworthy people who would not transgress against other citizens.

Perhaps the most visible and renowned effort of U Nu's revitalization program was the convening of the Sixth Buddhist Synod, or Sangayana, held between 1954 and 1956. Following the example of King Mindon, who convened the Fifth Synod in 1871, U Nu sought to unify the sangha and the purification and propagation of sāsana. But like King Mindon before him, he was destined to fail in the task of uniting a fractious sangha. Ironically, this would only be accomplished under the initially reluctant and thereafter dubiously devout Ne Win in 1980.

Significant to the current discussion, however, is that the Sixth Buddhist Synod was seen as marking off a new period in history in which the sāsana would be universalized. Burma was retrospectively regarded in much of Theravadan Buddhist Southeast Asia as having been the protector of the faith during the time of colonial imperialism. Burma's self-proclaimed role or service to the rest of the world was to reintroduce the true teachings of the Buddha in terms that were not culturally or nationally specific but universally applicable.[30]

According to political analysts, U Nu's program for reestablishing sāsana for the welfare of the country contributed to the fall of his government and the country's succumbing to military rule in 1962. As Manuel Sarkisyanz relates, Buddhism was amalgamated with nationalist sentiments in the quest for a Burmese identity, creating a great deal of uneasiness among various ethnic minorities whose identities were constructed according to different religious traditions.[31] In any event, at least between 1947 and 1962, actions taken and institutions formed for the revitalization of sāsana were placed under the special protection and patronage of the government. This pattern would be repeated in one form another by every postindependence government.

Systematization of Practice and Routinization of the Institution

Among the most remarkable achievements and characteristics of MTY is its expansion beyond the U Nu period and the death of Mahasi Sayadaw in 1982. The center has continued to expand up to the present; its expansion is an engine to and a mirror of the growth of the movement itself. To explain how this has occurred, one must refer to two separate contexts: first, the state's involvement in Buddhism and its response to the mass lay meditation movement in general and its most popular institutional locus, MTY, in particular, and second, the internal dynamics at MTY, particularly since Mahasi's death. I take up the former topic more fully in chapter 5, where I discuss rulers subsequent to U Nu and their pursuit of legitimacy in the idiom of or in reference to kingship. The internal causes of the center's continuation are of only moderate interest here, since they refer principally to organization factors or to the modern evolution of the institution of the sangha, both of which I discuss more fully elsewhere.[32] What I want to review here as a prelude to a discussion of the phenomenology of meditation and its relationship to the construction of potency and, ultimately, state power is the systematization of the technique of satipaṭṭhāna vipassanā meditation, the original impetus for which came from the writings of Mahasi Sayadaw. This will lead us to an understanding of the scope of the meditation movement and why its practice has such consequences as I claim for the behavior of rulers in Burma.

MTY has thrived during recent decades, and the instruction and practice of meditation in accordance with what is known as the Mahasi method has likewise expanded well beyond MTY. Mahasi drew attention away from arahat cults and helped sublimate the spiritual energy into the formation of a rationalized, formalized method that could be transmitted by monks who had not attained enlightenment themselves but who were trained in the pedagogy of vipassanā. By contrast, the monasteries built up around other famous (arahat) monks, such as Mogok Sayadaw and Sunlun Sayadaw, have gone the way of traditional cults focused on a charismatic monk. On the death of the monk, the moral community surrounding him is typically disbanded and his monastery may become, at most, a site for memorialization and pilgrimage.

The success of the center and the attraction of the movement altogether derive from the efforts and beliefs Mahasi himself held. A reconstruction of his enterprise begins, I believe, with the description in the Pāli canonical texts of how, at the time of the Buddha, individuals had so perfected their pāramī that hearing a single verse spoken by the Buddha could open their minds to arahat-ship, or sainthood. As the enlightenment of the Buddha recedes in time, the teachings as they are transmitted orally and in writing are said to become less accurate and more obscure to common understandings. This is held to result from the overall decline in morality of the present World Age, which cyclically declines and regenerates according to the law of moral action, or kamma. For the sangha, this decline is the result of disagreements over how to adhere to the vinaya, or monastic code. These disputes create schisms in the sangha as well as moral laxities in the adherence to vinaya rules. Concomitant with these events, there is a decline in the number of individuals who realize the teachings of the Buddha, that is, attain enlightenment. For the present period, it is held that attainment of any of the stages of enlightenment is only possible if exertion is made through satipaṭṭhāna vipassanā meditation.

In his investigations, Mahasi Sayadaw determined that in the present era of the Buddha's dispensation (sāsana), it would take an average of two months for individuals whose pāramī were "ripe" to achieve *nyanzin* (vipassanā insight, the precursor to the first stage of enlightenment, known as *sotāpanna* [in Burmese, *thotapan*]). Mahasi tried to rediscover, through analysis of texts and commentaries and through meditation, the most direct method for attaining enlightenment "in this very life." His determination of the two-month time frame was also based on his empirical observations of many thousands of yogi practitioners. He focused on a line in the Dhammadāyāda Sutta that he interpreted as the assertion of a guarantee given by the Buddha for how to achieve sotāpanna. There, it is stated that exerting unbroken, moment-to-moment mindfulness for seven consecutive days can result in enlightenment.

The texts describe four types of individuals who can become enlightened. These types are distinguished according to the time within the dispensation of the Buddha that they are born. At the time of the Buddha, as I have said, hearing a single verse spoken by the Buddha was sufficient to open the mind of an individual to enlightenment. At present, listening is not enough; the yogi must practice meditation. I am uncertain of the source for the idea that at the twenty-five-hundred-year mark of the current sāsana, which is around now, there will be a resurgence of paṭipatti sāsana and many individuals will attain first-stage enlightenment. It is also believed that in the present era, arahats, though extremely rare, will develop. As the sāsana proceeds toward the end of its predicted length of five thousand years, it is supposed to become increasingly difficult or impossible for people to achieve enlightenment or even nyanzin.

The degeneration of the direct path to enlightenment is accompanied by the slow disappearance of the teachings. The disappearance is said to begin with the most abstruse of the "three baskets" (Tipitaka) of learning—namely, the Abhidhamma, referred to earlier in the quote by U Ko Lay, and within those texts the Patthana, or "system of relations." To counteract this prediction that the Patthana will be the first text to be lost in the sāsana, a circular diagrammatic representation of the twenty-four causal relations described in the Patthana is reproduced as a visual symbol all over Burma—on calendars, monks' fans, signboards, and so on. Even the youngest novices must commit to memory the twenty-four conditions of relations. Finally, it is believed that, coterminous with the decline in the sāsana, there will also be a decline in the cosmic cycle of life span and lifeworlds until finally, with the decline in moral purity, this world and all the worlds in the cosmos will be destroyed by the four elements of earth, air, fire, and water.

The belief in the decline of the sāsana configures, in its counteraction, an essential feature of Buddhist practice in contemporary Burma: the preoccupation with preserving the Buddha's teachings in as exact a way as possible is evident everywhere. This emphasis colors the expression of every aspect of practice, from donations (dāna) to the pursuit of enlightenment (nibbāna) through meditation (bhāvanā). Further, the belief in the decline of the sāsana also results in a preoccupation with individual soteriology, which in turn characterizes the New Laity. The social environment within which the pursuit of individual soteriology becomes possible is the consequence of a collective participation in mutually shared and confirmed perspectives. These shared perspectives must be contextualized within the totalizing cosmological schema and metahistorical project that delineate the preservation of the sāsana. Situated thus, we can observe how phenomenological understandings underlie the causal conditions and relations between cosmos and world, individual and society. These phenomenological understandings, to which I devote chapter 2, may be most concisely described in terms of the revitalization of a particular epistemic assertion about the constitution of reality.

LAITY: WHO MEDITATES?

At the annual Mahasi festival in December 1994, sangha representatives from each of the 332 branch organizations around the country convened and compiled the figures for the total number of yogis who had attained insight (nyanzin) and perhaps enlightenment in their centers since the opening of MTY in 1947.[33] The number came to over a million (1,085,082). Further demographic research is required to determine the composition of meditators at all of these centers. However, one thing that seems evident from the numbers—a thing the center's executive committee members and teaching sayadaws all insist on, as well—is that meditation is not narrowly restricted to any one class of people, such as the urban middle class, farmers, or elderly people. Interest in meditation, they say, is widespread among all sectors of Burmese society.[34] The higher visibility of middle-class people in the movement, at least in Yangon, results from their being better able to afford the opportunity to practice meditation and to do so at unrestricted times of the year. (Their intellectual preoccupations and the roles they play in their institutions' support and hierarchy are also more visible.) Farmers, by contrast, may be limited by the seasonality of their work. Nevertheless, in their off-season, many farmers also visit centers to practice for shorter periods of time.[35] Indeed, during the off-season, busloads of yogis travel from the countryside to practice together. If it is at all possible to meditate at MTY, this is what people prefer because the main center affords comforts that the others do not. The Hititi Voluntary Organization helps people of more modest means pay for their stay.

Paralleling the model for monks mentioned earlier, there is a traditional Burmese formulation that in the last third of their lives, laypeople should also turn their attention to the monastery. There, they are to take precepts and meditate in anticipation of setting up auspicious conditions for the next life.[36] In this context, the older people have always tended to be concerned with meditation in a wholehearted way. Though I was unable to procure statistics for male yogis visiting the center, I was able to get precise data regarding the characteristics of women yogis practicing there between December 25, 1993, and July 22, 1994. Contrary to the expectation that meditation would be the preoccupation of the elderly, I found that at MTY, slightly more than half of the women yogis who came for practice (624 of 1,236 in my sample) were under the age of forty. A total of 466 women yogis were under the age of thirty, and 174 were under the age of twenty. To practice at MTY, the lay individual makes a formal request at the Nuggaha office. Typically, laity must be sponsored or recommended by an individual who has already practiced in the Mahasi system. This requirement, I was told, is intended to keep out "insincere" people, meaning those who are interested in the practice and the Yeiktha only as means of status enhancement or who come for other cynical reasons. Also, the center refuses individuals with a history of mental illness. Applicants fill out a form detailing such information as name, age, sex, and place of residence. A strict bookkeeping is made of the numbers of yogis who visit the center in order to maintain records for fund-raising efforts (particularly the solicitation of monthly dues), to track the areas in Burma from which yogis come, and to compile statistics on the number of yogis who have achieved nyanzin or even *magga phala,* the final insights that culminate in enlightenment. These two categories of achievement, called path and fruit, are blurred for purposes of the statistics, since the ability to know the degree of attainment in the practice of satipaṭṭhāna vipassanā is believed to be the purview only of an omniscient Buddha.

As the prospective yogis walk into the administrative office, they find on a chalkboard to the right the number of yogis, monks, and *thilashin* (nuns) presently at the center. Also listed is the number to date of yogis (monks and laity) who have attained nyanzin or enlightenment since the opening of the MYT and its branch centers, arranged by district. (Jokingly, I asked a senior member of the Women's Welfare Association, which shares a desk with registration, how it was that the Shan District had the largest number of enlightenments. The woman replied, somewhat sardonically, "Well, the Shan are very devoted Buddhists! But of course they may be building up their numbers . . . so that they can look better. Probably, here [at MTY] there are more people passing the course.")

An important demographic detail concerning meditators is the fact that the large majority are women: the ratio of women to men is quoted as roughly five to one. The president of the MTY Nuggaha explained to me that women are more involved in all religious activities at the center, not just in meditation; as she put it, "At a funeral sermon the first two or three rows will be men and then the next ten will be all women." The reasons offered to explain this by some influential women donors and by monks I interviewed on the subject varied from practical to psychological to theological. I devote space in chapter 4 to the nature and consequences of women's involvement in meditation and its relation to political issues, so I will not explore that subject here. I wish to recount, however, one important event in the history of meditation at the center that relates to the number of women practicing.

In the early 1980s, a glamorous movie star by the name of Ma Canda sensationalized the practice of meditation by shaving her head and taking temporary ordination as a thilashin at MTY. This is said to have caused a tremendous upsurge in the number of young women pursuing both vipassanā courses at MTY as well as temporary ordination. The *nahtwin* (ear-boring ceremony), traditionally a girl's rite of passage that parallels a boy's *shinpyu* (novice ordination), became less interesting to urban middle-class families. They began, in large numbers, to have their daughters ordained temporarily. At MTY, this resulted in instituting summer meditation courses, held for some two hundred children at a time. Girls of high school and college age also went in groups to the center.

Finally, beginning in the late 1950s, MTY became popular among foreigners from both Buddhist and non-Buddhist countries: Australia, England, Germany, India, Korea, Malaysia, Nepal, Singapore, Sri Lanka, Sweden, Thailand, and the United States are among the countries named in the registration records. Two residence complexes were built for foreign visitors and VIPs. In some cases, these visitor/practitioners became channels for later MTY missionizing work abroad. Invitations offered to monks to visit these yogis' home countries often resulted in the establishment of branch organizations in those places.

Significance of Satipaṭṭhāna Meditation Practice for the Organization of the Sangha

The appearance of Mahasi Sayadaw, the existence of the institution that bears his name, and the new orientation of the laity with the rise of the mass lay meditation movement have had significant consequences for the organization of the sangha as well. This structural change—in conformity with what I have been calling the restitution of the ternary order—can be recognized at three levels in the monastic order. The first is the level of the institutional arrangements at MTY itself, which is an important microcosm of all that has constituted the general trend. At MTY, we can see the dynamics of relations between lay associations (kopaka apwe) and monk's interests. The second level concerns the theological basis for a new kind of sect formation within the sangha. Here, we see the new distinction between those monks who concentrate on scriptural studies (pariyatti) and those specializing in meditation (paṭipatti), which spells out the reorganization of traditional sectarian patterns. The writings of Mahasi Sayadaw as well as the choice he made regarding his own sect affiliation were instrumental to the new arrangement's establishment. Finally, the government's participation in sangha purification is key to understanding both the ways in which the sangha relates to its patrons within the sangha-state-laity pattern and how the sangha can act as a clearinghouse for resistance movements by monks and laity.

Among the first notable characteristics of the Yeiktha as an institution is the situation of the Nuggaha relative to the order of monks at the center. Hanging in a prominent position in the administrative hall of the Yeiktha, which is the gateway to further access into the activities at the center, is a painting depicting the Buddha. In this painting, numerous laypeople surround the Buddha most closely, evidently listening to a discourse from him. At the periphery of the scene are a few monks, whose positioning indicates the artist's intention to depict them as occupying a secondary rank. The Buddha is preaching to the laypeople, and according to the scriptures, hearing the Buddha's teachings conditions one for enlightenment.

The connotation extends directly to the founding situation at the Yeiktha, in which the monk and chief preceptor (*ovadacariya sayadaw*) who established the institution, Mahasi Sayadaw, is the teacher at whose side stand the laypeople who benefit from his teachings. Mahasi is the most revered teacher for this age, and among the learned at the Yeiktha and outside it, one hears the expression "Mahasi thathana," which mirrors the idea of the "Buddha sāsana." Indeed, the establishment of MTY as an institution reflects the contemporary mythical interpretation of how the Buddha established his own sāsana. The emphasis is on an exemplar: the Buddha taught by example, and he responded to questions put to him by laypeople. When the Yeiktha was being formed, rather than the kopaka apwe proceeding on its own authority in the establishment of rules, schedule, and internal associations, the laypeople would approach Mahasi Sayadaw and request permission for what they desired. For instance, Mahasi was asked to give permission for buildings to be offered, to allow old yogis to take up permanent retirement and residence at the center, and endorse the formation of voluntary associations to attend to the needs of women yogis and to provide for indigent yogis unable to pay for basic meals and medicines while undertaking meditation courses. In responding favorably to such requests, Mahasi accommodated simultaneously the needs of the center, the requests of the laity in pursuit of meritorious actions, and the requirements and restrictions of monks living at close quarters with laity.

The premise for this kind of formative pattern at the center drew, as I have suggested, from the example of how the Buddha reputedly established vinaya rules. Those rules were meant to promote higher sīla for monks, for purposes of cultivating the requisite pāramī. Many of the rules were created in response to the laity's petitions of the Buddha regarding the behavior of monks. At the Yeiktha, Mahasi also adjudicated over practices concerning lay yogis.

A monks' organization emerged following the passing of Mahasi Sayadaw, who had been responsible for nearly all aspects of the center's development. Through the monks' organization, the lay Nuggaha committee negotiated changes and made decisions at the center.

Though I have never seen it, I understand that the Mahasi monks' organization owns a separate building in downtown Yangon, where they conduct their meetings . . . away from the center. The political tug between the lay executive committee and the nayaka sayadaws (senior monk teachers) concerned issues such as monk assignments, expulsions, and how to manage the coresidence of laity and monks in the same compound. Although monks may resent being under the thumb of the laity, the arrangement invokes legitimacy from the structurally similar role kings assumed toward the sangha in classical Burmese Buddhist configurations. The laity, for their part, are anxious for the Yeiktha to remain clear of scandal and infamy. A scandal at the Yeiktha would surely invite the government, ever suspicious of the center, to attempt to "purify" MTY by replacing the existing monks with its own members, as well as installing its own kopaka apwe.

Members of the lay kopaka apwe not only combat a government takeover of their association but also seek to counter critical popular conceptions of the Yeiktha. MTY is a hybrid institution, holding together contradictory purposes and populations. Though the center is widely known and has many branches and though other lay meditation institutions are modeled after it, it remains a new invention from a certain perspective. All nine sangha sects are represented at the Yeiktha, but the Mahasi *nee* (division; that is, the Mahasi division within the sangha) is not, strictly speaking, a sect but a new kind of sangha grouping.

MTY counteracts most negative public opinion by virtue of the fact that it attracts respected monks to its midst. Good monks draw the devotion of laity—and the wealth of the dāna that follow. Mahasi monks are well-off indeed. The fame of individual Mahasi monks also grows in the context of vipassanā training, which, though highly systematized, is very much an art as well. Individuals flock to the center to be associated with monks who embody the dhamma and through whom they may participate in the radiating quality of protection, insight, wisdom, and merit.

There is tremendous competition to become a supporter of a famous monk—a fact not missed by monks from outlying areas, who vie fiercely for permission to stay at the center. In the eyes of the center's critics, these monks are growing spoiled on the donations of the laity and becoming entangled in worldly materials, all of which portends a decline in their purity. This is where the kopaka apwe is expected to mediate. The Nuggaha is supposed to handle the wealth donated for the monks, but it operates under a slight conflict of interest in this regard. On the one hand, members of the Nuggaha are involved in making their association the chief donor to the monks, but on the other hand, the lay association that they strive to build up is intended to be independent of the monks. In the early years of the center, Mahasi Sayadaw forbade the kopaka apwe from soliciting funds for the institution because he felt the external fund-raising approach was antithetical to the ideal of dāna. Soliciting donations in the marketplace, he thought, was unseemly: people who wished to donate were to do so freely through their own intentions so that the cosmic benefits would accrue to them directly. More recently, the purportedly healthy financial status of MTY evokes resentment in some quarters and questions as to the sincerity of the center's administrators and monks. At the Ministry of Home and Religious Affairs, where I spent some of my research time, antagonism and even animosity toward MTY was palpable. This attitude, it was sometimes revealed, also stemmed from existing divisions between former members of the U Nu government who "took refuge" at the Yeiktha following the coup and members of the present regime.

On a number of occasions, the Nuggaha committee has expelled monks from the center because of unseemly conduct. The decision is taken by the chief nayaka sayadaws, often with the recommendation of the Nuggaha. It was stressed to me that laity do not make such decisions, although they stand behind the process; only monks can decide matters of expulsion, in accordance with technical-legal considerations and interpretation of the vinaya. A carefully organized network of *wunzao* (working) monks (those who perform various administrative and upkeep tasks at MTY) is responsible for assuring that no impropriety occurs at the center. Yogis and monks are kept strictly to their schedules of meditation. Movement within the compound is extremely restricted, and in every corner, there are lay-persons and monks responsible for observing the activities in their building, floor, or area between compounds. The sounds of the iron stick bell mark the times for meditation in couplets—*chak-chak, chak-chak, chak*—announces the five o'clock hour, while the deep resonant tones of the log striker call the yogis to their two daily meals. No superfluous activity is indulged, and silence is upheld.

A NEW SECTARIAN ARRANGEMENT: SACRED PROPERTY AND PARIYATTI VERSUS PAṬIPATTI

In 1980, the government's Sangha Purification and Unification Act led to the expulsion of many sangha members and the imposition of a limit on sangha divisions to nine *gaing* (sects). At that time, Mahasi Sayadaw was asked by the Burmese Socialist Program Party (BSPP, in power from 1962 to 1988) if he would like to be the head of his own gaing—to be included in the nine permitted. Mahasi declined, with the rationale that vipassanā was not relevant to sectarian distinctions. All monks, irrespective of sect affiliation, were welcome to practice vipassanā at MTY.

With this proclamation, Mahasi was distinguishing a different logic by which the sangha ought, in his view, to be organized by the state—according to the monks' engagement either as scriptural (pariyatti) monks or as meditation (paṭipatti) monks. For Mahasi, sectarian distinctions based on disciplinary interpretations of the vinaya—the most common cause for sectarian disagreement—had the potential of limiting the vipassanā movement to the activities of a single cult. Emphasis on the pariyatti-paṭipatti distinction serves to crosscut the strength of gaings as the primary organizing principle of orthodoxy in the sangha. The very logic of purification is affected because meditation rather than observance of the vinaya becomes the focus of the effort and outlook.

This new arrangement was nothing short of revolutionary for its time. And Mahasi Sayadaw's own trajectory within the sangha shows us why. Mahasi was originally ordained as a Shweygin monk. But the Shweygin raised a number of valid objections that resulted in lingering controversy over Mahasi's methods and the center—principally, the suitability of laity and monks living in close proximity. In time, the acceptance of the lay claim to the penultimate practice of meditation overshadowed this objection and became a new kind of orthodoxy in itself. A related issue that rankled the Shweygin with regard to the Mahasi movement concerned the Buddha Sāsana Nuggaha Apwe organization itself. According to convention, monastic grounds offered to a monk became sect property (*ganika*). In this case, the Shweygin wanted the Yeiktha to belong to them. Thus, can we see not only the emergence of new practices and institutions that absorbed the laity and helped reorganize the sangha but also the development of a new institutional space within the overall sacred geography of Burmese Buddhism. The new classification of landownership strengthened the kopaka apwe pattern and impacted state taxation and the devolution of religious property. The laity could claim more legal control of religious space, which worked to the detriment of the state as well as the sangha because religious lands are not controlled by the state and are not easily subject to nationalization and taxation.

CATEGORIES OF SACRED PROPERTY AND THE STATUS OF MTY

Sacred property categories classify religious holdings according to several determinations. Whereas the monk's code of conduct prohibits him from owning anything more than his requisites (robes, alms bowl, umbrella, and needle and thread), the sangha is the primary locus for lay donations. Dāna is considered the minimal practice for the Buddhist laity, and the greatest portion of the sangha's discourses and remonstrations to laity concern its importance, as discussed in chapter 3.

I will prefigure the discussion there to address property donation germane to the present context of MTY's institutional founding and growth. Lay practices directed at proximate and ultimate soteriologi-cal goals become intermeshed with the practical and penultimate goals of the sangha and the perpetuation of the sāsana more generally. The meritorious status or standing of the dāna recipient impacts the results accruing to the donor and is part of the logic by which sacred property is classified into four categories: *sanghika* (the Sangha of the Four Quarters; that is, all the members of the order in every direction), *ganika* (a division or grouping within the sangha), *poggalika* (an individual within the sangha), and *sāsanika* (relating to all residual types of donation that are offered on behalf of the sāsana more generally, as, for example, pagodas). The most meritorious category is sanghika, as it refers to property that belongs to the sangha in its abstract entirety, undifferentiated by individuals or groupings within the order. The sangha-as-institution is considered the most meritorious category because it represents the Buddha's teachings in time and space. The individual accomplishments of the particular monk-recipient do not impact the merit location of the dāna if the donor intends to give to the Sangha of the Four Quarters. Intention is critical to these considerations.

In a dhamma discourse given at Mahasi Yeiktha, a monk explained to the assembled laity the importance of intention (*cetanā*) in donating and the importance of designating one's donations as sanghika. The story involved a monk in a village monastery who did not keep strictly to his code of conduct. In that village, there was a pious donor who worked hard to scrape together money in order to make a donation. He had observed this monk's poor conduct on various occasions and had even scolded him for his bad behavior. On the day the donor was ready to make his donation, he approached the monk with great reverence and made his offering to him with the utmost respect. The following day, the monk saw the donor and approached him, expecting to receive the reverence and respect he had been accorded the previous day. Instead, however, the donor chastised him. Surprised, the monk asked why the man treated him so differently on this occasion. The donor explained that the day before, he had made offerings to the robes and not to the person. The story concluded with the admonishment to have right intention (*samma sankappa*) while performing donations and to have clearly fixed in one's intention the whole of the sangha as the object of one's giving. At Mahasi, monks may ask donors to verbally designate their intentions as to the categories of their offerings, encouraging them to offer sanghika in order that the most benefits will redound to the donor. In practice, individuals and groups within the sangha become associated with particular resources of religious property holdings, since the sangha is not organized as a church but rather as a number of independent monads.[37] Poggalika, or individual property, represents the least meritorious category from a doctrinal perspective because the merit basis for the donation depends entirely on the particular spiritual development of the individual monk-recipient. Since ordinary human beings can only guess at enlightenment—only a Buddha truly knows what an individual has attained—the uncertainty involved in offering to an individual makes poggalika donations less desirable in this light. From the donor's perspective, giving to virtuosi monks, especially allegedly enlightened monks, tends to outweigh any uncertainties about their actual achievements. Moreover, individual status accrues to the donor of a virtuosi monk, particularly if one has established himself or herself as a monk's chief donor. In accordance with a logic I describe more fully in chapter 3, establishing oneself as a key donor for a famous monk is an extremely competitive undertaking, often entailing bitter rivalries among the laity.[38] Assuring one's status as a *pongyi-daga* (monk supporter) can be tricky. I spoke with a number of donors who explained with disappointment how they were not pongyi-daga because the monk to whom they had made poggalika offerings had disrobed.

Another reason why poggalika property is less meritorious than sanghika or even ganika property is related to the way in which a monk can use or dispose of individual donations. A monk may transfer this property to whomever he chooses. At issue for the lay donor is the question of whether the donation leaves the sphere of the sāsana and becomes profane. In such a case, the donation loses some of its metaphysical leverage to return merits in a future life.

How do monks dispose of their individual donations? One of the ovadacariya sayadaws at MTY claimed that kinship is the most critical factor in a monk's donation of individual poggalika property. Most often, property transfers from a monk to his monk nephew, he said, or to laypeople, typically relatives.

U Zitilla, a renowned meditation monk at the Yeiktha, explained to me how he is offered many poggalika donations, especially by laywomen who practice meditation under his guidance and feel personal gratitude to him. He sends some of this money to the village monastery in Pyinmana, where he is the abbot. The larger portion stays within the central MTY branch, where he resides most of the time. The donations contribute toward building construction, the festival for Mahasi Sayadaw's birthday, electricity, and other needs of the center. Nephews, nieces, and a few close disciples make up the kopaka apwe at his village monastery and decide all the affairs of the monastery according to U Zitilla's wishes. His nephew and a student friend handle the money.[39]

Ganika is property owned by a division within the sangha. Such corporate groups are typically organized around a charismatic monk or descend from the lineage of a charismatic monk. E. Michael Mendelson's account of sectarian rivalries in the sangha in the nineteenth and early to mid-twentieth century describes the centrality of gaing affiliation to the organization of the sangha and its relation to politics and the king.[40] Sectarianism is a problematic category for orthodox Burmese Buddhist practice, since creating a split within the sangha is considered the highest offense (a sanghadisesa). A schismatic monk must disrobe, and the kammic retribution for his actions is as heavy as that meted out for drawing the blood from a Buddha.[41]

The last property category, sāsanika, appears to be a category in the making, for the term sāsanika is not commonly employed; educated laypeople and monks often express confusion over what exactly it refers to. Mendelson makes no mention of sāsanika property, although, following May Oung (1914), O. H. Mootham (1939), and Sisir Chandra Lahiri (1951), he identifies a category of property "vested in the public at large and . . . made up of pagodas, rest houses, ordination halls, and religious edifices not defined by the other classes, together with their structures and lands."[42] This "category of the remainder" is not identified by name. Its salience as a donation category was not yet relevant in the late 1950s, when Mendelson did his fieldwork. Utility of the sāsanika category became relevant only in the aftermath of the mass lay meditation movement in response to the new institutional arrangements represented by centers such as MTY. The following account by a ministry adviser in the Department of Religious Affairs points up the logic by which this "residual category" of "property vested in the public at large" is identified as an object for donation and as an object for lay trusteeship:

> If a donor states that he wants to give to Shwedagon Peyah, it can only go to Shwedagon [the most sacred and prestigious pagoda in Burma]. There are no two Shwedagons so there is no confusion. It is inanimate—a religious edifice. How can it accept their donation? A lifeless object cannot accept. So on behalf of the pagoda someone takes possession for the insentient thing. These are called "treasures belonging to an edifice." The problem is this. One man taking care of one pagoda is okay—the pagoda is always silent. If the individual is faithful and sincere it is all right. But, if there are two or more trustees in the kopaka apwe the problem comes out of the trustees not out of the pagoda. So many donors from different parts of the world, especially cosmopolitan cities, come to give to the pagoda. So all these offertories go into the hands of trustees. So management is important. If one person betrays—a dispute and case arises. About 90% of vinicchaya cases involve members of a kopaka. . . . Executive committee members' behavior may be to take something.

Edifices and other "insentient" things have only to be named as belonging to the sāsana. What makes the lay meditation center different is the fact that it is lay *owned*. This matter has been a source of consternation for both the sangha and the state. From both their perspectives, the lay kopaka apwe at MTY exercises too much control over the institution. Monks do not like to take orders from laity or be overly implicated in their projects.[43] Yet, because the institution caters predominantly to laity, monks are constrained by their *pātimokkha* rules of conduct from engaging in lay affairs and must therefore succumb to the directives of the lay Nuggaha committee. The state, for its part, is never happy to see monks and laity living together in close quarters for fear they will align themselves against the authorities. To check these tendencies, various spies (monks, wardens, kappia, and yogis) are planted at MTY to oversee the goings-on there. To protect its arrangements, the Yeiktha's trustee association, Buddha Sāsana Nuggaha Apwe, has been successful in carving out a new religious category status for laity, as can be observed through such materially tangible demonstrations as receiving state tax-exempt status for the center. However, the Yeiktha must perpetually renegotiate this status for various items donated to the center. In 1995, for instance, there was great consternation over attaining government approval to own a copy machine, which is usually against the law.

The stability of this category seems especially fragile, and I have heard monks and laity identify the Yeiktha grounds as being alternatively Mahasi ganika, sāsanika property, or simply lay owned. MTY can be viewed as a complex of donation *intentions*. A building may be sanghika or poggalika or sāsanika. Even individual floors of multi-level buildings may be owned by the sangha or by a particular monk; I was assured that if a monk wanted to leave the center, he would be allowed to remove every brick of the story donated to him. I have heard the sāsanika category referred to, on one hand, as the uttermost superior category of religious property (for example, when alluding to the Shwedagon) and, on the other, as the most inferior religious property category (when describing property owned by laypeople). The confusion arises over conflicting notions about sacred potency. The laity is an inferior donation category, and this adds to the confusion over the sāsanika religious property category. Despite these ambiguities, however, the religious affairs adviser at the ministry defined sāsanika religious property for me in unequivocal terms:

From the outset at the time of donation, if laymen and monks can use the donation for the sāsana as members of the sāsana—if everyone is eligible to use the offering—then it is sāsanika property. Examples of things that belong to the religion are pagodas and cetiyas [stupas]. Things a person is entitled to use, practice and avail themselves of in order to go after the teachings of the Buddha. Mahasi Yeiktha is classified as sāsanika property. It is not a monastic compound. You can wear shoes, plant, use umbrellas—it belongs to the whole religion. Sāsanika is the superior most category it is not only for Buddhists but for everyone in the world. Monastic rules and regulations cannot interfere with sāsanika religious property.

He then proceeded to explain to me how it was the government's job to make sure that MTY was maintaining the purity and orthodoxy of the institution on behalf of the sāsana.

We are keeping watch on this Nuggaha. If there is any misconduct at the center then we will take over the kopaka apwe. It's only a matter of time before they slip up. . . . The ruler decides about sāsanika. They decide the lives of their subjects. They are the lords of all. There are no rules against a king killing or committing homicide. The raja is owner. He can take it back by order or confiscate *sāsana wuduka* [land property]. Rulers are final authorities. Only rulers cannot interfere with the *sima* [ordination site]. That can be removed, canceled, or constructed only by the sangha, not kings. So only the sima is outside the king's rule. The Burmese mentality of government is still that of kings.[44]

MTY is sāsanika property. Monks, nuns, laymen and laywomen, children, and non-Buddhists may all use it. This is "property vested in the public at large." However, the function of the meditation center as a property held in trust for the public is of an entirely different sort than previously found in Burma. It is not a monument or edifice for the recollection of the Triple Gem, or Buddha-Dhamma-Sangha (which is usually the work of kings), nor is it an institution strictly in support of ordination and perpetuation of the sangha (activities in the realm of monks). The lay meditation center is preoccupied with a universalizing ideal about the possibility of enlightenment for any person from any walk of life or any place in the world, whether Buddhist or not. During the Ne Win period when the regime closed the country, meditators from all over the world were still permitted to enter Burma on meditation visas. Gustaaf Houtman reports that meditation was the country's largest export for a time.[45]

PARIYATTI VERSUS PAṬIPATTI INSTITUTION

The emphasis on MTY as a paramattha (ultimate reality) institution—because of its focus on nibbāna—became iterated in all sorts of ways at the Yeiktha. In many respects, the Shweygin sect pressure on Mahasi Sayadaw helped spur and shape the development of the center as it struggled to define the basis for its claims about conforming to orthodox norms. The final break with the Shweygin occurred following a miraculous claim made by a yogi who had practiced for two months at MTY. The young and uneducated peasant woman from the countryside reportedly became the "channel" through which a devā (celestial being) began to speak in Pāli, in a high-pitched and wavering voice. She requested an audience with Mahasi Sayadaw. Over the course of a few days, Mahasi is said to have engaged in conversation in Pāli with the young woman/devā before witnesses. The conversations were reportedly tape-recorded.

When the devā spoke, the yogi's voice became high and squeezed, and it undulated melodiously, producing an eerie effect. The conversation with the devā finds its parallel form in the canonical texts where the Buddha expounds the dhamma to the benefit of devās and men. Mahasi's teachings are verified in this account in the heavenly as well as the human realms. Devās come to hear the teachings when a profound teacher emerges.

News of the event became a sensation, and laity and monks flocked to MTY in the belief that the conversation with the devā was a special sign of Mahasi's enlightened accomplishments. The Shweygin demanded that Mahasi resign from their sect—not because the appearance of the devā in this fashion was incredible to them but because it was an unorthodox sort of involvement. Mahasi left the Shweygin sect and was reordained into the Thudhamma sect. Lay critics I spoke to claimed that this had been a publicity stunt, for it put Mahasi and the Yeiktha firmly on the map as a center of lay veneration.

There is another story about why Mahasi was rejected from the Shweygin sect, this one coming out of the Buddha Sāsana Nuggaha Apwe at the Yeiktha. The real issue, according to this account, had to do with a different sort of conflict altogether: the Shweygin wanted a board put up at the entrance of the Yeiktha proclaiming the center to be a Shweygin center. Mahasi was, after all, a Shweygin monk, and the sect felt the center should therefore be considered Shweygin (ganika) "property." Unlike other sects within the sangha, such as the Thudhamma sect, the Shweygin sect is distinguished by its emphasis on hierarchy rather than loose autonomy for its member groupings. Thus, its involvement in the center would create another dimension of oversight and control there, which the Nuggaha wished to avoid. Here, we see the ways in which crosscutting claims to religious property may be made. In many cases, these conflicts wind up in the vinicchaya (sangha) courts.

Mahasi's insistence that the meditation center not be considered ganika—the property of a gaing—reiterated the founding logic of the center as conceived by Sir U Thwin and U Nu. According to accounts from monks, MTY trustees, and ministry officials, the classification of an institution depends on the wishes of the original donor. Sir U Thwin was the original donor of the land on which the center would be built, and he contributed the center's first building—the dhammayone (the meditation and discourse hall). He stipulated that the property would belong to a lay trustee committee formed with the help and inspiration of U Nu and several other key cabinet members in the newly independent government. The lay association would be called the Buddha Sāsana Nuggaha Apwe, and Sir U Thwin would be the Nuggaha's first president. From the start, the BSNA was designated as a lay-owned institution, which meant that members of the executive committee would make decisions about which monks would be invited to the center and about succession issues; they even reserved the right to expel monks who did not conform to the code of conduct. The third president of the Buddha Sāsana Nuggaha Apwe, U Hla Kyaing, attributes the vision for the center entirely to Sir U Thwin and adds, "You do not find this kind of center previously."[46]

Mahasi's emphasis on paṭipatti, as compared with gaing-related distinctions, would have significant implications during the purification of the sangha (thathana thanshin ye) by Ne Win's socialist government. The year 1975 would mark the beginning of a period for the redress of sangha laxity by Ne Win. After thirteen years of attempting to secularize the government from all involvement in sāsana activities, Ne Win reversed direction and undertook to purify and unify the sangha. Vipassanā practice had made a great leap in popularity, and there was no sidestepping its influence. Remarkably, Ne Win succeeded where U Nu failed. Beginning in 1980, the unification of all the orders of the sangha began with the requirement that every monk register with the state as a member of one of the nine official sects. All monks were issued identity cards containing this information.

From 1981 to 1987, Ne Win's purification of the sangha would have important implications for Mahasi Sayadaw and for the mass lay meditation movement as a whole. It was during this time that Mahasi's paṭipatti sāsana became affirmed by the government as solidly orthodox. The government went so far as to ban discussions and publications that spoke out against the vipassanā method and its orthodoxy in relation to the canon. Controversy and criticism of the vipassanā method arose concurrently with its rise in popularity.[47] One famous case involved the monk Shin Okkata, who did not accept the so-called paṭipatti sāsana and therefore did not accept the possibility of achieving nibbāna in this life. The government tried him in a vinicchaya court, and he was disrobed.

Scholarly monks, lay religious scholars, and religious affairs ministers I have spoken to all aver that the practice of vipassanā meditation is consistent with the teachings found in the canonical texts. Where there tends to be disagreement is in the smaller details of meditation practice itself—for example, whether one should observe the rise and fall of the breath at the tip of the nose or at the abdomen. Vipassanā is not a nonorthodox sectarian movement, they explain. Its populist appeal coincides with the most orthodox elements within the sangha.[48] A conversation that I had with the head of the Shwegyin sect—Mahasi Sayadaw's original sect and one of the most orthodox divisions in the Burmese sangha—is revealing in regard to the movement's status even among its potential antagonists.

At 103 years of age (the headship of a gaing or monastery is accorded to its oldest living member), the Shweygin Sayadaw was extremely clear and mentally energetic. When I asked him about the lay meditation movement, he explained:

Paṭipatti sāsana was spread by Mahasi. U Nu brought Mahasi and he led people. Other sayadaws did too. Meditation became popular after WWII. They all had their own way, but none was so popular as Mahasi. Before they had Ledi, Mohnyin, SunLun, Taung Pulu. Before WWII every monk preached for dāna and sīla. At monasteries monks give you sīla and they accept dāna. But, according to the teachings, there are three practices to be fulfilled: dāna, sīla, bhāvanā. But, bhāvanā had been left out. Because everything was prospering, they didn't see dukkha [suffering]. So they left out bhāvanā. War broke out. The people suffered and they repented to find a solution for better living. Mohnyin Sayadaw made a meditation center to find a solution for better living. Mohnyin Sayadaw made a meditation center on the verge of WWII. Mohnyin expired around 1940–41 and left no successor. After the war Mahasi and U Nu established the Yeiktha.

This account leaves no doubt as to the orthodoxy of the mass lay meditation movement. It asserts that revitalization of the Buddha's teachings emerges in the aftermath of war and suffering by the people, and it is the monks who lead the people in finding "a solution for better living." U Nu's role is portrayed as that of a facilitator. He finds the exemplary monk and brings him to the political center in the classical pattern of Buddhist kingship. The meditation movement is not the invention of Mahasi and U Nu but a broader movement already in motion; Mahasi is only one of several exemplars teaching meditation and leading the people. Shweygin Sayadaw also signals the causes for the shift in practices by sangha and laity according to orthodox understandings of suffering and delusion. The desire to achieve liberation through vipassanā meditation arises with wisdom about the nature of suffering. Many sangha discourses emphasize to the laity how prosperous times can make one complacent and deluded about the nature of suffering (and salvation). Preliminary practices of dāna and sīla are oriented to soteriological concerns over future auspicious life circumstances and not the ultimate goal of attaining nibbāna and exiting the suffering round of rebirths (saṃsāra).

I would argue that an important shift was implied when the emphasis became placed on meditation. As compared with the system of scriptural learning and vinaya observance that contributes evidentially to sāsana perpetuation, meditation implies the cultivation of *individual* soteriological goals—cultivation of what Burmese Buddhists refer to as ultimate reality (paramattha). Meditation is also, per the traditional pattern, associated with purification. As a combined result, purification has come to conform more explicitly to a logic of intention and motivation, and it is applied everywhere in the same way: to monks, laity, and, most consequentially for the argument of this book, to members of the political regime.

The evidence for the increased importance of meditation relative to scriptural study is hardly obscure. In the early 1990s, the Ministry of Home and Religious Affairs under the State Law and Order Restoration Council (SLORC) government was bifurcated into the Department of Religious Affairs and the Department for the Promotion and Propagation of Sāsana. The Religious Affairs Department concerns itself with monks' affairs (vinaya adherence) and scriptural study. It also oversees a monks' university at Kaba Aye. The Promotion and Propagation Department, as the name suggests, is the government arm for conversion efforts, especially in the hill tribes region. It is also responsible for overseeing and scrutinizing activities at the various meditation (*kammaṭṭhāna*) centers, including MTY. Members of the Promotion and Propagation Department told me directly, "We are concerned with paṭipatti [meditation]." On one wall of the headquarters hangs a huge portrait of Sir U Thwin, lay founder of MTY and now credited with having sparked the widespread establishment of lay meditation institutions throughout Burma. The efforts of the Promotion and Propagation Department to export Buddhism outside of the country to South and Southeast Asia, East Asia, and the West involve meditation almost exclusively. And it is for its renowned meditation teachers that Burma is famous the world over.

The pattern of the alliance of religion and politics that emerged during the Ne Win years and continues today is the basis, as I will show, for the public discourse over sincerity. The public asks: Are the rulers acting sincerely (that is, with pure intentions) when they build pagodas and serve on kopaka apwes and on and on? Or are they being manipulative? This and other questions will be advanced with an investigation into the phenomenology of meditation itself, to which I now turn.

Chapter 2

THE PHENOMENOLOGY OF
SATIPAṬṬHĀNA VIPASSANĀ
MEDITATION

Methodological Considerations

From an ethnographic point of view, meditation presents a challenge as a subject of study. Vipassanā meditation is a private technique for the observation of psychophysical experience. Although the conditions for this practice are carefully structured at MTY and one can refer to this structure in a tangible way, the inward encounter is less accessible. The challenge to the ethnographer is immediately obvious on entering a meditation hall. Dozens or perhaps hundreds of people sit in long rows—straight-backed or slightly bent over, their eyes shut. The hall is utterly silent, save for the twittering of birds and sounds that come in over the private walls of the Yeiktha. When the bell clangs to signal the end of an hour, the yogis (meditators) carefully rise from their sitting positions and make their way to the exits. They do so silently and in slow motion. Every extension of torso, arms, legs, hands, and fingers is done with excruciating precision. As the sayadaws (meditation teachers) admonish, "The yogi should move as though he were an invalid—slowly, slowly, slowly."

Walking meditation—or, rather, pacing in infinitesimally small steps—immediately resumes for the next hour. The process of walking now becomes the object of meditation. "Lifting, moving, placing, shifting, lifting, moving, placing, shifting . . ."—the yogi relies on these labels initially to draw his or her attention and mindful observation to the physical sensations experienced in the body. Every aspect of daily activity, whether the taking of two meals before midday, bathing, attending to personal hygiene, or arranging one's clothes, becomes the material of vipassanā practice at the center. Four hours are allotted for sleep, and the yogi is enjoined to maintain continuous awareness up to the final breath before falling asleep and to observe mindfully the first breath on awakening. "Did you awake on the in-breath or the out-breath?" the sayadaw may inquire.

Apart from brief interviews with a meditation instructor (which comprise one crucial setting where an ethnographer could witness narrative aspects of the structured interiority of meditation), the yogi is admonished to maintain complete silence. The sayadaws explain that proper observation of psychophysical phenomena can only occur if the yogi refrains from speech and slows down bodily movements in order to train the mind to observe mental and physical phenomena distinctly. The mode of kinesthetic comportment is a training tool that assists the yogi in more clearly observing the experience of physical sensations and other sensory inputs. When this is practiced by a large community of meditators continuously throughout the day and night, the environment at the center produces what might be called a collective space of concentration. In fact, even nonmeditators attest to the palpable sensation of this mutually projected state of leaden concentration and perceptive acuity. Reflexively, nonmeditators gingerly navigate around the yogis, bowing their heads and crouching in respectful submission.

Two considerations frame the analysis of this unusual environment and intensely social yet private activity. The first is how to connect our own models of social scientific research to the phenomenon at hand for purposes of comparison and, for lack of a more graceful term, scientific expression. I refer to my subject in this pursuit as interiority. The second notion is Burmese and Buddhist in orientation.

It conforms to the distinction made by practitioners of vipassanā between conventional (*sammuti*) and ultimate (*paramattha*) reality. In its most compelling aspect, the two "systems" of analysis are intertwined, as I will explain more fully.

Anthropological research has yielded a number of theories as to how interiority is reflected in communicative and structural features of observed society. Examples of interiority studied by anthropologists include ritual, embodiment (of suffering, identity, or skill, for instance), artistic expression, and classification patterns. For the most part, phenomena that begin with internal experiences are seen to end in specific collective experiences and representations of or in the world. Ultimately, norms and social orders mirror, metaphorically or otherwise, these representations. Thus, to choose an example that stands close to mine, Stanley Tambiah analyzes a Thai Buddhist meditation practice as a performative ritual in which the yogi is taken through a guided meditation and enjoined to imagine, or create mental visualizations of, sacred geographies and experiences.[1] These performative rituals evoke in the meditator a first-person experience of social representations of cosmic realities and in turn become "blueprints for social action."

Although it is true that the realization of meditative insights (suffering, impermanence, and so forth) is dependent on the enactment or performance of meditation, this is not the only or even the principal site of realization. I would argue instead that in seeking to interpret the interiority of meditation practice, at least in Burma, one must take account of the fact that intervening between the experience of meditation practice and the cultural norms or symbolic or linguistic representations that apparently stream from that practice, there stands a complex native theory of interiority that classifies and sorts meditative experiences into a distinct way of knowing. An anthropological treatment that ignores this native philosophy/psychology, as it were, and its effects on individuals' interpretations of their meditation experience would be incomplete. In this respect, I propose to depart from the implicit objectivist position embraced by many anthropologists who seek an understanding of the relationship between mind and society. Though not the latest representative of the approach I am departing from, Claude Lévi-Strauss was most concise in its expression roughly fifty years ago:

[F]acts can more easily yield to structural analysis when the social group in which it is manifested has not elaborated a conscious model to interpret or justify it. . . . For conscious models, which are usually known as "norms," are by definition very poor ones, since they are not intended to explain the phenomena but to perpetuate them . . . the more obvious structural organization is, the more difficult it becomes to reach it because of the inaccurate conscious models lying across the path which leads to it.[2]

Invoking another classical scholar, I propose taking seriously Emile Durkheim's suggestion that religion is a "theory of knowledge."[3] I will not, however, *pace* Durkheim and many later anthropologists of religion, quickly locate the public or collective representation of that "native theory" in either ritual or symbolic facts and declare it a mere cultural epiphenomenon of a rational truth to which only the scientist is privileged. "The discovery of irrationalities everywhere," Bruce Kapferer comments in the introduction to his book on sorcery in Sri Lanka, "is one of the pastimes of anthropologists."[4]

But to return to the mind-society trajectory, I do not mean to deny that, grossly speaking, something like this (that is, a passage from private experience to public meaning) is what happens—if that were the case, it would be folly to pursue explanation in the current venue. One might sooner construct a tone poem or some other art form to evoke the private but universal experience of meditative insight: for this sort of evocation, art is uniquely suited. I want only to introduce a layer of subtlety in the analysis of the gap that exists between experience and communication or between percept, which is privately experienced (in the refrain of Maurice Merleau-Ponty, for example),[5] and concept, which can only be publicly held (as described in Durkheim or Clifford Geertz).

This way of stating my intent puts me more meaningfully in opposition to another great anthropological theorist, of more recent vintage. Marshall Sahlins has declared on a number of occasions, "There is no immaculate perception." He cites Franz Boas, with great approbatory finality, as saying that "the seeing eye is the organ of tradition."[6] This is meant to imply an automatic and immediate transition from percept to concept or, rather, a prefigurement of the former by the latter—what Charles Hirschkind describes as a "tradition-cultivated mode of perception."[7] Hirschkind goes some distance toward presenting a processual view of the way perception plays into the formation of belief and ideology in Muslim Egypt. Bruce Kapferer goes a step further in his inclusive analysis of sorcery in Sri Lanka, where, he says, "[s]orcery often takes the human body and its *primacy of perception* as foundational of sociality and of the paradoxes of social existence. Among Sinhalese, the senses through which human beings extend and realize their existence in the world—those of sound, smell, taste, touch, and sight—become, in the notions of sorcery, the processes whereby human beings are disrupted and inhabited by others to ill-effect."[8]

My departure from these three worthy formulations, each to their ethnographic and philosophical context, comes directly from my field experience. In the context of Buddhist Burma, an entire philosophy of mind, equivalent in scope to the disciplines of psychology or existential phenomenology, is devoted to the relationship between percept and concept. Situated as it is within a religious cast of interpretation—in Burma, at least, it is Buddhist principles that are affirmed, per Boas's golden rule—its analysis remains germane to ethnological objectives. But it does so by means of a conveyance of concepts that are evaluative rather than predetermined, that are the sorting and proving grounds for two rather different kinds of truth than the terms *tradition, performance, practice* or *blueprints for action* might suggest.[9] I refer to the Burmese Buddhist interpretation of meditative experience as a kind of native epistemology, and it is to this subject and its relevance to political constructions or meanings that I devote this chapter.

Satipaṭṭhāna Vipassanā Meditation:
The Mahasi Method and Its Orthodox Foundations

Vipassanā meditation is a first-person, empirical investigation of cognitive procedures and mechanisms. It is made up of rigorous procedures for evaluating truth claims concerning the nature of the relationship between knowing and being. Vipassanā meditation is a theory of knowing that asserts a claim for knowledge over the causal relations between material and mental phenomena as they arise in first-person experience. The ultimate purpose of vipassanā meditation is to discern the conditions for human suffering—a preoccupation it shares with all religious traditions, in a departure from the quasi-utilitarian or normative orientation of the sciences. Vipassanā meditation is a practical technique and method for a *moral* empirical theory of knowing, praxis, and being.

In vipassanā meditation, the objects of evaluation are not inferred. Inductive and deductive logic are not the operative conventions; indeed, these are shunned as improper tools with which to access the intrinsic properties of consciousness or, more methodologically put, the ways in which the knowing can know itself. Furthermore, the method (that is, insight meditation) for assessing how false belief formation comes about is simultaneously the technique by which the systematic process for belief revision is accomplished as an intuitive and universal progression of insights. This progression of insights is held to culminate in an irrevocable epistemic break with former ways of perceiving and knowing the world, simultaneously resulting in an ontological reconstruction or transformation of being.

In the meditative process, the individual's mode of perception is drawn away from conceptualization, which produces the sense of wholes, schemata, representations, and conventional understandings of space and time. The transformation is toward the perception of a disaggregated experience of such wholes in which the object of consciousness and the mind that knows it are simultaneously apprehended at the moment of their arising and immediate disappearing—

for thoughts, feelings, and sensory perceptions are observed in meditation as transitory. To accomplish this, the meditator is trained in fine-grained observational techniques. Apprehension of experience becomes centered on the point of knowing, which is momentary and directed at single focal points (seeing, hearing, smelling, touching, feeling, and so on). Conception, in contrast with perception, is concerned with organizing experience in coherent, consistent, and enduring ways. This is the realm of conventional reality. In addition to being the "place" where arbitrary wholes are constructed in conventional reality, experience is formalized, through conception, into discrete units situated in broader schemata of the world as it is known, marked, and named in processes of or for purposes of communication. This too is made up of arbitrary conceptual divisions of space and time. These are the habits of thinking and experiencing that the yogi attempts to depart from.

As the momentum of concentration builds, the observational ability to train one's attention on the rapid succession of single focal points becomes accelerated, making the discernment of phenomena, external and internal, ascertained on the level of process only. This becomes the basis for deeper and deeper intuitive insights into the nature of *anicca* (impermanence), which is the first fundamental recognition in the path leading toward enlightenment.

With the development of the factors of enlightenment, the yogi experiences stages wherein the perceptions of phenomena become systematically and naturally directed toward a particular mode of knowing. This mode of knowing takes the momentary arising and disappearing of phenomena (*pyit pyit* in Burmese) as distinct occurrences in a causal chain—voluntary (that is, intentional) and involuntary (such as unintended physical phenomena, the spontaneous arising of thoughts, and so forth). In other words, the volitional and operational arisings within consciousness are observed as a process in which the observer notices, on the one hand, the relationship between intention and its result (for example, having the intention to move the arm and then extending it) and, on the other hand, how unintended conditions within the mind arise as a process independent of volition (for example, a moment of unintended anger arising or consequent on an unintended thought or memory). These experiences become the foundations for insights into the universal characteristic of *anattā* (the insubstantiality of self), since the yogi recognizes that there is no doer in the doing; there is merely the process of cause and effect going on without end, whether the yogi intends it or not. Finally, this leads to recognition of the ubiquity of *dukkha* (suffering). Where there is no permanence or substantiality, there can only be unsatisfactoriness and suffering.

Intuitive comprehension of the three universal characteristics (anicca, anattā, and dukkha) is experienced differently according to the particular stage of insight in the progression. However, comprehension of one of the three characteristics is said to be inherent in each and every moment of conscious arising and passing away. These characteristics are comprehended more and more profoundly as the practice progresses. Ultimately, the individual's perceptions of the insubstantial, impermanent, and suffering nature of reality (as a truth arising in each and every moment of the individual's psychophysical process) are seen as transforming his or her speech and actions in the social world through the unprompted, free, and spontaneous mental intentions preceding these agential procedures. In other words, percept and concept are drawn into a correspondent relation in which conceptual modes of representing experience follow and are dependent on a new perceptual foundation.

The deepening awareness about the nature of anicca, dukkha, and anattā constitutes the whole of insight practice. Following attainment of the first stage of enlightenment, the same procedures are again applied, and the progress of insight unfolds once more. However, the building up of the intuitive insight into these three characteristics becomes progressively more difficult as the individual systematically abandons prior (conceptual) "wrong views" about the nature of reality. In their place, the meditator aligns his or her intentional and practical actions in conformity with the wisdom won through this difficult process of epistemic reconstruction and ontological transformation, meaning future rebirths.

Through the repetition of the procedures for intuitive knowing, experience creates a direct knowing in the yogi that is said to be unshakable and irreversible. Realization of the teachings of the Buddha is understood to mean, in its fullest sense, the realization of the four stages of enlightenment: *thotapan, thakadagam, anagam,* and *arahatta* (in Pāli, *sotāpanna, sakadāgāmī, anāgāmī,* and *arahat*). For yogis practicing at the Yeiktha, realization of one or more of the sixteen insights leading up to actual enlightenment is, in itself, said to be experientially transforming. Yogis express greater confidence in the method and goals of vipassanā meditation and are able to intuitively grasp many of the more difficult teachings found in the highly abstruse Abhidhamma text. Since the mid-1960s, the subject of monks' dhamma discourses has reportedly changed to meet the new demand of an enlightened laity. An MTY monk explained to me that laity, especially educated laity living in the urban areas, prefer to have monks expound the most difficult and esoteric teachings found in the Abhidhamma because they have had experiences in their vipassanā training that allow them to grasp these teachings. Moreover, in the 1990s, lay Abhidhamma classes (taught especially by *pothudaw* [lay religious scholars]) began to spring up all over Yangon and other large cities. The concordance between vipassanā meditation and the Abhidhamma has become a form of first-person verification of the texts for the laity. A Mahasi monk, U Aggadhamma, related, "This nyanzin [insight] approach got started in the Mahasi period. Previously, people would not measure their practice by nyanzin. Vipassanā-kammaṭṭhāna is a chapter in Abhidhamma and there is much written about it in the Visuddhimagga [The Path of Purification]. Vipassanā was not so widespread in the days before Mahasi."

According to Buddhist cosmology, the individual reconditions the spontaneous procedures of intention and action over the course of many lifetimes until he or she has come into alignment with the law of dhamma. At the penultimate stage of arahat-ship, all roots of greed (*lobha*), hatred or anger (*dosa*), and delusion (*moha*) become eradicated, not by restraint or temporary suppression but by removing their causes—craving and ignorance. A Burmese aphorism describing this universal truth says, "Unknowing we seize. Knowing we release." The cultivation of wisdom is viewed as a process of releasing or letting go of attachments. Suffering and freedom from suffering are ultimately in the hands of the individual alone. "You are the owner of your own actions," the esteemed meditation teacher U Pandita Sayadaw says, quoting the texts. "Doing unwholesome deeds is like swallowing a ball of molten hot iron."

Vipassanā, or insight contemplation, is the method of meditation prescribed in the Mahasatipaṭṭhāna Sutta and described in greater detail in Buddhaghosa's fifth-century commentary, the Visuddhimagga. Although the Visuddhimagga is not part of the orthodox Pāli Tipitaka canon, Burmese Buddhists consider this classical commentary orthodox. Mahasi Sayadaw's book is a subcommentary on Buddhaghosa's work. It elaborates in greater detail the stages of insight and the textual justifications for a more practical and formalized pedagogical approach to vipassanā practice. What distinguishes the Mahasi method from other techniques of vipassanā meditation, and what has been the basis for controversy over its orthodoxy, has been the taking of the rise and fall (*poun dey pin dey*) of the abdomen as the object for sustained and repeated observation and focus.[10]

Mahasi stressed that because materiality is easier to discern than are mental states, emphasis for the beginning meditator should be on the tactile manifestation of the rise and fall of the breath as it is experienced as pressure and movement. Because breathing is involuntary, the yogi is able to focus on a natural and independent (that is, nonvolitional) process as the object for comprehending the characteristics of one of the four elements—here, the wind element—as it is subject to the laws of impermanence, suffering, and insubstantiality (anicca, dukkha, anattā).[11] Initially, yogis employ conceptual labels to draw their attention to precise objects for observation. Eventually, these labels are dropped, and the yogis come to experience physical sensations, for example, in terms of their sensate qualities (of hardness [earth element], heat [fire element], movement [wind element], and so forth). Mahasi says he selected the satipaṭṭhāna vipassanā method because it is the fastest way for a yogi to establish himself or herself on the path to realization of the nibbānic (enlightenment) goal.[12]

It needs to be reiterated strongly that one of the meditation teacher's primary concerns is whether the yogi is describing an authentic experience or just narrating conceptual knowledge about an experience. In the Mahasi pedagogical manual, determination of whether the yogi has experienced a true level of insight is the greatest preoccupation. The manual is kept secret so that inexperienced persons will not read it and be hindered by attempts to anticipate what is to come next. The type of advice a monk gives is based on his estimate of the yogi's progress. The sayadaw's skill in determining authentic experience is thought critical because an incorrect interpretation could lead the yogi to falsely believe she has finished the meditation course. At the same time, however, a sayadaw can never know with certainty whether the yogi has attained enlightenment—only Buddhas are said to have this knowledge. According to the monk's Pātimokkha (the 227 rules of monastic life), a monk can be disrobed for making declarations of attainment. This taboo is not incumbent on laity, although it is considered gauche and uncharacteristic of a person with true achievement. Making a claim on behalf of a yogi is only cautiously done by monks and usually only in the context of discussing the yogi's progress with other teachers.

At MTY, a tape of Mahasi Sayadaw discussing the stages of insight outlined here is played on half-moon and full-moon days. It is reserved for those yogis who have been determined by a sayadaw to be sufficiently deep in a number of the insights. The yogi listens to the tape and decides for himself what has been experienced. Mahasi developed this "know by yourself" procedure to avoid the dilemma of making declarations. (This does not mean that yogis do not try to communicate their accomplishments to each other and to the outside world after their meditation course. Questions such as "Did you listen to the tape?" or "Did you pass the course?" were common signals referring to having attained the first stage of enlightenment. So too was the polite request after a long meditation period, "Did you get the insurance policy?"—referencing the idea that rebirth in lower realms of existence is forever cut off to the sotāpanna.) The tape is of a discourse Mahasi Sayadaw gave from time to time when there were yogis who had progressed in the practice. The discourse was intended for those who had sufficient insight so that their confidence in the teachings was not clouded with doubts. Hearing the lecture would only inspire greater confidence for further practice.

THE IMPORTANCE OF "SEEING THINGS AS THEY ARE" IN MAHASI PEDAGOGY

Mahasi Sayadaw kept a record of the meditation experiences of his yogi interviews, and he asked meditation teachers under his guidance to do the same. He compiled and analyzed the results with the aim of determining regularities in mental patterns experienced en route to the attainment of nyanzin, or insights leading to enlightenment. His empirical findings became the basis for a manual that would be used to guide "future teachers in interviews with their students or yogis. . . . [I]t will also be useful in judging the yogi's level of vipassanā (insight) knowledge attained."[13] Following the advice of Mahasi and his successors, the Nuggaha controls the distribution of these materials to the branch centers, and only on the advice of a nayaka sayadaw are monk teachers issued a copy of the manual. The president of the Nuggaha told me that these are "very strictly controlled" and that as of 1995, 90 of the original 100 copies of the document were still in the Nuggaha office. It is significant to note that it is the Nuggaha and not the sangha that controls the distribution of this book (although monks have told me that monks make copies and when a monk who has been given the manual dies, the manual disappears). This situation demonstrates how the lay kopaka attempt to assume responsibility for the Mahasi legacy.

The purpose of the manual is described in its introduction:

This book is meant to help the qualified vipassana teachers who had practiced according to the Venerable Mahasi Sayadaw's method and had practiced long enough to appreciate the 16 levels of knowledge. Therefore those who have not practiced the vipassana meditation or those who have not practiced long enough to attain the full 16 levels of knowledge should not be allowed to look at this book. For, if they had known the contents of this book, they might form ideas or concepts on them, or they might not understand and begin to have doubts about the practice. Furthermore they might make condescending remarks which could only cause harm for them. Even if one understands the points made out in this book, one may think about these while meditating. That person's mind would be vulnerable to complex ideas or thoughts. Then the knowledge will not be a pure one (but one with pre-existing knowledge gained by reading) also it can be a hindrance to improving the level of knowledge.[14]

The manual then proceeds to discuss how the teacher ought to evaluate the accounts yogis give of their experiences. It describes three types of yogis, in keeping with a classification based on the level of clarity and ability with which they are able to describe their experiences. The manual provides a means for discerning the differences between accounts given by yogis who relate experiences they have heard about from other people and those given by yogis who have had the experiences themselves. For the first type of yogi in this typology, it is not necessary for the sayadaw to probe with all sorts of questions or to ask leading questions, since such yogis are able to clearly describe their experiences in a systematic manner. For these yogis, it is only "necessary to listen to what they say, giving instructions when necessary, correcting wrong concepts or wrong ways of noting. Sometimes when the yogis are slackening in their practice, lectures or discourses should be given accordingly at an appropriate time" (5–6).

Yogis of the second type are unable to describe their experiences as discrete moments of perception noted at the time they occurred. They are also incapable of describing what they observed step by step, that is, in sequence. The manual explains:

This may be so because of their shyness. In such cases leading questions should be asked when necessary. When such questions are made, the yogi sometimes admitted that he could remember or otherwise. The yogi honestly admitted about his experiences. To test whether the yogi was speaking the true experience or not we asked about the sort of experiences which could not be met as yet; and also which do not relate to the condition of the yogi's experience or sometimes said the wrong thing as if it was right. Sometimes we asked questions that could give two types of answers. From time to time the teacher could ask the honest and frank yogi about things which could have been missed out in the yogi's description of his experiences. (6)

Yogis of the third type cannot "explain well but when the teacher ask[s] some leading questions, they give a reply which they had learned from other people":

Leading questions or hints should not be said to such yogis. Instead the teacher should just listen to his account. If there were points that you would like to know from him, ask questions which could give two types of answers. Or ask for example, "When you were noting on the arising process what did you know, how did you know it?" Ask in such a way that the yogi could not guess what you wish to know. Then only you can know the yogi's true level of concentration and knowledge. This gives you a general idea of interviewing the three type of yogis at each level of knowledge. (6)

This classification of meditator types clearly emphasizes the importance attached to having the yogi approach the practice without preconceptions and with honesty as to what is truly observed. The techniques for confirming that the yogi is really experiencing what she says she is are meant to create as much certainty as possible that her experiences are truly vipassanā insights and not mere conceptualizations. If the yogi should incorrectly assume that she has achieved the first stage of enlightenment, she might become complacent and consequently not secure herself on the path to nibbāna. In her next life, she could be born in states of woe. The meditation teacher would be responsible in large measure for this kammic catastrophe and would himself reap the kammic consequences of having misdirected the yogi by encouraging her to believe she had attained what she had not. Apart from the Buddha's unique ability to discern with certainty another person's attainment, one can only know for oneself by honestly examining one's experiences. Mahasi's successor, U Pandita, writes:

> As yogis practice vipassanā meditation under the instruction of a qualified teacher, they become able to perceive different truths about reality not accessible to ordinary consciousness. These meditative insights tend to occur in a specific order regardless of personality type or level of intelligence, successively deepening along with the concentration and purity of mind that result from proper meditation practice. This list is provided with a strong cautionary note: if you are practicing meditation, don't think about progress! It is quite impossible for even the most experienced meditator to evaluate his or her own practice; and only after extensive personal experience and training can a teacher begin to recognize the specific, subtle signs of this progression in the verbal reports of another meditator.[15]

DHAMMA STRIVING AND THE YOGI-TEACHER RELATIONSHIP

A nayaka sayadaw at Mahasi provided the following Pāli aphorism to emphasize the need for a teacher in meditation practice: "*Yathabhutam nanaya satta parivesitabba*" (To achieve the true and correct knowledge, one should seek and rely upon a teacher). The relationship between sangha and laity is iterated in the relationship between the kammaṭṭhāna (meditation) sayadaw and the yogi. The sangha is the legitimate institutional embodiment for the teachings of the Buddha—that is, the dhamma—and the Buddha's representatives as the repository and perpetuator of those teachings over time. Monks are teachers in the manner that the Buddha was a teacher. They comprise one of the facets of the Triple Gem (Buddha, Dhamma, Sangha). Without the sangha, there can be no perpetuation of the teachings across time. Furthermore, there is the issue of purity. Monks are in a superior position vis-à-vis the yogis because of the number of precepts they observe. In this context, the term *precepts* relates to the degree of moral purity that constrains the individual. The monk who is neglectful of his Pātimokkha is referred to by the laity as "a man in yellow robes." He is a counterfeit monk, an imposter.

The teacher's role is considered essential for the progress of insight, for there are many pitfalls along the way and the path is sometimes discouraging. One must learn the correct way of practice: even monks who retire into the forest begin their training under teachers. For this reason, lineage is of great concern even at MTY. Paṭipatti is ultimately transmitted through a teacher's line. Despite the Nuggaha's control over the Mahasi sāsana in the distribution of the manual and Mahasi books and relics, in sending monks out on dhamma missions, and even in expelling monks who do not keep their sīla, members of the association cannot nor do they want to take over the sangha's unique role.

New yogis attending a meditation course at the Yeiktha are instructed in the manner for reporting at interviews with their teachers. First, they report how many hours of sitting and walking meditation they have performed since their last report. In the beginning, the yogis experience great difficulty in maintaining continuity in the sitting and walking meditation. Only once practice has become firm and concentrated are they able to maintain a continuous, twenty-hour schedule of mindfulness. Before that time, however, the yogis are beset with distractions, classified as *nivarana,* the "five hindrances" (sense desire, ill will, sloth and torpor, restlessness and worry, and skeptical doubt),[16] that obstruct their practice. Becoming "established in mindfulness" is a difficult and arduous task, and in the beginning, the yogis are unable to find the object for observation or to notice when the mind has wandered. The yogis become drowsy or uncomfortable sitting in one position for an hour without moving, or they experience doubt that the practice will amount to anything. The sayadaw attempts to guide them to focus more exacting attention on the characteristics of direct perception experience.

The following is a typical example, drawn from a yogi interview. On the first day of the course, the yogi reported that her back ached. The sayadaw instructed her not to label the place from which the feeling originated but just to note the sensations. In a subsequent interview with the sayadaw, the yogi reported: "I experienced a lot of pain in my back. Then I remembered what the sayadaw instructed and I tried to focus on the sensations of pain. I felt the sensations of heat and hardness. As I observed, these sensations moved around. They didn't stay at one place. When I observed the sensation happening at one place it disappeared and a new sensation came up." From the report of the number of hours a yogi has spent in continuous sitting and walking throughout the day, the sayadaw is able to determine how much effort (*viriya*) the yogi is exerting. This helps the sayadaw gain a rough idea of how much concentration (*samādhi*) the yogi has been able to achieve. He can then evaluate this as one piece of evidence in judging the yogi's reports. With noncontinuous practice, it is difficult to build up the momentum of one's observational skills. Kammaṭṭhāna sayadaws direct the yogi's progress according to an understanding of balance in the yogi's efforts. The seven factors of enlightenment are mindfulness, investigation of states, energy, joyful interest, tranquility, concentration, and equanimity. When one of these factors is missing, the yogi's progress is impaired. It is in this regard that the meditation teacher plays an essential role in directing the yogi. Once the sayadaw has determined that one or more of the balancing factors are missing, he will seek to correct the imbalance by directing the yogi to overcome its opposite. For example, the yogi may find that he has too much concentration and consequently becomes sleepy. The sayadaw will instruct the yogi to increase his effort, since energy is the balancing factor for concentration. He may recommend that the yogi practice more walking meditation rather than sitting meditation. Mindfulness is the most important factor of all because it develops and balances all of the other mental factors. This is the reason why Mahasi stressed mindfulness as the paramount undertaking, since it is a direct path to enlightenment and therefore the most accessible to the laity.

Insights arise systematically as the result of continuous mindfulness. Consequently, the pedagogical emphasis is placed not on the yogi's descriptions of anicca, dukkha, and anattā, for example, but on the quality of the yogi's observational precision and continuity as evaluated by the degree to which he is able to note the object and observe what happens to it following the noting. Sometimes, the yogi may declare that he could see "arising and passing away"—the fourth insight (for example, "the rising of the abdomen and the falling was changing all the time, thus it was anicca impermanence"). However, since this is the fourth insight, it would not be possible without the accompanying level of concentration, effort, and exacting mindfulness. In such instances, the sayadaw gently chides the yogi that these are merely thoughts and imaginations and that he should note "thinking, thinking" when these arise. The experience and the idea-of-the-experience are distinguished according to the depth and exactitude of the yogi's cultivated observational skills.

Because the manual is precise in its instructions and because teaching monks refer to it, I will cite it at length:

> Reporting is a three-phase process. First, the yogi must give the fullest commitment and accuracy when one is looking at an object that has arisen. The yogi must direct their whole attention to penetrate and note objects. Automatic noting, like repeating a mantra, is not correct. Mental notes are intended to direct the yogis attention to what is happening so that one can see clearly what is going on there. The yogi must observe the three phases of observation: observation of the occurrence of the object, noting of the object and describing the sensations occurring during the process (of the rise and fall of the breath and the lifting, moving, placing of the walking). Although the yogi may try there hardest, the mind may still

wander off away from the object of primary observation, at which point a new object has arisen. At this point the yogi must note, "wandering, wandering." They must then describe to their sayadaw what happened after noting in this way. Did the object disappear? Did the mind keep wandering? Did thoughts reduce in their intensity? Did the object disappear? In the event of the disappearance of the wandering mind the yogi is instructed to come back to the basic object of the rise and fall. Invariably after some time of sitting, the yogi encounters unpleasant sensations—a pain, or ache. This should be handled in the same way. The yogi should note, "pain, pain." Now there is a new object arising. The yogi must observe what occurs after noting it. Does it continue to get worse? Does it remain as it was, neither increasing nor decreasing in intensity? Does it disappear? These are the things that should be described to the sayadaw as precisely as possible.

In the process of meditation the yogi will also encounter a wide range of objects beside the basic object of rising and falling, wandering mind and unpleasant sensations. The yogi will also encounter visions, sights, sounds and tastes, sensations in the body like heat and cold, tightness and vibration, tingling sensation and so forth. There is an unending procession of such objects. All you have to do is apply the same principle, the three phase system of reporting: "What occurs? How do you note it? What happens? Occurring, noting, describing. Try to be as precise and accurate and frugal as you can in a description of your experience." It is not necessary to go into anything more than that.

The yogi must demonstrate whether they can express their experience in a competent way. There is an actual task here. Can the yogi do it or not? The yogi can only express their experience provided they have been able to follow the object. The yogi must be precise and concise. Assuming that the yogi is not able to note the basic object, then something else must be happening. If they cannot note the rise and fall of the breath then the mind must have gone elsewhere. So it is now up to the yogi to describe what has happened. If the yogi is not watching the rise and fall, where is the mind? Has it strayed? Or fallen upon some painful sensations that have suddenly occurred?

The sayadaw aims to guide the yogi to understand when his observations are conceptually based and when they are experience based. Eventually, the yogi will train himself to perceive experience as it arises as "raw" experience at the "sense doors." The experience of hearing, for example, is at first separated from the concept of, say, a dog barking or a person coughing. But hearing is itself conceptually bound. One hears the sound coming from somewhere—outside or elsewhere in the room (a spatial concept). In time, this subtle level of conceptualizing is shed, and concentration moves closer to the experiencing subject—to his sense doors, where seeing, hearing, touching, smelling, tasting, and mental objects occur. The lag between percept experience and concept formation describes the difference between conventional realities that are experienced in everyday life outside the intensive meditation setting and the penultimate truth uncovered by vipassanā meditation.

THE PROGRESS OF INSIGHT

The individual's practice at the Yeiktha kinesthetically removes him from experience of the psychophysical process in its ordinary condition of competencies, behaviors, dispositions, and understandings. This is not a psychological project. The yogi is asked not to "think" or conceptualize while undertaking practice. This break with ordinary conceptualization allows the yogi to observe mind and body in relation to each other and in relation to a complex of explicit and nonexplicit intentionalities. The yogi should arrive at the point where it is clearly seen that mind and body work together and that preceding each movement in the body, there is first a mental intention. The taken-for-grantedness in the everyday competencies of the body—the "residing within the body"—is scrutinized outside its regular framework and conventional modes of interaction. These modes, which anthropologists conceptualize as mediating conditions between the individual and his social and natural environment and which the yogi now separates as the "conventional" world, are temporarily abandoned. The mind-body complex as might be situated outside of these defining conditions is roughly described in the pages ahead.

GETTING STARTED:
ATTAINING PROFICIENCY IN THE EXERCISES OF
MEDITATION AND CONFIDENCE IN THE METHOD

Mahasi Sayadaw described the progress of insight in a short book (translated into English) called the *Progress of Insight.* What follows is a paraphrase of the general outline of the sixteen stages in the progress of insight, including the characteristics of yogi interviews, interspersed with my own comments.

1. *Nāma-rūpā paricchedda ñāṇa,* or the knowledge that distinguishes between mind and matter. Once the yogi has begun to focus his attention and to build concentration, the first insight that occurs to him is that all phenomena can be divided as either mind or matter.

2. *Paccaya pariggaha ñāṇa,* or the knowledge that distinguishes between cause and effect. As the yogi observes more closely, he begins to observe the relations between cause and effect. This is usually experienced as the relations between an intention and the being of the action.

3. *Sammasana ñāṇa,* or investigative knowledge. Following these observations, the yogi is said to find that his observational powers become stronger. He is able to note objects distinctly and also to label them (for example, "seeing, seeing," when an image occurs to him).

4. *Udayabbaya ñāṇa,* or the knowledge that is aware of the arising and passing away of phenomena. At this stage, the yogi becomes excited. His noting seems easy. He observes how all phenomena (mental and physical) arise and disappear—nothing stands still.

Yogis who have attained these first four stages of insight are technically called vipassanā strivers (in Pāli, *araddhaviritya-vipassaka*). At this stage, the yogis are proficient in the exercises of meditation and have full faith or confidence (in Burmese, *thaddha*; in Pāli, *saddhā*) in the vipassanā method. Sayadaws describe yogis at this point in the practice as willing to exert vigorous effort and exhort others do to the same. The yogis become filled with a strong desire to propagate vipassanā meditation practice among their friends and families. A nayaka sayadaw at the center said that this was one of the main ways in which the Mahasi sāsana has spread. If one person experiences this, then they come back with another person. (It is probably significant in this regard that permission to meditate at the center requires [though obviously does not depend on] the recommendation of someone who has already practiced as a yogi at the center.) A Nuggaha executive member explained to me that the guardian association needs to be certain the people who come to practice at the center are sincere; otherwise, they may cause trouble for the center.

Experiencing insights is exhilarating for yogis, who speak enthusiastically of them. For example, one remarked, "I wanted to move, but before I moved I observed that there was an intention to move. The intention was nāma [mind] and the sensations of moving were rūpā [matter]. In this way I saw that there was cause and effect between nāma and rūpā and there was no I. It was just anatta. Just mind and matter." Another yogi stated, "The thought arose all by itself and then it disappeared again all by itself and there was only the observing of it. And then a sound arose and I noted it and it too disappeared by itself and I returned to the breath. As I continued noting in this way I realized that there is constantly going on this process of cause and effect, cause and effect, cause and effect . . . without end. Now I know that the law of dhamma is true and that nothing happens without a cause."

During this phase of practice, yogis describe their experiences as filled with *piti* (joy). It is common to hear them speak of the experience of sparks or flashes of light or of dark rooms becoming illuminated. This phase is also a time, according to the sayadaws, when yogis experiencing chronic illness and even life-threatening diseases become healed.[17] It is with real pride that a layman or laywoman will describe how they *experienced* for themselves the nature of these truths (of seeing things as they are). Yogis frequently report that this "experienced-based knowing" has produced within them a greater sense of equanimity toward the vicissitudes of everyday life. These direct experiences give active, potent meaning to the daily disappointments and genuine hardships of life through expressed resignation to the inevitable laws of impermanence, suffering, and insubstantiality, which are commonplace in any conversation. For the yogis, practice makes it possible for these concepts to become knowledge of a different sort than it was before.

The yogis' experiences of the processes of arising and passing of the object simultaneous with the noting of these at the moment of their arising and passing are said to constitute an experience-based knowing, as compared to that sort of knowing which "reobserves" the experience and therein conceptually frames perception. The yogis realize that because objects are arising and passing away, they are impermanent and unreliable and therefore a form of suffering. Seeing that there is no person in this process but just the arising and passing away of natural phenomena, the yogis come to realize the insubstantiality of self. It is common for yogis at this point in the practice to think that they have attained enlightenment. The sayadaw's role is to remind them that their attachment to this state is also temporary.

INSIGHT

5. *Bhanga ñāṇa,* or the knowledge that is aware of dissolution. In the previous insight level, the yogi was aware of the arising of the object and its immediate disappearance on noting. But at this stage, he perceives that his noting abilities are deteriorating, and he becomes disheartened. The sayadaw encourages the yogi at this time, letting him know that this is a sign of progress and that all yogis

feel despair at this point. The yogi no longer sees the arising of objects, but due to the quickness of the "knowing mind" and the quickness of the disappearance of objects, he only observes the disappearing of objects and not their arisings. For example, while listening to sounds, each sound appears broken up.

6. *Bhayatupatthana ñāṇa,* or the knowledge of awareness of fearfulness. As the aspect of disappearance becomes more prominent, the yogi begins to feel sadness and fear over the realization that life has this characteristic of disappearance.

Many yogis become so overcome at this stage of the practice that they flee the Yeiktha. As observations now take only the rapid disappearance of objects into awareness, the sensation of stability, unchanging self-identity, and contentedness evaporates. Instead, the yogi experiences the rush of disappearing moments in the psychophysical field that is the object of all direct knowing. The sayadaw may then send his kappia (lay attendant) to fetch the yogi back and encourage him by stating that his practice is progressing and that he should carry on with his noting. Indeed, it is so common for yogis to want to end their practice at this point that the Women's Welfare Association even has a committee member whose job is to chase after other committee members and promising yogi practitioners who have fled the Yeiktha. They try to encourage these yogis to return to the Yeiktha and their practice so that they can overcome this obstacle.

7. *Adinava ñāṇa,* or the knowledge of misery. At this stage, the yogi's observational powers exactly fit with the arising of objects. However, every object is perceived as miserable and suffering. The sayadaw encourages the yogi to continue noting the mind that knows and thinks everything is miserable. In other words, the yogi is encouraged to see the mind in its aspect of knowing and not as an essentialized and personal locus to whom experience happens. The yogi is being trained in how not to identify with the objects of knowing.

8. *Nibbida ñāṇa,* or the knowledge of wearisomeness or disgust. Now the yogi's experience of the continuous process of arising and passing away and of the emptiness of all experiences leads to feelings of weariness.

One yogi whose insight progress stopped at this stage described how this experience stayed with him even after leaving the Yeiktha: "I felt like there was nothing to be interested in. Everything was *loki nyingway* [a feeling of weariness for things of the world]. I would go to the theater and listen to the music, but all these pleasures felt empty to me. In fact, I felt a kind of disgust for them even though I used to love to go to the theater in the past." Another yogi described how she felt the desire to be left alone and separate from other people. This, too, is considered a common experience.

9. *Muncitu kamyata ñāṇa,* or the knowledge of the desire for deliverance. The yogi's observations now become focused on the disappearance of the noting mind and the object simultaneously. Even if he decides not to note, the noting is said to happen automatically, by itself. At this stage, the yogi has the sensation of being a prisoner to the noting process, which he cannot escape. This leads to a strong desire to be free from all these sufferings, and the yogi expresses this as a strong wish to attain nibbāna and extinguish all these miserable phenomena (*sankhāra*).

10. *Patisankhanupassana ñāṇa,* or the knowledge of reobservation. At this stage, the yogi is reported to experience with greater intensity the arising and passing away of phenomena and the unsatisfactoriness (dukkha) that each moment of knowing brings. Every experience begins to feel amplified in its aspect of misery. Some yogis described the sensation of intense burning and pain. And associated with these feelings is the intense desire to put an end to all sensate experience and all knowing. The sayadaw gives special encouragement to the yogi at this time. He may give short dhamma talks to try to inspire and encourage the yogi that he is perceiving the universal characteristics of anicca, dukkha, and anattā.

11. *Saṅkharūpekkha ñāṇa,* or the knowledge that can view psychophysical phenomena with equanimity. This is the final stage of insight, leading to the edge of the experience of nibbana. Now the yogi's observational powers are said to be smooth and proceeding rapidly. The yogi finds that he can stay in one posture for hours at a time with no experience of pain. Reflection on the happiness of this smooth noting is also recognized as impermanent. Yogis describe how they feel no preferences. Eventually, the noting becomes extremely fine, nearly imperceptible. The sayadaw warns the yogi about becoming complacent and encourages him to continue ardent noting.

As the yogi continues, one of the three characteristics of anicca, dukkha, or anattā becomes apparent to him without special effort and without any associated feelings of disgust or fear and so forth. The prominence of the perception that everything is either impermanent, insubstantial, or suffering is considered to be the result of one's prior practices over many lifetimes. Associated with each universal characteristic are said to be particular characteristics that describe the person's psychological profile.[18]

TRANSFORMATION OF CONSCIOUSNESS:
THE FINAL STAGES OF INSIGHT

12. *Anuloma ñāṇa,* or the linkage moment immediately leading into the next insight.

13. *Gotrabhu ñāṇa,* or the extinction of the object, the noting mind, and sankhāra (phenomena).

14. *Magga ñāṇa,* or path, referring to the knowing mind just before the experience of bliss.

15. *Phala ñāṇa,* or fruit, referring to the knowing mind catching a final glimpse of the moment of bliss of the "null phenomenon," nibbāna.

16. *Paccavekkhana ñāṇa,* or the knowledge of the recollection of the formation of magga phala (the *path* leading to, and the *fruition* or experience of, nibbāna).

These last five insights occur "automatically" after the momentum of swift noting has, as U Pandita describes it, "ripened" the pāramī of the yogi. Magga phala ñāṇa, the path and fruit of the practice, are the final realizations of the goal in the experience of nibbāna. This linkage to the null phenomenon (nibbāna) in consciousness describes the experience whereby the extinction of the object and the knowing occurs, followed by the realization of an experience outside all sense and conscious experience. These are the insights leading to the realization of nibbāna. But the perception of them can only be experienced on taking "resolves" (*aditana*) to recollect or reobserve the processes culminating in nibbāna. By making these forceful intentions, the yogi undertakes these resolves to review and verify his experiences for himself. The sayadaw then asks the yogi to resolve to reside in phala (the null experience of nibbāna) for extended periods of time. It is claimed that some yogis at the Yeiktha have made these resolves and remained for two days in the sitting position without moving. Before taking such a resolve, U Pandita Sayadaw instructs, the yogis are to include in their resolve the caveat that if the place where they are meditating should catch fire, they should automatically come out of phala even if the full time of their practice has not been completed.

With the insights of magga phala ñāṇa (path and fruit insight), the momentary experience of nibbāna is attained, after which the ontological status of the yogi is forever altered. With these two insights, the individual is transformed from a *puthujjana* (worldling) to a *thotapan* (literally meaning "stream winner" [*sotāpanna* in Pāli], a reference to the metaphor of "crossing the stream" from saṃsāra to nibbāna). The thotapan is believed to be a radically new kind of moral individual, incapable of breaking the five Buddhist precepts against killing, stealing, lying, committing adultery, and taking intoxicants. (Hence, as described in chapter 1, U Nu released from prison all those who meditated to this stage.) Although thotapans are naturally constrained to keeping the five precepts, their behavior is otherwise considered to be indiscernible from that of worldlings.

There is a dispute regarding whether the thotapan is freed of all manifestations ("arisings") of the mental state of jealousy. However, it is not disputed that the mental state of doubting with respect to the method of practice and the goal of nibbāna has been uprooted for all time. Also eradicated is the belief in a soul or an abiding self. Finally, the thotapan is said to never again be born in the hell, ghost, or animal realms and is destined within seven lifetimes to attain full and final enlightenment. With the final attainment of nibbāna following arahat-ship, the infinite cycles of rebirth are forever ended.

SOTĀPANNA:
PRIVATE INSIGHT AND PUBLIC ACKNOWLEDGMENT

As recounted earlier, those just back from a meditation course might signal to each other about their attainments. Referring to someone as an "old yogi" is one way of signaling that an individual's practice is accomplished, although this term also blends ambiguously with the relation of a yogi to the center as a donor or volunteer for more than ten years. Verification of status distinctions also occurs through the collective practice of meditation, which is perhaps most evident in the procedures by which executive committee members are selected for the Nuggaha and the Women's Welfare Association. "Passing the course" is required for members of the executive committees of both organizations.

Meditation is a requisite for involvement in the center's kopaka apwe. Further, there are so-called proofs of one's attainment, such as listening to the nyanzin tape mentioned earlier. At one point, it was gossiped that proof of one's attainment was signaled in the gift from Mahasi Sayadaw of a few tiny pearlized relics (*dalone*) from an arahat. Mahasi had been given these while on a visit to Sri Lanka. He was at first unaware of the significance being attributed to his gift, that is, that it was a sign of his recognition of the yogi's attainment of enlightenment. He thereafter stopped giving the dalone and disclaimed any significance of a yogi's practice by his or her receipt of them. Just the same, making claims and securing proofs of one's attainment became a competitive engagement among that sector of the institution that aspired to achieve the highest donor status at the center—and, of course, access to official roles in the voluntary lay administrative organization. These posts offer a leveraged source of merit making and social status inside and outside the center, as I will expand on in later chapters. Thus, social status, economic network, and merit are all tied up together in this single location for action.

Vipassanā Insight as Moral-Causal Knowledge

Lay enlightenment cannot be identified in any specific embodied way other than by the practitioner's observance of the Buddhist five precepts, which are said to be inviolable once the individual has attained enlightenment. In this sense, we can see how lay enlightenment becomes an indeterminate or inexplicit form of social action taken toward the purification of self and society. Through the mass lay meditation movement, classical political conceptions about how the well-being of society is dependent on the king's morality are inverted to form a theory of how the well-being of society is dependent on the morality of its citizens.[19]

The belief that laity can gain insight into the most difficult and penultimate insights of the Buddha's teachings through meditation and not through study of the scriptures has meant that a new source of verification for the teachings has arisen outside scriptural orthodoxy. To be sure, meditative insights are verified against the texts, but they nevertheless remain an independent source of the truth of the Buddha's teachings and the universal law of dhamma. In this sense, the laity have laid claim to the penultimate understandings of the teachings without either renouncing the world or studying the scriptures. This has not meant the laicization of the sangha in any way. It has instead resulted in a kind of epistemic reconstruction of lay consciousness by means of vipassanā techniques, in which the universal constitution of reality is given empirical proof. It further demonstrates that the goals of the Buddha's teachings can be achieved here and now—or, as U Pandita says in the title of his book, *In This Very Life*—through "seeing things as they are."

The development of vipassanā as a movement to create an "enlightened citizenry" has meant that the laity has assumed the responsibility for the welfare of society. It is their sīla on which the cosmic conditions depend, just as during the time of kings, the natural and social conditions depended on the king's sīla. The nonobservance of dhamma is seen to create calamity within society and nature. Whereas the king used to be the "coordinator of Nature's and Humanity's orders in society, in the institution of kingship and in the morality of the head of state,"[20] the laity has now undertaken moral purification through "purification of view." In part, this is the gist of the project of verifying empirically the epistemology of the Abhidhamma texts through vipassanā.

The act of purification through epistemic reconstruction constitutes the yogi's conversion experience. This conversion is said to alter the individual on a number of registers affecting his or her mental position toward life outside the meditation context. Individual experiences vary on the basis of personal circumstances and psychological profiles. However, they are similar according to the degree to which the individual has "learned" how to take up an attitude with which to experience the vicissitudes of everyday life with forbearance and equanimity. This characteristic, called *upekkhā* (equanimity), is the penultimate mental disposition of the vipassanā practitioner.

The cultivation of this mental state toward any and all formations arising in the individual psychophysical process either may be developed as a *temporary* insight borne out of a limited experience of the comprehension of the three characteristics of anicca, dukkha, and anattā or it may be more thoroughly comprehended as an indisputable perceptual modality through which life is experienced, as though in a cognitive transformation. For the enlightened individual, insight is no longer a momentary glance into seeing things as they are; it is a total psychophysical transformation of individual ontology as part of the kinesthetic extension of the individual within the environment. That the enlightened person now sees things as they are constitutes not only an individual statement of perspective on the phenomenal world but also a universalizing truth. The enlightened person is a transformed and impersonal psychophysical phenomenon within the total social, natural, and cosmic field of the phenomenal world.

The first assertion of the essential conditions of knowledge and being is, in other words, said to be an empathic knowing. Compassion (*karuna*), loving-kindness (*mettā*), and sympathetic joy (*muditā*) are wholesome mental states that may be cultivated as the bedrock of the system of moral purification. These are the mental dispositions leading one to feel motivated to give charity and keep one's sīla. They are the empathetic qualities of mind borne of the fundamental condition for comprehending the nature of social reality and bound up in the concept that "just as I suffer, so too do others suffer." Morality is held to be a condition that first and foremost exists as part of the conditions in the relations between sentient beings. These are articulated in terms of basic principles of restraint, and they form the foundations for a theory of purity essentialized for the layperson as the five precepts. It should be noticed that these are precepts directed at the social plane of interrelationships. They are not directed to the abstract plane of purification as a condition of the individual's own deliverance.[21]

Though social relations are articulated in terms of this basic theory of restraint, these ideas are justified in terms of a causal logic and not in terms of a normative code of ethical conduct that should be undertaken because a god or Buddha has commanded it. Knowledge is constituted on two registers. The first is the conventional reality (*sammuti*) register, which describes the comprehension of one's experience of social embeddedness. It is on this register that the low ethics of the layperson are articulated as restraints protecting individuals from suffering caused by the lack of empathy toward their existential condition.

Once again, the empathic perspective is not experienced as a theoretical assumption; it is constituted as a basic condition of knowledge. People do not simply follow rules, blueprints for social action, representational mappings for the comprehension of order, or even a Wittgensteinian-like linguistic contouring of the dimensions of reality as the primary conditions of knowledge as rule-governed epistemic knowing. Knowledge production necessarily implicates empathy in advance and thus is a moral reflex automatically produced in the cognitive moment of compassion, loving-kindness, and sympathetic joy. The absence of empathy and the pursuit of one's own desires and cravings without regard for the potential for suffering that it might cause another being produce negative actions within a total field. Associated with this empathic theory of knowledge is a causative component as well—the theory of kamma. Kammically, the condition of suffering is a *universal* condition caused by the trespassing of one sentient being's intentions, speech, or actions against another. The theory of kamma cannot operate as a theory unless the total field within which actions take place is *assumed*. Vipassanā meditation practice invokes the total field—a condition of knowing in which one's perception is not subjectively separate from an objective world, as in the Western framework, but in which one's perceptions are empathically grasped as part of a shared world of knowing and being.

The epistemic "shift" that occurs for the yogi even in early stages of insight is the realization of "position" toward experience and knowing. The extension of that comprehension to practical social realities becomes the foundation for a moral theory of restraint based on the dislocation of identity with a singular position (the self) taken up in the world. The yogi now acts in relation to a moral field coextensive with the regulation of her or his own mind-body processes. The external world has been internalized in the cognitive act of registering experience closer to the sense data of perception, while simultaneously accomplishing the experiential engagement with concept- and emotion-driven cognitive processes as distinct phenomena. The cognizer has taken up a relationship to experience that reclassifies experience according to new categories. These categories distinguish the kinds of phenomena being observed at the moment of their arising. In so doing, the yogi has reconstructed the categories through which he or she takes in the world of experience "at the site of their arising." The yogi has also established an impersonal relationship to feelings that color the arising of phenomena at each of the sense doors.

Inasmuch as feelings become the object of observation at the time of their arising, the yogi identifies desire and aversion as conditions to be dealt with separately from the phenomena in the world at large that may have been the cause for their arising. The yogi is thereby emancipated from the impingement of sense, cognitive, and emotive phenomena. These are taken as things in themselves and not as things set apart—that is, not as forces on the singularized identity of a self alienated from the world at large. This epistemic reconstruction reorients experience away from practical actions conceived as the will to act on the world by an individualized force (the self). It reorients experience toward a theory for social action in which the proper observation of phenomena (things as they are) becomes the constituting modality from which intentions, speech acts, and physical acts are motivated. The dhamma constitutes the ultimate terms of reality, whereas conventional reality remains a "metaphor."[22] The Buddhist trusts that full understanding of this process was comprehended by the Buddha and interpreted for the benefit of ordinary worldlings so that they might cut through the veil of delusion that holds them prisoner in a vision of false reality.

This entire progression is not only or merely an ideological battle over orthodox religious views and their implication for individual soteriology.[23] Rather, it is a competition over the objective and potent materializations of dhamma. Struggle for control over these objective, potent sources as well as individual mastery over the conditions leading to future propitious life circumstances and eventual escape from saṃsāra (the continuous cycle of coming into existence) constitute multiple threads for action in a tapestry of apparent realities. In this logic of purification, truth is a reality to be perceived, acted on, and existentially experienced as a condition of being. Purification is a procedure for individual cognitive realization pursued in order to effect ontological changes in the individual, society, state, sangha, and World Age.

The mass lay meditation movement represents a newfangled and, in a sense, rediscovered rationalization and intellectualization of the Buddha's teachings, moving away from representational modalities of understanding and comprehension and toward a precise mechanics of causal working. A Buddhist praxis for efficacious acts taken toward the world and the individual's taking up of a position in it—a theory of being and knowing—has become iterated in an intellectualist and rationalist mode. Hence, we can observe the rise of a Burmese Buddhist praxis directed at ameliorating the causes of suffering through precise Abhidhammic understandings of the workings of the mind and the exercising of greater control over mental forms and their arisings. And for once, this is a mass phenomenon, not something sequestered off for scholar virtuosi monks.

Outside the intensive meditation context of the center, practice looks very different, and it is different for different people. Some individuals may continue to meditate an hour a day or perhaps an hour in the morning and at night. Most yogis find that devoting any substantial amount of time to vipassanā while remaining involved in the everyday affairs of worldly life is difficult—a few short minutes in front of the altar at night when they take refuge in the Triple Gem (Buddha, Dhamma, Sangha) may be all the time they find for meditation. Vipassanā practice is soon reduced to a bare-bones effort to apply the technique of mindfulness to the vicissitudes of daily life, as well as the moral implication and the afterglow of the insights.

Outside the intensive meditation practice setting, the *conceptualization* of the practice becomes organized in terms of a discourse about the true conditions of suffering. Events in one's life are related as to a false view of self—that the perpetuation of the causes for one's suffering is evident in the fact that one continues to cling to the notion of an "I" consciousness. Nevertheless, in general parlance, one is far more likely to hear the phrase *Dukkha-beh!* (there is suffering!) as the reiteration of a self-evident fact of universal suffering in all phenomena and not just unique instances of suffering: "there is suffering," not "I suffer." In response to a change in circumstances, one also frequently hears *Aneisa!* (impermanence!). The self-evidence of reality is perpetually iterated as a fact verifying the truth of suffering in everyday circumstances, for in response to these exclamations, there is a resigned nod of the head or affirmation that a true and wise thing has been spoken. These expressions have not originated with the New Laity. However, they are discharged as expressions that have been understood as firsthand experience and not as mere conceptual intellectualization or customary wisdom.

Meditation, History, and the Foundation of Sāsana Society

A sāsana society, by which I mean a society concerned with the perpetuation of the Buddha's teachings, is structured by certain premises that limit the range of possibilities for social action and contain the system for its adherents as a coherent, meaningful whole. I consider two important propositions that may be thought of as part of the *cosmological rule set* accepted by Theravadan Buddhists regarding the perpetuation of sāsana society. The first is the proposition that the perpetuation of the Buddha's teachings is inevitably doomed. Slowly, as time moves away from the period of the living historical Buddha, the teachings and practices will gradually become corrupted and their original meanings and interpretations lost. Such, of course, is one of the senses behind the term *sāsana,* which is the *dispensation* of the teachings. The prediction that the Buddha is said to have made—that his dispensation would last for five thousand years—remains one of the fundamental parameters that are meaningful to contemporary practitioners. These people see themselves as participating in the project of sāsana's perpetuation in order to cultivate their pāramī and enrich their kammic stores for the long journey to nibbāna. The temporal and spatial dimensions of sāsana locate the individual within a historical stream, imparting the sense of immediate purpose and future destiny. Moreover, it is a historical vision that has been readily grasped as the justification for a number of political forms, the most impressive of which is the Ashokan paradigm.

In Burma, this has served as the predominant model for the organization of the state. It is noteworthy that kingship is given its own strand of history (*min win*) and destiny that intersects with sāsana history (*thathana win*) but remains distinguished from it. A third strand of history, *maha win*—the great or universal history—relates the history of enlightened beings (*samma sambuddha*, or fully enlightened Buddhas; *pacceka*, or silent Buddhas; and *arahat*, or individuals enlightened through the teachings of a Buddha). Together, these three strands of history form in the Burmese system a totalizing picture of the cosmological, metahistorical, and historical dimensions that make up the indisputable and mutually apprehended and shared "horizons of the life-world," in Maurice Merleau-Ponty's apt expression. A second proposition is contained in the other sense of the term *sāsana*, which is *a teaching*. The Buddha sāsana is, first and last, a teaching intended to help individuals transcend the conditions leading to perpetual rebirths and suffering. The preoccupations and practices for perpetuating these teachings are of secondary importance.

According to a popularly held folk belief, as we have seen, it is precisely at the halfway point in the Buddha sāsana—the twenty-five-hundred-year point—that a resurgence in the number of individuals achieving the first stage of enlightenment is prophesied. For the present period, it is held that attainment of any of the stages of enlightenment is only possible if exertion is made through satipaṭṭhāna vipassanā meditation. What were the historical circumstances permitting this particular interpretation of the trajectory of the sāsana and of the roles of laity in perpetuating and realizing the goals of the Buddha's teachings? How did orthodox canonical ideas become actualized in new practices and ideologies? And how did these new practices become justified as orthodoxy and orthopraxy?

It is by considering the historical circumstances leading to the rise of the so-called New Laity that we begin to understand the significance of vipassanā to the revitalization of the sāsana in Burma. Revitalization of the techniques for attaining the penultimate goal of nibbāna was a socially and politically germane movement. This point has been overlooked, probably because the political bearings of the vipassanā movement do not correspond to the modern Western calculus of political action. What was ultimately being conveyed in the mass lay meditation movement was, first, a normative *description* for state-society relations (in particular for the relations between the three orders of the sangha, the state, and the laity) and, second, a *justification* for specific ideas about the role of kings or rulers, the sources of their power, and the conditions for the legitimacy of that power. In short, the meditation movement has promoted a Burmese Buddhist theory for the social contract between state and society. Although individuals try to attend to their own personal salvation by striving for nibbāna, they are simultaneously enacting broader social ideas about the arrangements of the state, the structure of cosmic time, and their participation in a metahistorical project of sāsana perpetuation.

By undertaking practices for the purification of the self, especially through mental cultivation of such dispositions as renunciation (*nekkhama*), nonattachment, forbearance (*kanti*), and mindfulness (*sati*), and by undertaking as subsidiary activities the "guardian" practices of loving-kindness (*mettā*), compassion (*karuna*), sympathetic joy (*mudita*), and equanimity (*upekkhā*), the laity's practices define the limits of reality in individual, worldly, and cosmic terms. These practices describe the attempt to enclose the world of experience—individual, social, and cosmic—in a framework that encapsulates the whole of reality in a single theory of knowing. That is why the mass lay meditation movement has intrinsically been a political movement because it refutes, out of hand, the primacy of the nation-state as the geospatial boundaries of the Buddha world. It refutes theories for the bureaucratic arrangements of the state that do not take into consideration ideas about what the sources of truth/power are and how these are morally caused. And it refutes especially Western modernist theories of personhood that do not situate an individual's actions, speech, and intentions in terms of both conventional and ultimate contexts for the production of knowledge and being.

Vipassanā-centered practice represents lay and sangha attempts to assert the validity of the outermost limits of a cosmological vision of reality—the limits of ultimate reality within which a conventional interpretation of historical events is possible. It is also a theory for what the structure of relations between state and society should be. The orthodox and popular verification of vipassanā-centered practice, especially the Mahasi technique of vipassanā practice, has become the vehicle through which the objective terms of ultimate reality are asserted. The New Laity and contemporary monks are claiming it to be the most encompassing umbrella under which all other connected and ancillary patterns of practice and belief might be covered.[24] Vipassanā practice has become the center of a movement to verify the coherence and continuity of the Buddha's teachings as a particular kind of episteme—a particular way of knowing, being, and becoming and of asserting what are the true grounds of reality.

Transmission of the teachings is simultaneously an individual project and a societywide project. Verification of the dhamma is accomplished through a confirmation of perspectives that are text based (pariyatti) and experience based (paṭipatti) and through realization of a particular epistemic position taken toward realization (paṭivedha). The three classical components—pariyatti, paṭipatti, and paṭivedha—are dialectically engaged verification procedures.

The newly iterated theory of the concordance between text and practice has been increasingly reflected on by the intellectual guard of the laity, particularly since the early 1990s. There has been a tremendous interest in Abhidhamma study by the laity in this period. This interest is mostly confined to the urban, educated middle class, although, due to widespread practice and the consequently altered environment of religious thought, it is of relevance to all Burmese Buddhists. Part of the reason for the lay interest in the most difficult and abstract texts of the Tipitaka is that they provide a theory for what was experienced in practice and a rational underpinning for the possibilities of practical attainment. It is a theory of causality and of the interdependence of the conditions of mind and matter that ideologically oppose scientific, Marxist-socialist, capitalist, and other ideologies that underwrite systems of social welfare and governance.

Yet another register of procedures for confirming the Buddha world as undertaken by the sangha involves its role in sāsana perpetuation. Preoccupation over the perpetuation of the sāsana is an implicit element in the relationship between the lay donor and the monk recipient, for instance, because they are coparticipants in the project of sāsana continuation. On this register, it is typically the continuity of the sangha institution that is focused on as the legitimate location from which perpetuation of the teachings is accomplished. Within the sangha, vinaya discipline is the primary focus. Pressures on monks to maintain their vinaya emerge as much from the laity as from within the sangha, since it is the laity's merit fields that are put at risk when monks do not remain purified fields of the dhamma. The dhamma as universal cosmic law also affects the processes by which sāsana is perpetuated, for the purification process is understood to occur as a phenomenon in nature.

Meditation and its "realization" (paṭivedha) are the primary and experiential objects of all of these procedures for verifying the constitution of reality. Through the exploration of the mass project of meditation, I argue not only that Buddhism should not be viewed solely as a totality of social, economic, political, and ideological beliefs expressed in a religious key but also that a unique epistemic position is being reproduced through a historical process of verification. Vipassanā meditation deconstructs the social categories and meanings of pragmatic life in order to assert a mode of knowing and perceiving in which the actor/agent takes up a position in the lifeworld that is fundamentally skeptical of the objectivity of the structures of social space. The individual's practical activities are directed to another level than the conventional one, while he or she simultaneously acknowledges common life experiences as conventional reality within which cosmic forces are played out. The actor/agent is trained to adopt a practical position that asserts the continuous relationship of the individual vis-à-vis the environment and not opposition and separateness from it. The location for practical involvement with the world then remains within the individual's own psychophysical process.

The difference between the practice orientations of the urban population and the rural population is most evident in terms of their interests in the Buddha's teachings. Although members of the urban middle class are greatly preoccupied with merit production for purposes of securing better life conditions for themselves and their families in the future, these practices are situated within the longer view of pāramī production for the purposes of attaining nibbāna. For the Mahasi disciple, the best of all conditions for approaching practice is to attain the first stage of enlightenment, after which it is guaranteed both that one will have only seven more lifetimes at the most before attaining nibbāna and that one will never fall into the lower realms of *apaya* (hell), or *peta* (ghosts) or animal realms. In addition to meditation, they are assuring for themselves better future life conditions through their enormous dāna contributions, and they are industrious on this point. The pervasive practice of dāna bridges the soteriological and practical political realms quite overtly. This is the subject of the next chapter.

Chapter 3

SACRED GIVING AND THE
POLITICS OF SINCERITY

The Giving Junta

Burma's military regime is widely counted among the most brutal and oppressive governments in the world today. Freedom in the World, a human rights watch group, describes the junta as

> having imprisoned or driven into exile most of its vocal opponents; severely restricted freedoms of speech, press, association and other fundamental rights; and used a tightly controlled mass movement, the Union Solidarity Development Association, to monitor forced labor quotas, report on citizens, and intimidate opponents. The army is responsible for arbitrary beatings and killings of civilians; the forced, unpaid use of civilians as porters, laborers, and human mine sweepers under brutal conditions, with soldiers sometimes killing weakened porters or executing those who resist; summary executions of civilians who refuse to provide food or money to military units; arrests of civilians as alleged insurgents or insurgent sympathizers; and widespread incidents of rape.[1]

Although these brutal facts are verified in reports from many sources, a brief sojourn in the country is sufficient to reveal that the junta, known as SLORC/SPDC,[2] is also ardently engaged in what appears to be quite a peaceable enterprise of making and sponsoring lavish donations to Buddhist institutions and to monks throughout the country. The military (*tatmadaw*) government's participation in what I will call the dāna economy is made broadly public through the conspicuous projects it undertakes (such as pagoda building), as well as through its influence over networks of civilian donors.

The apparent contradiction of these two images—SLORC/SPDC's highest officers parading in honor cavalcades between popularly attended libation-pouring ceremonies (which consecrate donation events) even as all the repression of rights bluntly continues—has led many journalists and foreign academic researchers to conclude that the regime is "playing the religion card."[3] That is, they see the military rulers as attempting to engage in an elaborate charade, a manipulation designed to deceive or, at best, appease a devout public.

No one is in a position to outright confirm or deny this interpretation, but my ethnographic research in Burma, supplemented by reflection on historical antecedents, suggests a more complicated scenario. To begin, it appears far from clear even to highly educated and connected Yangonites, among whom I have conducted research most intensively, that the government is engaged in a simple pretense of Buddhist devotion for the purpose of (somehow) maintaining its hold on political power. The lively and nuanced character of the internal debate—always framed in terms of sincerity—suggests that the true meaning behind the government's actions is by no means widely deemed self-evident. But even to confront the question directly in this manner is to inadvertently prefigure the outcome in terms of one or the other of two common modes of explanation. One scheme conceives of the military regime as standing in a relation of mystifier to mystified vis-à-vis the Burmese populace—a kind of Gramscian hegemony. The second scheme also treats the regime as a monolithic agent with conspiratorial intent, but the junta's donation activities are seen less as conspiratorial and more as pragmatic and rational components of its attempt to achieve power and legitimacy in a majority Buddhist country.

These interpretations notably exclude the fact of the participation of military *and* government bureaucracies as well as individual personnel therein who seem to be competing to control the personal moral assets associated with donation rather than the collective political or economic ones. The giving junta is far from a monolith of intention. The presumption of explaining its actions in this way, moreover, calls our attention to what might be the theoretical underpinning of such an interpretation, since the same theory of action has presumably been applied to more than the phenomenon of government dāna. The unquestioned assumption here is the methodological individualism of formalist economic anthropology, in which strategizing, maximizing, rational decision making characterizes economic activity of any kind. But this model cannot account for the *systemic* complexity of donation activities, nor does it benefit us to reduce Buddhist cosmological principles to instrumental plots, economic or soteriological. Dāna does have micro- and macroeconomic components. But its perception as a practice leading to purification and nibbāna, wherein the goal of donation is to achieve a state of mind in which generosity emerges in the individual's intentions as unprompted volitional acts, is more prominent. It is this native "calculus of intention" that may most beneficially be applied to the regime's donation activities.

These logical intricacies are addressed in a theoretical critique developed by Maurice Godelier in relation to classical infrastructure/superstructure theory.[4] Godelier's ideas are particularly relevant to a consideration of dāna and its role in Burma, since his overarching goal is to account for the "mutual compatibility"[5] of ideology, politics, kinship, and economics rather than rendering one or the other of these subordinate to the next in a hierarchy of simple causality and/or manipulability. In an insight whose import will become apparent later in this volume, Godelier concludes that "at the heart of the 'material' infrastructure of societies, lie active mental realities, in other words realities stemming from the mind. Productions of the mind could therefore not be a by-product, the superstructure of an infrastructure, since they were already present deep within these material infrastructures."[6]

The relation of "material infrastructure" to "mental realities" is a particularly suitable framework to employ here because I wish to decipher the relationship between the sincerity, the purity of intention (cetanā), and, at a higher reserve, the soteriology of donations, on the one hand, and political economic realities, on the other. To foreshadow my conclusion, I will trace the outlines of a complex system of donation involved in the redistribution of resources between the spheres of civil society, the state, and the religious order.[7] Dāna is embedded in a native theory of moral Buddhist causality. I suggest the materialization of its effects in social, economic, and political relations as the "social organization of intention," and I support this conclusion by relating incidents and opinions expressed to me by Burmese government bureaucrats, monks, and lay donors. Material to this exposition are discussions of the phenomenology of dāna and the politics of sincerity in association with it.

Dāna: The Ethical Foundation of Purification

Mingun Sayadaw, who memorized the Pāli canon in its entirety and served as the *vasajjaka* (respondent) at the Sixth Buddhist Synod, commented that generosity

has the quality of making the mind and heart pliable. When someone makes a generous offer of some gift, the very act of giving serves as a decisive support (*upanissaya-paccaya:* life immediate support) to make the mind more pliable and ready for observance of the precepts, for cultivation of concentration and for development of insight wisdom through practice of vipassana meditation. It is within the experience of every Buddhist, that a feeling of awkwardness and embarrassment [*anade*] arises in him whenever he visits, without an offering, monasteries or temples for the purpose of keeping precepts, of listening to the dhamma talks or for the practice of meditation. Therefore it was customary for the noble disciples like Visakha to bring an offering such as rice, sweets or fruits in the morning, and beverages and medicinal preparations in the evening whenever they went to visit the Buddha.[8]

Mingun Sayadaw's description of generosity draws out both the psychological and the social aspects of the performance of dāna. Dāna (moral charity), sīla (dhamma morality), and bhāvanā (mental development through meditation) constitute a threefold hierarchical and progressive purification process marking the road toward individual enlightenment and a moral and ordered society. The three are also practices linked indexically to a cosmological, hierarchical, representational map of the thirty-two planes of existence, in that thought, speech, and action produce the ontological grounds for rebirth.[9] In the Buddhist framework of cause and effect, dāna, sīla, and bhāvanā are the moral causal acts that result in attainment of nibbāna, rebirth in higher realms of existence, rebirth in more auspicious conditions in this world, or better conditions in this life. From an individual's standpoint, they are perceived as ethical practices that create one's merit store for future lives and are the basis for one's present merit status as well.

For the Burmese Buddhist laity, the "free will act of giving,"[10] as one scholar puts it, is considered the foundational practice on which other practices, in pursuit of the final soteriological goal of nibbāna, can develop.[11] Through repetitive acts of giving, the donor is understood to be cultivating a mental disposition toward the world characterized by a lessening of attachment to material wants. In the native cosmology, donation acts motivated by the desire to receive material sustenance and abundance are considered inferior to those acts motivated by the aspiration to cultivate a proper disposition toward material circumstances. One should cultivate a disposition in which loss of material wealth and pleasant circumstances can be accepted without attachment and therefore without sorrow and suffering. One strategic component of dāna—the aim of inviting future material abundance—conforms at least partly to the religious interpretation of the matter, since it is by means of kammic principles of retribution that such wealth would accrue. Ideally, however, the worldly goal is subsumed under the more totalizing conception that the ultimate goal of dāna is to transcend dependence on worldly material and social circumstances altogether. Because these two registers—the worldly and the transcendent—can intersect in the same deed, the criterion of sincerity of intention emerges as a public preoccupation in Burmese Buddhist society.[12] The individual's cultivation of the dānā pāramī is directed at training the volitional inclination of the mind toward spontaneous and unprompted thoughts and acts of generosity. The mind should become unhesitating, uncalculating, and freed from clinging to notions of "me" and "mine." Among the great donors at Mahasi Thathana Yeiktha, this ideal was expressed to me in terms of "never refusing anyone at least some amount." The great donor is recognized as a *kind* of person—a rare individual worthy of admiration, awe, and emulation. The charismatic quality of such donors is not measured simply by how rich they are now or will be in the future, that is, in terms of their merit potential. Rather, their charismatic quality is evaluated in terms of the kind of moral perfection of the dhamma they embody.

Great donors perpetuate the Buddha's teachings by virtue of their endowments. In Buddhist Burma, it would be impossible to have high social status *without* participating in sāsana-directed donation. As F. K. Lehman has pointed out, there is something of a relationship of proof of pāramī and merit store that demands the positive demonstration of one's high moral standing along the path to nibbāna. This is why dāna events are so publicly visible. From an emic perspective, the public aspect of donation is important because through it, others may share in the merit making and therein produce within their own minds feelings of mettā (loving-kindness), saddhā (faith), and so forth. This emotional facet of mental participation in acts of devotion and generosity is a critical underpinning to the way in which moral communities emerge out of like-minded participation in collective rituals.

Sincerity in the act of donation is valued because it is the foundation for one's merit base in a system of moral causality in which intentions are the final determinants of what one will reap in the future. The meritoriousness of the gift (that is, the strength of its "return") is dependent on the state of mind of the donor at the time of the donation, the state of mind of the monk recipient, the type of gift, its value or appropriateness to the recipient, and so forth.[13] Intention is the single most important criterion for the evaluation of the cosmic return of the gift.

The sangha is popularly viewed as the best field of merit for the laity's offerings, for two reasons. First, monks are exemplars who have renounced their worldly lives and pleasures and are prohibited from owning anything other than bare requisites, such as an alms bowl, robes, needle, and umbrella. They therefore embody the ideal detachment from materiality that the dāna is intended to induce in the giver. Second, wealth donated to the sangha (which is looked after by lay guardian committees or personal attendants) is seen as serving the sustenance and reproduction of the Buddha sāsana, or the teachings and dispensation of a Buddha.

Classifications of the meritorious value of dāna acts are not just monkly preoccupations over kammic returns. The religious schemata are also legal categories. Acts of dāna are sorted according to how many people are donating and whether the dāna is given to a single monk, a group of monks, or the entire Sangha of the Four Quarters (all monks within the sangha, irrespective of their sectarian differences). This concept is meant to invoke the Buddha's resolve that the sangha not be split by sectarian rivalries. Thus, as reviewed in chapter 1, a donation directed to the legal property category of sanghika—the Sangha of the Four Quarters—is considered a higher form of merit making than others, for sanghika encompasses the entire order and not just the individual into whose hands the donation is immediately offered. This fact has repercussions for how monks may use these donations. Only donations given to individual monks (poggalika) can be used according to a monk's individual will (in accordance, of course, with the sangha disciplinary code).

In 1996, I interviewed a renowned monk at the Mahasi Thathana Yeiktha. The copious donations to this monk were transferred to his natal village to provide funds for a meditation center as well as a school and other public works benefiting the village. Because poggalika donations are easily "profaned" (in instances when they flow back into civil and lay domains), the sangha orthodoxy views them as less meritorious. However, from the layperson's point of view, donations to individual monks are often preferred because the donors seek to establish privileged relations with monks. Such relations help a donor exert influence on potent merit fields. They also demonstrate the donor's cosmic affinity to a monk in the classical monk-donor relation that is thought to be evidence of prior kammic affiliation and therefore a shared path in spiritual striving. Rivalry over who will count among the close supporters or even as the chief donor of a monk often turns bitter. At the same time, from the government's point of view, these arrangements are seen to draw monks and laity together in opposition to the state, for in times of need, it is to the sangha rather than to the state that people turn.

Another critical feature of dāna is its centrality to Burmese Buddhist ideas about power. Prior meritorious actions (in this and previous lifetimes) are attributed to an individual's present endowment of power and influence. In the Burmese Buddhist scheme of moral causation, the mental intention contained in the act of donating is critical for the creation of substantive political power. The pursuit of exchange relations based on sincere and wholesomely intended transactions, as characterized by loving-kindness, compassion, and equanimity, is evidenced by the ubiquitous discourse on these subjects surrounding dāna activities. Indeed, the system for creating and evaluating sincere intention strikes the ethnographer as such a pervasive preoccupation as to seem to lie at the logical core in the production of general social relations and mental realities, thereby also subsuming the strategic component of what I have, due to the scale and scope of the phenomenon relative to the economy overall, called the dāna economy.[14]

A Government Aspect: The Mingala Society

The practice of dāna is seen as foundational to the creation of a *mingala* society, (prosperous and morally ordered) as based on the ideal portrayed in the Mangala Sutta (*mangala* means "good" or "auspicious").[15] The sutta is commonly recited by monks and is one of the first lessons schoolchildren study.

Beginning in the 1990s, the SLORC government attempted to co-opt ideas of a mingala society for their own state-sponsored version of a welfare society.[16] Making state projects the focus for donation has been one of the central aspects of this campaign. Wealthy lay donors at MTY and elsewhere are frequently contacted when the government is in need of funds for such things as schools, road repairs, and the construction of water reserves. In exchange for lay patronage of state-sponsored welfare projects, SLORC offers these wealthy individuals concessions to build hotels, access to rare resources such as cement at government rates, and other privileges. Reluctance to participate in these projects may result in harassment of various sorts, especially surveillance and bullying. Juliane Schober reports that in the late 1990s, SLORC began approaching renowned donors at their homes on their "birthdays" (that is, the day of the week on which they were born), telling them this was an occasion for them to go to the monastery and make offerings.[17]

Two things are to be understood in the structure of this request/demand. First, the volitional component for undertaking a donation has been removed from the lay donor, and hence, the kammic merit of the gift had been mostly nullified. Second, the military official who pressures the donor into making the offering himself accrues the merit of the dāna because the volition originated with him. I often heard wealthy donors bitterly complain about this dilemma. One explained how the government demanded that he make donations at a state-sponsored event. Angrily, he recounted that he had his own places he wanted to donate to and that he had limited resources. The pressure to donate with the junta created bad volition in his mind; he said: "What I must do is meditate before I donate so these thoughts do not arise. I must keep a wholesome intention in my mind and forget about this government. It is still dāna if I give with the right intention."

The following excerpts are taken from *A Guide to the Mangala Sutta,* published by the Department for the Promotion and Propagation of Sāsana under the SLORC government. I reproduce a rather lengthy set of quotations here to impress on the reader how the regime, which carefully oversees the publication of documents such as this one, is situating its actions to mimic the virtues recounted in the sutta.

The Buddha had condensed all moral virtues into 38 rules, or modes of conduct. If these Mangala rules are obeyed, or adhered to, one can become a good son, a good parent, a good citizen, a good administrator, or even an ideal head of state. These Mangala rules are therefore very important in the making of a nation of good citizens, and the building of an ideal state, or a Mangala country. . . . (xi)

Dana Mangala: In the ancient days people were not very greedy as they only needed enough to support their parents and to feed their own families. But in this world, there are people who cannot earn enough for their needs. They are the poor people, and there are also some bhikkhu sangha, who live purely on donations. That being so, should we think only of the family? No. We must share with others. This is dana Mangala, or act of charity. After seeing to the needs of your parents and your own family, if there is still some surplus of what you have earned, do not consume or use up all by yourself. Give away some in the form of donations or gifts to the poor and the needy. Some people think that only offerings of requisites such as food to the sangha, or donations towards building of monasteries or such things are dana. But dana is much more. The Buddha, in his exhortations, has expressed strongly that there should be no one who is so poor that he has nothing to eat; for this reason, the rich must give something to the poor. In any country there can be peace only if there are no poor people. Dana is indeed, very important in the building of a country. Nowadays, help given to the poor and the needy is getting less; and as their number is increasing, the problem of help has become more difficult. In the Pitika, about the time of King Cakkavati there were no poor people in the country. If someone were poor he would be given the necessary help out of the treasury of the king. In the olden days,

Myanmar was a Mangala country. People built monasteries, dug wells and tanks, built roads and bridges on their own initiative and on their own expense. As the people in the Mangala country adhered to the Mangala rules and principles, and built the necessary works for public welfare, the government had to spend little on such works. Out of their own free will and generosity the people subscribed liberally to all works or projects concerning education, economy and social welfare. This shows just how important is dana Mangala to the people of those days. Indeed, any gift or donation given for the welfare of the country is dana Mangala, an act of charity. (34–36)

The propagandistic motive behind these statements is apparent. Cast in the idiom of Buddhist hortatory rhetoric, the goal is to encourage the citizens of Burma to help subsidize government projects. However, as I will argue, the actions of the state officials in supporting this point of view demonstrate that they are also reiterating a shared causative logic in which moral order is achieved through the aggregate and held-in-common views and practices of its citizens. With regard to the question of how SLORC has attempted to "capture" the discourse about moral purity, I seek to demonstrate the way in which Buddhist civil society ultimately holds court over the political legitimacy the regime so desperately seeks.

Cliques and Moral Communities around Monks

Acts of dāna result in merit for this and future lives. This aspect of dāna exposes a practical or economic dimension that initially concerns the individuals' assurance that they will create generous conditions for their own and their families' future lives. But one's generosity also can serve as a marker of social status. Dāna cliques, in which groups of lay donors share in each others' merit-making events, also form the backbone of commercial networks among women, and they convert into patron-client relations among men. The ubiquity of patron-client relations in government bureaucratic institutions is a meaningful connection to male dāna clique arrangements, since government co-optation of both political and economic influence in fact transpires according to the same logic and conditions as lay participation in sangha purification.

The social dynamics of dāna cliques would be hard to convey without some direct reference to examples of how they form. Lay organizations in the past typically raised funds on an ad hoc basis for various religious activities, such as temple repair, the provision of requisites for monks, and the celebration of religious festivals. However, contemporary lay organizations such as MTY, a potent field for donations, have created endowments for various religious objectives. Favorable state interest rates for savings account deposits and savings certificates, introduced in 1975, encouraged this trend. (I was informed that the government required the Yeiktha to open a savings account and keep its money there. A committee member from the Women's Welfare Association explained how members of her group were afraid to remove any money from the account.) In 1994, the center had assets of 10 million kyats,[18] on which it earned 10 percent interest. It also owned government bonds.

Further resource flows into the center include a fixed monthly donation from active members, daily donations for the offering of food to the sangha, large individual endowments (among them solicited donations for specific projects such as constructing buildings), and endowments typically made by a permanent coterie of older women who retire to the center to practice meditation for the remainder of their lives. There are many other sources of income for the center that are not of specific relevance here, such as membership fees, wedding banquets, the Mahasi festival, and so on. The daily output of the Yeiktha is also considerable. Not including the two hundred meal takers at the Hititi (a voluntary organization providing free meals to indigent yogis), from seven to eight hundred monks, thilashin (nuns), and yogis dine at the center each day, creating the need for a steady income not entirely dependent on the spontaneous pattern of most donor activities.

In the summer of 1994, donations substantially diminished in the wake of an indefinite announcement by the government that, in the interest of its modernization program, buildings on the main road in the jewelry district would be torn down and replaced by an eight-story structure. The jewelers would not be compensated for their loss of property but would instead be forced to purchase space inside the new building at market rates. As many of the center's biggest donors were jewelers working on that street, rumors as to the extent of the financial impact on their businesses directly affected donations at the center. For ten days during *waso* (Buddhist Lent), there were no donors for meals.

Subsequently, the center organized a special money tree fund, bequeathed by specific donors, that is designated for subsidizing the cost of meals, the most persistent and largest outlay. The cost of one of these "feeding funds" is 10,000 kyats a tree. On each tree, 1,200 kyats in interest are accrued in one year. The Women's Welfare Association's goal was to assemble ten donors to donate ten trees, which would yield 12,000 kyats from the yearly interest—the cost of a meager meal for the large eating hall at the center. The virtue of donating a tree is that it is a gift that keeps on giving; the laws of commerce (interest) are employed to effect merit returns. Each year on the anniversary of the donation, the donors return to hold a water-libation ceremony for the sharing of merits. If donors have passed away, their children attend, and the merits transfer to the deceased in whatever life form they have taken.

There are ten notable donors to the center. All of them are women, and the majority are jewelers. The most generous donor, Daw ———— Kyi, has multiple business involvements, including jewelry and construction. I have been told that a fair number of Burmese herbalists also support the center. Big donors are not determined by the number of times they have donated or the amounts they have offered. Rather, they are the individuals who can be called on at any time to help the center with donations, ranging from offering the monks and yogis food when there is no outside donor to offering substantial chunks of cash for large projects, such as the construction of buildings. A Women's Welfare Committee member explained, "Whenever you need funds you just ask them and they provide them. If Mahasi announces that there is an event coming such as *kathein* (robes offering), *waso* (Buddhist Lent), or other *bwe* (festivals) the big donors need to donate at least 10,000 or 15,000 kyats each [US$100, US$150]. Then they need to collect all the funds for these events. They give for buildings—like this new building. One room with a bathroom costs three and a half lacs [US$3,500]—they donate for these things." My interviews with donors demonstrate some of the dynamics and motivations surrounding dāna cliques. I will begin by describing something of the social context in which women in donor cliques interact, as taken from my field notes.

February 10, 1995: In the dining hall (*sala*), when the monks and yogis eat, there is total silence, collective, somber mindfulness, even for lay observers who curtail their movements in studied observance of restraint and mindfulness. After the monks and yogis have completed their silent meal and have returned to their rooms, the somberness lifts and the room is instantly transformed into a gay hall with clattering dishes and friendly banter, amid calls to come and eat. Sitting at the lay women's tables (since the men's tables are separate), the conversation turns to gossip about family, friends shared in common, the danas they have organized, social scandals and discussions about monks and the laity associated with them. In contrast to the monks and yogis, the lay donors discuss with relish the quality of the various dishes served and are particular in their selections. As the hall clears out, a few ladies straggle behind enjoying le peh [pickled tea leaves] and conversation. The thilashin [nuns] and lay volunteers are busy clearing the last of the dishes and collecting the mats to be wiped and aired. Now the empty hall echoes with sound and the laziness of the heat of the afternoon begins to descend. Outside the crows gather cawing in anticipation of the last specks of rice and curry offered to them after the remaining food has been packed up to take home by the donors to be offered at home that evening to the rest of their families. Nothing is saved.

January 19, 1995: I had lunch at the Yeiktha at the invitation of one of the "old yogis" offering dana to the monks and yogis. A number of donors were invited to come. They were bedecked with their "everyday jewelry" which consisted of 10 karat diamond ear bobs, gold bobble buttons on their angies [blouses], sapphire, emerald and ruby bracelets where the stones are set side by side to form the complete circle of the bracelet. Rings of the same are set in rows. One woman, a renowned donor who received a title from the SLORC government for her generosity, had a huge pearl set among diamonds as a necklace. A two-year-old child came in a flouncy white frock and she wore a gold chain with a square amulet and a gold bracelet (which I priced later at the market at US$60.00). The ten-karat diamond earrings are ubiquitous and Daw T. —— says that they cost about 7 lacs [700,000 kyats or US$7,000]. She added that on festival days and bwe then they [that family] wear the "really big ones." She remarks how in the old days the diamonds weren't so expensive. Everybody used to wear them—but, now, not so much any more.

March 6, 1995: Donor Daw Kyi —— from Moulmein is today's meal donor. Various committee ladies from Mahasi show up for her dana as well as many guests who are natives of Moulmein. Lots of jewelry is worn. About 50–60 guests sit in the back of the hall to observe the monks eat. The offering today is only to monks, and also to one table for Ladies Welfare Committee volunteers. Daw Tun —— remarks after the meal how, "Those Moulmein people can talk a lot. They really can chat!"

March 9, 1995: U Chit ———'s daughter's wedding at the Yeiktha.[19] The vice-president of the Nuggaha busies himself with all the details of the event. Ordinarily it is the Women's Welfare Committee that is concerned with arranging a *suhn chwe* [monks' repast] and wedding. I discover that U Maung ——— is the captain of a ship—a very important person. Between monks, yogis, guests and workers 910 people are offered food. I am told that the cost of the affair is about 100,000 kyats or (according to the black market rate) 1,000 U.S. dollars.

February 5, 1995: Bogyoke Tun Tin, ex–prime minister during Ne Win period, gave dana at the Yeiktha.

April 6, 1995: After the donation by Daw Than ——— the ladies all chat together. One of the ladies gives Daw T. ——— (a volunteer at the Yeiktha) some money as she is collecting for the waso robes. Daw T. ——— puts the money in her purse. Another lady has brought her own tiffin tin filled with *ngapyi kyaw* (small fried shrimp) which she passed around and which everyone relishes. Comments are made about the difficulty of getting *nagpyi kyaw* these days, whereas before it was the most common food that any person could afford. The nuns are careful to be sure that our table is replenished with all the curry and soup dishes. There was soup, fish curry, chicken and potato curry, fried gourd, "smelly fruits" (that's as much as I know of them), fresh cucumber, cucumber carrot salad with dressing (Western-style, the first and only time I saw it), green bean curry, dried salty fried beans, lepeh (pickled tea leaves), oily tapioca cakes, mangoes, bananas, plain tea and sweet and milky coffee. Most of these very rich women are jewelers and have shops at Scotts Market (now Bogyoke Aung San Market). One wealthy woman has a material shop in addition to a jewelry shop and is extremely wealthy, according to Daw T. ——. Recently, on account of her being considered a big donor by the government (she is proud to tell me that when the government needs something, she is the first to be called on the phone), she has received exclusive concessions for hotel building, in preparation for tourism year 1996. To build her hotels, she is given access to purchase cement at the government rate.

May 20, 1995: Interview with Daw —— Kyi, Mahasi Thathana Yeiktha's biggest donor. Daw —— Kyi tells me how she has recently donated to the building fund at Mahasi Thathana Yeiktha. Because the buildings are very small, each donor had to give 50,000 kyat to one lac to help extend the buildings. She donates to the sangha [that is, she offers her dana as sanghika, meaning it is offered to the Sangha of the Four Quarters]. She boasts how Mahasi was her Sayadaw and now U Thawara [Mahasi's close disciple and nephew] is her Sayadaw. She reminds me that U Thawara is the eldest of the ovadacariya [Pāli, from *ovada* (advice) + *cariya* (teacher)] and therefore chief ovadacariya among the three. [By such reckoning, he is the greatest field of merit at the center.] She says she donates Sanghika— "Mahasi sanghika" [which is to say that she actually donates ganika, for the Mahasi division within the sangha; her statement is meant to emphasize her status as one of Mahasi's chief donors]. She also donates with the Buddha Sasana Nuggaha Apwe, Hititi [a charity internal to MTY] and Women's Association [meaning she participates with them in collective donations]. Daw —— Kyi donates mainly with women whom she met at Mahasi and not with women she knows outside of this setting. She gathers funds from Mahasi members and from people she knows through her business. She is in the gems and jewelry business and collects from friends there—especially in Scotts Market. From Mahasi she organizes funds from about 20 people. Some of these people she met at the Yeiktha and some in her businesses. She has a lot of friends through the jewelry business and through the Yeiktha. Her friends introduce her to other donors. Her husband is the director of finance at Petro Chemical Industry Corporation (PIC). Daw —— Kyi is the Yeiktha's biggest donor. She is a Mahasi Executive Committee member, Jivitidana Hospital Executive Committee member, Mingun Tipitaka Nikaya Apwe Executive Committee member (for the Yangon area), Jivitidana Hospital Committee member (for Sagaing), and *Theravada Sasana doh twin ka: pyan pwa: ye,* lifetime donor at Panditarama [the center U Pandita founded after splitting from MTY]. I ask her, "Do other gems dealers come to you [that is, ask you to donate in their cliques]?" Daw —— Kyi: "All those ruby dealers are disciples of Mogok Sayadaw." [This is another famous meditation monk and alleged arahat, now passed away.]

There are 27 people at the Yeiktha formally in charge of collecting dana and who are asked to bring donations from the "outside." Daw —— Kyi says that she gets donors to give out of friendship and wanting to do dana. They also in turn ask from her. [The implication is that she is sincere and that the moral community with which she is involved is also sincere in its sāsana practices.] These are close friends with whom she works. She tells me how there is not a person who doesn't know her. . . . She deals in diamonds there. But, she knows all connections with rubies and gold people. [The donor's "name and fame" is itself a sign of the superior paramis that he or she has cultivated and therefore also a sign of his or her moral purity. It is only when these transcendent characteristics are recognized as the causal underpinnings for the donor's prosperity in this world that mere wealth and networking get transformed into actual social status and reverence.]

Many gems dealers have meditated, she tells me. Merchants and companies all have connections with Mahasi. Nevertheless, she is not drawn into other circles than the Mahasi. Sun-lun Sayadaw's kopaka apwe and others don't ask funds from her because from the beginning she says, she has always been a Mahasi devotee. [Daw —— Kyi asserts here how she is discerning about the proper method of practice. This is intended to show the mature development of her pāramī.] Her husband doesn't solicit donations because he's a government worker. If the Yeiktha needs petrol oil for lamps, he gets it through the government at the government rate. It depends on how many gallons they need and he applies for it. He's in the Nuggaha Apwe Executive Committee and also the Jivitidana (sangha hospital) Executive Committee family.

Daw —— Kyi met Mahasi Sayadaw for the first time in 1975 . . . through another donor. In 1985, Daw —— Kyi did meditation for one month, a little more. She claims to have "finished the course." [Other women in the Women's Welfare Association sniffed at this claim: "Daw —— Kyi may be the wealthiest and best-connected donor at the center but she is *not* enlightened!" Daw —— Kyi has had ongoing problems securing her big donor status to the cosmic plane in the eyes of her contemporaries.] U Lakana was her teacher. [U Lakana is one of the renowned meditation teachers.] She donated 3 lacs to U Lakana's Kyaung in Sagaing. U Lakana conducts ten-day retreats there and there is also a *sa-thin-taik*—a center for the study of scriptures, so he is both pariyatti and patipatti. [She stresses the fact that he is well known both in scriptures and in practice, for this once again demonstrates her inclinations toward orthodox practice and therefore is a sign of her pāramī development.]

Before meditating she was an Executive Committee member, beginning from 1975. If you are to be an Executive

Committee member, you must first meditate but, because she was a big donor they let her be an Executive Committee member. In 1983 she tried to meditate for ten days. She couldn't stand it and she left. [Or as described by Daw T. ———, she "ran away."] Daw ——— Chan, an Executive Committee member (now expired) wouldn't let her quit and encouraged her to continue in her practice. Daw ——— Chan was a spinster. She was there to encourage Executive Committee members who are going to meditate. She offered her special food and encouragement so that the practice would be easier.

Daw ——— Kyi is the first in her family to be interested in vipassana and she describes how from an early age (11 and 12) she started fasting. Even today, she says, she takes only vegetarian food on the day of the week that she was born. [The suggestion of *dhutanga* purification—austerity— here once again is meant to signal the degree of her pāramī ripeness.] She describes her parents as traditional Buddhists—"born buddhists"—people who had faith because that was how they grew up. Her father and mother would give whatever they had cooked in the house daily to the *kyaung* (monastery), she says. [By contrast, Daw ——— Kyi distinguishes her own activities from those of her parents in terms of her active interest in the penultimate practices and the demonstrations of the ripeness of her pāramī.]

Kaba Aye [the place and complex of buildings where the Sangayana took place and where the Religious Ministries are located] makes requests of her to give raw rice and other dry rations for the State Sangha. The headman for her area may also request donations. So for example, the primary school was small in her area and so she donated a school 40 x 60 meters with mat walling and cement that amounted to several lacs. The headmaster requested this. The government couldn't donate to them so they said if

you could gather funds from students' parents, the
government would match funds. They asked her to
donate one lac, but no other students' parents could come
up with money so she paid for the whole thing—with
zinc roofing. She is not a government-titled donor.[20] But
she knows these ladies. She says dismissively, "Whoever
donates the most gets titled."

Daw —— Kyi's example demonstrates how dāna cliques organize around monks according to the kind of livelihood the donors
are involved in. Shared ties to natal villages also figure in (in this instance, the Mogok area, where rubies are found). In general, trust-
worthiness is measured according to the degree of distance from
one's immediate family and birthplace. The women with whom one
shares in merit making are also the individuals who make up your
moral community—a community that is founded on repeated acts
of dāna, grounded in sīla or moral conduct (and especially an expanded expectation for business ethics that includes expectations of
mutual support), and directed ultimately toward bhāvanā (meditation and wisdom). In the context of these cliques, bhāvanā can become a locus for a competitive jockeying for status. It is significant
that in the Women's Welfare Association, the eldest member of the
society holds the title of president—a mostly honorary post. One
might also note that she accrues the greatest merits for collective actions taken by the clique, since she is the foremost donor among
the rest.

I wish to reiterate that this is not only a competition for asserting
social status; it is also concerned with creating the grounds for one's
future *ontological* status. Furthermore, it is not simply one's individual kammic trajectory that is under consideration, for an individual is also building future social relationships—future societies,
even, and certainly the foundations for participation in certain lifeworlds, such as the devā, or heavenly realms. Most often, this implicit idea is expressed through making resolutions (*adeittan*) to
meet up with one's family in future lives.

Giving dāna forges networks, and there are certain dāna network cliques that women seek to join. To be in a prestigious network, one has to be able to give bountifully. One woman I knew who is in the Mahasi clique is invited to many outside dāna circles (formal invitations to donate are sent) thanks to her standing in the Mahasi women's executive committee. However, she confessed that she could not accept most of these invitations because it obligated her to participate in donation making beyond her financial means. Being part of a prestigious dāna clique is desirable because the well-connected individual participates in multiple moral communities centered around prestigious monks. Women compete fiercely to be one of the famous *dagama*s (female lay supporters) of a monk. A dagama's acts are multiply indexed—she makes merit in a leveraged way because she gets to be around the good monks.

There is great prestige associated with "discovering a monk" and becoming his chief donor, for in that position, one might have his ear and receive advice on personal problems, hear the dhamma from him, or learn meditation directly from him. Close ties between disciple and monk become more difficult to engineer once a monk becomes famous, for then he is absorbed into the patronage circles of the very highest segments of society as well as the government. Having had an earlier tie to a monk—having discovered him, so to speak—enhances the possibility of maintaining enduring ties with him. Having access to the great monks is taken as a sign of pāramī.

One might hear a layperson comment on how someone has the pāramī to be able meet up with good monks, to have the opportunity to offer them dāna, and to be able to listen to their dhamma discourses. Obligation does not obtain explicitly (that is, formally) between the lay donor and the individual monk recipient, since the monk is merely the vehicle or vessel through which the donor may participate in the dhamma at its embodied location. It is the donor who experiences gratitude, not the recipient. Reciprocity between monk and layperson occurs only at the most general level, and it is recognized in terms of the laity providing the material supports for the sangha.

Donation obligates individuals within a clique. Although the language used is that of offering someone the opportunity to donate or share in the merits of others' donations, it is evident that a woman's power to raise funds from her friends on behalf of a chosen cause makes her what might be considered the equivalent of the male "big elephant." (I will discuss this concept later.) Participation in the *ahlu* (donation event) of one person obligates the organizer to participate in future dāna events organized by her guests. It also creates the expectation that the donor can be counted on to provide other "profane" favors outside the donation sphere itself.

It is worth commenting on the distinguishing elements between male cliques and female cliques. Women exchange dāna participations and the sharing of merit within defined dāna cliques. Men seek to donate as the chief among other donors in a hierarchical arrangement of statuses. Men's donations thus tend to solidify patron-client relations and obligations and therein establish vertical relations of power. Women, by contrast, extend their power horizontally as a function of the extension of trade relations. Men's donations are seen to affect their *pon* (from *punna,* meaning "merit quality," where "quality" refers to pāramī). The word *pon* refers to the prior accumulation of merit toward the production of one's accumulated accomplishment, specifically in relation to charismatic power and authority. Women are not seen to possess pon. Their dāna practices are deemed to relate only to the economic sphere and the perfection of their dāna pāramī. It is the woman's prior *akusala* (demeritorious) actions that have caused her to be born female. Women assume the main economic role in the family—a familiar pattern throughout mainland Southeast Asia and one that, in Burma, apparently dates back to the eleventh century, for inscriptions of women donors in Pagan are in evidence.[21]

Though women enjoy a relatively high status and freedom in Burma, there nevertheless is, to use Melford Spiro's phase, an "ideology of male superiority" in the country:

> The masculine is much superior to the feminine. . . . It is irrelevant who wields the bigger stick or brings home a richer basket. The

important question is who wears the crown. And that mark of glory rests upon the man's head. And the whole of society is as sure about this as he is himself. As to what the wife thinks, there is hardly a Burmese woman who doesn't feel this deep inside her, brag though she might about every other ability of hers . . . this ideology is found in a society in which, as we have seen, women are the structural and jural equals of men.[22]

I think it is most profitable to consider the distinction between men and women in terms of key Burmese ideas about the *transferability of merit* and the *capturing of merit*. It is not that women are transferring merit to their menfolk. Men offer in their own network spheres. However, men's and women's spheres may not entirely overlap because women's and men's networks operate quite differently in regard to dāna. For a woman who is in the market business, for example, her dāna networks create the obligation of long-term support and reciprocity. The women one participates with in dāna activities are the same individuals one would turn to for a loan or connect with in a network of business supports. The integral link between dāna and business networks was illustrated to me when I came to know a Muslim jeweler in Bogyoke Aung San Market. This woman participated as rigorously in dāna, as did her Buddhist associates in the market. Asked why, she replied that by giving dāna, she made more money. Belief in kamma had no relation to or conflict with her Muslim faith.

The Politics of Sincerity

The laity's support of monks is based on their determination of his meritoriousness, reckoned according to a variety of criteria. The virtuoso monk who is thought to have attained sainthood is deemed the most deserving of the laity's veneration and donations.[23] Though it is recognized that a monk's inner states of consciousness cannot be evaluated by a third party, there has developed, nevertheless, an informal folk system of classification that the laity believe reflects inner states of consciousness. The virtuoso monk is mild, does not have strong desires, and is free from anger and delusion. He apparently evaluates worldly affairs from a place unclouded by personal investment. Laity search for signs in a monk's comportment—ennui in speech, a lack of animated curiosity that might be betrayed even by a darting glance, or the absence of food preferences. Even such gestures as a vigorous extension in opening a door or showing one's teeth while smiling can be considered as proofs that a monk still has a distance to go before achieving full enlightenment.

Monks are not permitted, by their code of conduct, to make claims about their own or others' inner states of consciousness and achievements. But a subtle register about who has accomplished what stage of insight or enlightenment, as described in the last chapter, reinforces conventions in assessing another person's inner consciousness. Sincerity is key to these assessments. The persistent and unflagging cultivation of inner mental states through the practice of monkly discipline is evaluated in terms of a monk's sincerity in striving for nibbāna. Likewise, Burmese Buddhists believe that achievement of the various stages of sainthood through meditation results in irrevocable transformations of consciousness, resulting in sincere or truthful dispositions in the world. The *materialization* of these evidences of sainthood and sincere striving for nibbāna can be seen in the support that the laity give these monks. A renowned monk becomes a center of intense donation. Zealous competition emerges over who will control the donation arena surrounding the monk—over who will be the primary donor. A good and sincere monk represents to Burmese Buddhists a highly leveraged field in which to sow the seeds of their future good merit.[24]

Renowned donors are persons of influence, and their status is closely linked to that of the monks. Monks and their daga (donors) indexically link the statuses of the worldly to the transcendent, for it is believed that they have cultivated their relationships over multiple lifetimes of support and striving. The pairing of a famous monk with an equally famous donor legitimizes the status of these individuals in both directions. The monk is validated by the attentions of the donor, who materializes (through lavish donations of temples and even cars, refrigerators, copy machines, and the like) the qualities of perfection (pāramī) cultivated by the monk over many lifetimes. Simultaneously, the donor is validated as the supporter of an exemplary monk around whom much donation and veneration activity occurs—a clear sign of his or her accumulated merit.

One need only observe the government's annual ceremony for presenting titles to scholarly monks and nuns to recognize this logic in action at the state level. The highest-ranking official presents the title to the highest-achieving monk and so on, down to the lowest-ranking official. This pattern is then repeated for the nuns, with the highest-ranking official's wife presenting the title to the highest-achieving nun and so forth. The indexical ranking of worldly power and status to the accomplishments of world renouncers in ceremonies of this kind are forceful, visual public assertions about who's who in the social, political, and religious arenas.[25] Claims to merit in this manner participate in a theory about moral intentions with causal generative effects in the material world. F. K. Lehman has observed that these affirmations share similarities with Calvinist assertions of election.[26] In the Buddhist context, the moral state implied by acts of dāna and the ability to carry them out is transitory or finite, in the sense that stores of merit may be depleted or replenished. Thus, is it possible to look to the donation and other religious activities of the generals today and ask, "Are these generals producing sufficient merit to offset the impending kammic results of their brutal practices?"

This stopgap to moral capital is an important feature, for it implies an added mechanism for questioning the junta's legitimacy in cosmological terms. To some degree, it is in the hands of the laity and the sangha to judge the level of sincerity of regime members' actions—or to doubt that sincerity. But as long as members of the regime carry out dāna with *apparent* sincerity, then, as with the mental state of the monk that can only be guessed at through surface indications, the people must go along. It is not that they believe blindly that the junta is sincere; rather, it is that there is a general acquiescence toward or a priori acceptance of the conditions set by their adherence to the cosmological principles. Thus, it was with a heavy mood that Yangonites told me in the summer of 2002 that the military had successfully accomplished the refurbishing and repair of Burma's most important pagoda, Shwedagon. They believed this to be an accomplishment that only a "legitimate" ruler could fulfill. (Legitimacy, in this instance, is based on the prior accumulation of merits and their conversion into power.) In the absence of inauspicious signs such as earthquakes and floods, which are predicted to occur in the event that a pretender to the throne seeks to act as a ruler without the requisite cosmic merit stores, many believed that the completion of such a monumental sacred task was evidence that the regime was destined to stay in power. At the close of the ceremony to hoist the gold and bejeweled finial on the crest of the pagoda, the rulers exclaimed, "*Aung Pyi! Aung Pyi!*" (We won! We won!), thereby demonstrating a recognition of their position.

In accordance with this logic, members of the regime maintain that the basis for their legitimacy is implied by the fact of their ascendance to power. Consequently, their donations and other pious religious acts can be reinterpreted not as being enacted to gain the support of the people in the pursuit of legitimacy—the manipulation hypothesis—but as evidence for that legitimacy.[27] SLORC/SPDC's merit-making activity may certainly be agonistic, an example of the negative imposition of the logic of the gift, and thus a form of strategic gifting.[28] But it is behavior that nevertheless lies within and not outside the cosmological framework for action and moral causality that is understood by the Burmese populace.

Again, so as not to be misunderstood on the question of actual and potential resistance to the regime, I do not imply that SLORC/SPDC's dāna behavior is never taken as a distortion of Buddhist practice, as the following report from the online Shan Herald Agency for News suggests:

Shans returning from Panghsang, the Wa principal town, after a religious ceremony presided over by Gen Khin Nyunt, Burma's #2 strongman, told S.H.A.N. they considered the general an adherent of black magic rather than a Buddhist. "Holy monks, especially invited for the occasion, were left to stand around the Razamat (lattice fence) surrounding the Pangkham pagoda," said a layman follower of a Buddhist priest from Kengtung. "Instead, it was him who ambled around the pagoda mumbling incantations and hoisted the hti (bud) and panzak (vane) atop the pagoda." The worst insult, they felt, was when Gen Khin Nyunt, from the top of the pagoda, shouted, "Gawng Khan Ja!" (Bear with your heads) three times. Others, meanwhile, said they thought they heard him say, "Kong Khan Ja!" (Bear with your backs arched). "Whatever he said means we people have to take everything that is meted out to us by the military," one interpreted. "He even brought his own Namyard (libation water) from Lashio," added another. "He must be a sorcerer, that guy."[29]

The internal debates—what Foucauldians like to call discourse and counterdiscourses[30]—are rife. The popular differentiation between "government monks" and ordinary monks, the refusal of some famous monks to go to the capital to be honored by the regime, and, still more damning, the refusal of many monks to accept donations altogether are further evidence that there is no simple acceptance of the regime's actions. However, the ultimate *terms* of these actions are not cast in doubt, since they are the mental tools, as Godelier might call them, with which the religiopolitical reality is engaged. Godelier's reflection on the notion of "consent," as he expressed it in an interview with Paul Eiss and Thomas Wolfe,[31] is suggestive of the situation I am trying to depict:

[C]onsent means the sharing of the same representations, even with different interpretation of the same ideas, with opposed interpretations. But if you live within the same circle of ideas, you reproduce them even with an opposite attitude, so that dialectic of opposed interpretations of the same representations is crucial to the understanding of many things. . . . And so it needs a very complex theory of what is a representation and what is a sharing of representation, conscious and unconscious.

The point is that dissimulation may have moral causal consequences, but even dissimulated actions can retain a measure of positive kammic result. A monk at the Mahasi Thathana Yeiktha heightened my awareness of this fact when he related to me the following folk story:

> At the time of the Buddha, a huge crowd of people gathered to listen to the Buddha's teachings. As the gathering swelled, a man who at first had been sitting in the front was pushed back by successive waves of new listeners until he found himself at the very back of the gathering and unable to hear the Buddha's words. He thought to himself, "Why is it that I have the good pāramī to meet up with a Buddha but then am unable to hear his discourse?" Perceiving the man's thoughts, the Buddha came to him and explained that in a prior life he had made an offering to the embryo Buddha. As the thought first arose in him to give a donation, his mind was glad, but he then hesitated, weighing his desire to keep the gift for himself. He overcame these thoughts however and began preparing for his offering. Again the thought arose in him that the embryo Buddha was probably not so worthy of a gift and that perhaps he should change his mind and not part with it. Again he overcame these thoughts. After many bouts of doubt and judgmental evaluation of the worthiness of the recipient he finally carried through with the act of charity. The Buddha explains that on account of having made that offering the man had the great fortune of meeting up with a fully enlightened Buddha. However, because he did not relinquish his gift with full and sincere intention to perform dāna he was pushed back in the crowd by wave after wave of other devotees who had better perfected their dāna pāramī.

To conclude this part of the discussion, I would reiterate that dāna participates in a larger system of ideas regarding intention and the reproduction of present political realities. Sincerity discourses are assertions about an actor's conformity to an already given moral order. In the political context, it functions as a civil demand, articulated at the level of rumor, for evidence of the military regime's "good faith" in abiding by the moral code. In a country where a paranoid government does not allow free speech and free association, it is fascinating and even puzzling that it is the people who claim the right to determine the regime's sincerity in acting the part of good Buddhists, whereas the government plays the role of chief donor to and purifier of the sangha—fulfilling, on some level, the role of a king who is responsible for the perpetuation of sāsana and support of the sangha.[32]

The regime's donative activities, whether construed as sincere or manipulative, are both *generative* and *reflective* of social and political hierarchy. I believe political analysts have overlooked the generative component of the way in which state and society are mutually engaged in the production of social, economic, and political arrangements in Burma. For Western analysts, the unquestioned assumption about SLORC's "sāsana activities" has been that the military regime has sought to legitimize its authority by merely looking and acting like Burma's Buddhist kings of yore. This theory that religious acts should only be interpreted as covert political acts—a theory of the symbolic legitimation of political authority—does not take into account several significant factors: the very real social processes that occur in the production of patron-client ties and obligations, the interdigitation of the common and black market economies in the so-called dāna economy, the devolution of lay-controlled property through the sangha, and the growth of strong moral communities organized around the monk-donor pattern. Of specific interest to me is the impact of the rise of the New Laity, which asserts through mass practices for enlightenment what the goals and values of society ought to be, how revitalization of civil society is to be accomplished, and therein also a claim about what the terms for political legitimacy are.

The laity are centrally involved in assuring the purity of monks by materially supporting those who are most purified in their practices.

The self-evidence of the sangha's purity is not ultimately affirmed by monks but by the laity. This is a coparticipation framework, of course, since the laity are not better arbiters than are the monks in matters of doctrine. Laity are simply the means through which endorsement and validation of the Buddha's teachings are made representationally available, that is, as materially expressed through institutions, requisites, buildings, lands, ordination, and so forth. What we see in the competition among members of the laity over fields of merit is the working out of this principle of moral endowments. The principle is a matter of personal influence and political power, as they are centered on the monk (who is the *pongyi,* the great glory). By participating with a monk, a layperson acquires something of the radiating glory that surrounds the monk like a nimbus.

Pon also amasses to leading donors. This is an important reason why the image of military leaders at donation events dominates television broadcasts and is the subject of daily reports in the newspapers. (Burmese say that they do not watch television in black and white, but in green and gold—green for the color of military uniforms, gold for the gilded pagodas.) A typical daily account in the newspaper, in which one can see the mingling of governmental and monkly personnel, is as follows:

YANGON, 18 Nov.—The families of Military Intelligence held the 12th Kathina robe offering ceremony at Tatmadaw Dhammayon on Arzarni Street this morning. Chairman of the State Peace and Development Council Commander-in-Chief of Defence Services Senior General Than Shwe and wife Daw Kyaing Kyaing attended the ceremony and offered Kathina robes and alms to the Sayadaws.

Present on the occasion were State Ovadacariya Sayadaws, Vice-Chairmen of the State Sangha Maha Nayaka Committee Maha Aungmyaybonsan Kyaung-taik Sayadaw of Bahan Township Bhaddanta Paninndabhivamsa and Myole Kyaungtaik Sayadaw of Lashio Agga Maha Saddhammajotikadhaja Bhad-danta Kavindacara, member Sayadaws and members of the sangha.

The recitation continues in the same vein for another two long paragraphs. The Burmese titles may be foreign to the general reader, but the point is that the massive presence of military brass at sacred donation events is both evidence of their status as "chief donors" and contributory to it. The logic of attraction (that is, why power accrues to big donors) is, in Burmese terms, that of pon and sacred potency. As in the radiating glory surrounding monks, here it is transferred to important laypersons. In anthropological terms, the big donors are patrons located at the top of a pyramid of clients who, voluntarily or otherwise, sanction the leaders to make offerings that are both cosmologically and economically redistributive. The true, unspoken currency is that of political legitimacy.

The mounting influence of big donor activities can be discerned again in the following quote taken in an interview with an executive committee member who was in charge of fund raising for new buildings at Daw Nyanacari Kyaung in 1995:

> We invited this Secretary 1 and Secretary 2—they came and received the donations and so the more people were interested in coming and they gave more money. Instead of three coming, four would come. U Khin Nyunt [Secretary 1] is the most honorary and most powerful person. And his number two is U Tin Oo and he is the second most powerful man. So when they come to receive the money, the people become more interested. Secretary 1 and Secretary 2 accept the money, so for example, if I am the donor instead of 10,000 kyats [US$100] I would put 20,000 [US$200], 70,000 [US$700] kyats in front of him. You have to please him—something like that. So when the other donors come they give more.

On the day of the ahlu (offering), Secretary 1 arrived and was ushered downstairs to the main hall. About a hundred people were present, and he offered the money on behalf of all the donors to the kyaung—he put it into the hands of the building committee. The building committee was headed by "local people," in other words, local government people, who administered the Saung Kyaung township, Mawata. These government officials volunteered their time on behalf of the building project and controlled the money, "so that there will be no mistake anywhere," said the doctor. (In fact, the government is involved in controlling the kopaka apwe.) "Whenever we want to buy something they [the military government people] will help us to buy it, and will procure the needed materials from the cheapest government shops," he said. By this, he was referring to the special prices available only to government people and not the rest of the market. But of greater significance even than price was availability itself. This committee, being part of the formal government bureaucracy, would be able to procure cement for the project—cement that was otherwise not openly available.

I asked the doctor whether these officials undertook these duties on behalf of their own devotion or on behalf of the government. He replied, "Both, because of the voice of the Secretary 1 and 2 and at the same time because they are devoted Buddhists . . . so there is no problem." I asked: "For the most part then, it isn't governmental polices, it's just individuals wanting—" The doctor interjected: "Of course, they are all individuals! Secretary 1 and 2 are coming just as individuals. They also donate something but they can't donate much, 1,000 or 2,000 kyats [US$10–20] by themselves. There is not a single institute that is directly subsidized by the government, but this one is one of the rare ones that is supported by the government. Only last week Secretary 1 and 2 donated 350 bags of rice. There is no government grant to any institution—except for those monks that received the Agga Maha Pandita titles and so forth and who get the *suhn* [rice] and some *wutu* [monks' money used only for requisites] amount such as 750 kyats [US$7.50] a year for the title."

Burmese skeptics cynically describe the water-pouring ritual that concludes donation events attended by the military as "bribery,"[33] since it is here that patron-client chains are formed between the regime and members (especially rich members) of the laity. Access to business concessions and difficult-to-obtain resources are offered by the government in exchange for privately funded support of various social projects, such as the building of schools, hospitals, and roads. The regime freely calls on these individuals whenever it requires financial backing for one project or another, and it is difficult to refuse the request. Dāna cliques of this sort are also a way for the regime to "capture" moral communities that would otherwise be donating together outside the influence of the government. These cliques are, in this sense, a form of control over the religion. Aside from explicitly instrumental and strategic governmental goals in religious giving, it must also be remembered that, as the doctor pointed out, military personnel are acting as individuals in pursuit of personal power created through acts of purification and the production of patron-client ties.

The intertwining of the regime's sāsana activities with secular authority, as evident in the relation between sacred giving and the profane economy, is worthy of further comment. Dāna is tied to redistribution streams between the spheres of the sangha, civil society, and the state. Many among the laity can be assumed to be offering dāna as a way of shielding their lands from a predatory government. Sacred land cannot be taxed or easily confiscated by the government, and there are various categories of sacred land that blend into laity-controlled properties on which monks reside. The monks' code of conduct forbids them and laypeople from living or staying on the same land together. However, as one pious bureaucrat at the Ministry of Home and Religious Affairs put it to me, "Out of compassion the monks allow the people to stay since during times of hardship they want to stay near the Buddha, Dhamma, and Sangha." It is a common practice for laity to donate private buildings to monks along with larger tracts of land with the stipulation (enduring for the life of the donor, for so many generations, or in perpetuity) that the family donors may occupy the private buildings. These donations are classified as sacred property and hence are exempt from taxation. In aggregate, these tax shelter–like arrangements also underpin a territorial competition between the regime and the sangha, a topic of considerable complexity and significance that awaits further investigation.

The tension between the military's command economy with its frequent attempts to nationalize private property and wealth, on the one hand, and the considerable informal economy and black market, on the other, tempts one to look specifically to the dāna economy as a potential repository for illegal wealth. The most notable example supporting such a strategic interpretation of the dāna economy may be found in the vast donations of land to the sangha following the government's refusal to transfer power to Aung San Suu Kyi and her National League for Democracy party in the early 1990s.[34] The regime's attempts to nationalize properties and relocate large segments of the urban populace were met with massive land donations. Some donors explicitly explained to me that they felt it was better to make merits by donating their lands to the religion rather than having them confiscated by the military government. According to statistics provided by the Ministry of the Interior, religious landholdings grew from 43 percent to 57 percent of the total inhabited land between 1989 and 1994, an absolute increase of 143,343 hectares. Taking title to the land, the monks nevertheless permitted donors to continue living on and enjoying sustenance from the donated land.[35]

Dāna as a System of Intention

As an opening caveat, I said earlier that too much focus on the regime as a monolithic entity was distorting, since the government is made up of different branches (the military and the administrative bureaucracies, to begin with) as well as individuals within those entities whose actions do not directly follow on the putative interests of their institutions. A review of a few instances of dāna will support this observation and suggest a new logic for ordering the activities.

Political officials in particular are in a position to leverage their opportunities to donate. Furthermore, there is an expectation that rulers and men of substantial political power (those individuals possessed of pon) ought to provide opportunities for their inferiors to make merits and to support the perpetuation of the Buddha sāsana. As I have reviewed in chapter 1, in the classical Burmese Buddhist state this worked out to a theory of moral causation that linked the king's actions to cosmic, social, and natural events. The well-being of the state and the people was understood to depend on the personal morality of the king.[36] Through an analysis of dāna patron-client obligations that crosscut the military and government administrations, it is possible to begin constructing a model that shows how the native theory of mind and intention is generative of power and legitimacy at the state level.

Government ministries are known to donate to religious organizations as a single group or clique. This is required by the central military government, and it is done in recognition of the fact that patron-client ties emerge from donation societies. In other words, by requiring donations to be organized hierarchically within the officially sanctioned channels of ministries, the government both secures loyalties stretching downward from ministers to their underlings and short circuits the development of relations of loyalty along nonsanctioned social pathways. Put another way, the government that donates together stays together. This activity is enforced by means of a compulsory skimming of bureaucrats' monthly salaries for the purpose of donation. One of the principal materializations of this ministerial donation activity in the 1990s was the construction of *dhammayone* (Buddhist discourse halls) at the base of Shwedagon Pagoda. The military provided each ministry with small parcels of land at the base of Shwedagon. In turn, each ministry was responsible for internally generating funds from its workers to construct dhammayone that would be affiliated with the ministry office. The dhammayone functioned as a location for government ministers and their subordinates to gather twice monthly (on full- and dark-moon days) and on other special occasions to make offerings to monks and to listen to their sermons.

Individual merit making within this political donation structure is also possible. In an example from the 1970s that was brought to my attention by an administrator at a Yangon monastery, the tax minister offered the state tax building to Mogok Sayadaw, a famous monk who was reputed to be a fully enlightened saint (arahat). The imposing colonial-period building is today mostly unused, following the death of the charismatic monk to whom it was offered. How had state property turned into religious property? Was the minister acting on behalf of the state? I was told that the tax minister had acted on his own, thereby demonstrating that he was a big elephant—a political person with true power.

In a similar case in the 1990s, a senior official within the Ministry of Home and Religious Affairs related to me how he had taken out a "personal" loan of US$4 million from the minister of forestry. That is, he borrowed money from another government bureaucracy in order to undertake a personal merit-making project. His aim was to build an escalator to the top of Shwedagon, enabling the elderly to reach the peak and undertake merit activities.[37] As a consequence of his actions, he explained to me, merits performed by the elderly would thereby also accrue to him as the agent responsible for their merit-making activities. Gesturing to the bare surroundings of his extremely modest home, he remarked, "You can see that I do not have very much. I donate everything to the sāsana. Though I may look very poor, actually all are given for dāna." Moreover, he explained that he was able to repay the debt to the forestry minister in half the time promised by exacting a small fee for the use of the escalator and by the pious donations of the faithful.[38]

Within the military itself, the head of a particular command will require his subordinates to give him sums of money so he can create a collection for donation. It is important to point out that in this case, he is collecting not just money but people, since his subordinates will show up at the donation event itself. The military commander donates "on behalf of" his subordinates as the "foremost" donor. In accordance with the logic of the system, the commander may not even donate his own money, or he may only donate a token amount. Nevertheless, as the charismatic magnet capable of drawing together people and resources in the dāna event, he is the main recipient of the merits for the collective donation.

Individual merit-making activities and the pursuit of proper intention by government personnel is evident in the system of golden parachutes whereby military officials would, on retirement, receive bureaucratic sinecures. This practice is common in many socialist countries, but in most places, political or military retirees might end up in a ministry or in a state-run corporation. In Burma, the golden parachute of choice took the retiree into kopaka apwe of major Buddhist institutions such as the Shwedagon Pagoda. The SLORC/ SPDC military regime following Ne Win continued this practice of controlling the most important religious edifices in the country. Golden parachutes provide benefits on two levels, personal and political. On the political front, influence over the management of key public institutions is indispensable. Effective control over religious sites permits the government greater control over the population. On a personal level, many military and government officials also take seriously the Buddhist dictum that one should devote one's final years to making merits and preparing for the next life. These posts are considered highly leveraged opportunities for merit production, and they are especially suited to high-ranking military officials because these men need to balance their merit base after careers of presumably demeritorious activities.

Finally, as mentioned earlier, the regime exploits existing patron-client ties implicit in independent dāna cliques by visiting the homes of wealthy individuals on auspicious days and pressuring them to give donations. By instigating the populace to do good in this manner, the government accumulates merit. This cajoling of the citizenry into acting morally also contributes to the redistributive coffers that radiate outward from monkly institutions. But in terms of the junta's actions to secure political legitimacy, this activity echoes the role of the classical kings, in which fostering a moral citizenry (through such acts as encouraging donation) redounded positively on the merit of the sovereign. The actual donor's merit is, in the process, diminished, for the mental intention (cetanā) for the donation can be said to originate with the cajoling state and not the donating individual. Some people will say, however, as a form of refuting this logic, that when they go to witness the donation being made, they conjure up the intention that they, not the state, are donating.

That the logic of political resistance is likewise expressed in the idiom of dāna is evident from an incident that occurred in 1990. Following the military's refusal to hand over power to Aung San Suu Kyi, whose National League for Democracy had won a landslide election, four monks were shot dead in Mandalay for rejecting alms from military personnel. This religious boycott, referred to as turning over the bowl (*pattam nikkujjana kamma*), represented a form of protest that monks, ordinarily not permitted by their precepts to participate in worldly political affairs, may undertake under specified circumstances. Several more monks were taken into custody, stripped of their robes, and sentenced to imprisonment with hard labor. The military threatened additional sanctions against the sangha. In the meantime, the monks' early morning alms route began to conspicuously bypass military homes. To protest being deprived of the opportunity to make merit through dāna, the wives of key military personnel refused to cook for their husbands. These cleavages within households speak to the profound regard in which dāna is held even by those in power.

The link between private intention and state legitimacy is tied to the fact that dāna is a preeminently public practice. Amounts donated are broadcast for all who might hear and in whom there might be produced the feeling of sympathetic joy (muditā) through vicarious participation in the donation act. (The television news station devotes much of its airtime to covering events of donations made by military brass.) The mental act of free-will giving is cultivated by the donor and simultaneously by his or her witnesses, who find the thought and inclination to donate are produced in their own consciousness as well. Consequently, donation is a social event in which invitations to "share in the merits" of the occasion may be sent out to family, friends, and acquaintances. These regularized groupings in turn form the basis of dāna cliques. The prominent givers in these more or less labile groups accrue greater amounts of merit and social status because they give more and because larger numbers of giving participants are drawn to their events as a result. There is, in fact, a functional reciprocity involved, as all of those individuals who participated in the donor's event will eventually invite him or her to participate in their dāna events as well. These networks of donors form latent action groups for activities extending outside the religious sphere. For men, donation networks develop into patron-client ties in political formation, as I have suggested. For women, donation networks spread horizontally to extend economic networks and supports.[39]

The existence of dāna cliques demonstrates how dāna shades away from being a personal act of individual relinquishment to being an act in which the goal is to influence others. We find in these cliques the location at which individual intention toward soteriological goals becomes transmuted into a system for the production of great men and great women.[40] Renowned donors are recognized by the government with titles that parallel the titles for accomplishment in learning presented to monks. The qualities of a great donor stem not merely from the amount he or she gives but also from the attitude that generosity is held to imply about the inner mental dispositions of the donor. This emphasis is intended to communicate that something more than giving is taking place. These donors are communicating that their dāna activities reflect more perfectly cultivated, foundational moral perfections and that they themselves are persons of a certain spiritual status worthy of awe and admiration. Their wealth is evidence of generosity in previous lives, thus demonstrating that they are deserving of their status in the present one. Monks devote most of their homiletics to the subject of dāna, encouraging the faithful to employ every opportunity in the present to secure the life conditions of the future.

In light of this, it is understandable why a wealthy donor virtually never donates privately or secretly. Donation events are concluded with a water-pouring or libation ceremony that ritually invites all present to share in the merits—even if vicariously through sympathetic joy. Donation thus brings people together. In Yangon, the very wealthy extend invitations to attend donation events. Issuing an invitation implies the reciprocal obligation to attend one's guests' donation events and to contribute something. A donor's status is based on how many people he or she can influence to attend, in addition to the ability to maintain membership in a wide range of dāna cliques.

The social phenomenological principle of dāna is epitomized by the way in which donation activities provide places and opportunities where virtuous private mental intentions may be cultivated and performed. On this level, we may interpret dāna as being directed outside the worldly sphere of exchange, and it is best interpreted in terms of Buddhist soteriological doctrine. However, as the materialization of dāna cliques would imply, the mentalistic domain of dāna is not independent but rather mutually constitutive of social, political, and economic realities.[41]

Dāna as Moral Validation of the Regime

In accordance, once again, with Max Weber's insight that political legitimacy can never be accomplished solely by means of violence,[42] the regime has been constrained to accommodate the framework for moral state action that includes dāna as one of its key features. When the military regime came to power in 1962 under Ne Win, the military dropped the prior government's overtly Buddhist agenda and sought instead to justify itself in socialist terms. This strategy was unsuccessful, and for a decade or more, it was lay guardian committees that attended to the perpetuation and protection of the sāsana. During this period, the "age of paṭipatti" grew rapidly. Mahasi branch organizations spread throughout the country. In these private centers, the sangha was "domesticated," to use Michael Carrither's term, and brought under the control of powerful trustee committees in a pattern reminiscent of the earlier ideal ternary order (sangha, state, laity)[43] in support of the sāsana. Eventually, the Ne Win government set out to purge these centers and bring the sangha under state control, drawing an official state sangha to its center at Kaba Aye in Yangon. Now, the Religious Affairs Department is the kopaka apwe for this sangha, one monk explained in 1995. All postindependence governments (whether parliamentary democratic, socialist, or military) have looked to Buddhism, in one way or another, as a common ground from which to define national identity and the legitimacy of the nation-state and its government. What makes the present SPDC regime's public interest in donation activities so significant is that it demonstrates the double effort on the regime's part to both secure control over the most prominent and important Buddhist sites and sangha members and to lead civil society in religious merit-making activities.[44] The military government's adherence to and participation in elaborate donation schemes attest to the influence of the Buddhist model over the question of political legitimacy as well as economic organization and hence the necessity to account for dāna in the explication of these.

I have argued that acts of sacred giving by the military regime are not best interpreted as mere strategic manipulations of symbols for purposes of legitimation. One reason for this is that legitimation entails a moral validation by the populace. In this instance, the Buddhist populace is in control of the criteria for sincerity; the regime, in search of legitimacy on these grounds, must conform. However, in a political environment characterized by the brutal suppression of regime critics and demonstrators, a politics of sincerity, articulated at the level of rumor, has emerged. Although ascertaining the inner psychological states of another person is neither possible nor permissible, inferring what motivates actors, including the regime actors, is an everyday affair. The politics of sincerity marks the recognition of the possibility of dissimulation in actions. What is most interesting for the Burmese case is that it is the people/laity who purport to make the final judgment about sincere actions.[45]

Dāna practices operate at a location where the transcendent and the worldly—the spiritual and the practical, or the "mental and the material," in Godelier's language (1986)—meet. Burmese Buddhism has retained its characteristic as a cosmological religion—that is, it remains preoccupied with reproducing a conception of the whole that Frank Reynolds (1998) has called the "Buddha world," a self-referentially conceived space for the perpetuation of the teachings of the Buddha, the production of moral society, and the foundation of the production of individuals' own ontological grounds of being. Political, economic, and religious institutions all "function" toward this end. In Godelier's terms, cosmology "dominate[s] the overall functioning of a society and organize[s] its long-term reproduction. . . . [It] functions as relations of production . . . constitut[ing] the social armature of the society's material base."[46] Because these two registers—the worldly and the transcendent—can intersect in the same deed, the criteria of sincerity of intention come to be scrutinized, by Burmese Buddhists and consequently by the social analyst. And thus, I speak of dāna as a "system of intention" lying at the nexus of both mental and material realities, extending into each other's sphere and necessitating a theory that can accommodate the social realities as—to borrow W. V. Quine's (1965) expression—"reciprocally contained."

Shinpyu procession initiating a boy into the Buddhist Order as a novice. His sister undertakes the *nahtwin,* or ear-boring ceremony.

Laity pay respects to new novices.

Young girls take temporary ordination during a school break.

Entrance to the Mahasi Meditation Center (MTY), Yangon.

Administrative office, MTY. Pictures of renowned meditation monks line the wall.

The seated women are two of the great donors at MTY.

Mahasi Yeiktha entrance and main buildings.

Dhamma discourse and meditation hall, MTY.

Main meditation hall, MTY. Yogis have left the hall for an hour of walking meditation.

Main meditation hall, MTY.

Yogis at MTY.

*Thilashin*s meditate at MTY.

This kitchen at MTY serves two meals a day for up to five hundred yogis, nuns, and monks.

One of the nuns in charge of the kitchen, MTY.

A volunteer offers food to stray animals after the main meal.

Memorial to Mahasi, MTY. The marble wall is inscribed with the names of donors.

Life-size wax image of Mahasi.

This photo of Sir U Thwin, the initial donor of the center, is displayed at MTY and at the Ministry of Home and Religious Affairs.

A life-size wax image of Sir U Thwin is encased in a glass hut at the front of the Yeiktha grounds. The image is a replica of the well-known photo.

These "old yogis" lived at the meditation center in small huts after having donated substantial property to MTY.

A *yeiktha* is "a place that is cool and cools the passions."

Accommodations for a meditator at MTY.

The author (*left of center*) with pilgrims visiting Thamanya Sayadaw.

Wedding guests eat after monks and yogis are offered food.

Monks take their midday meal at U Pandita's meditation center.

Department of Religious Affairs book distribution storeroom. A photograph of Aung San is at the back.

Office at the Department of Propagation, Kaba Aye, Yangon.

Mosquito nets protect yogis at an upscale meditation center.

Chapter 4

THE DOUBLE ORDER OF LAW

Monks, Gender, and Resistance

A Focus on Violence: Into the Field

To this point, I have not focused directly on what the Burmese political landscape is most famous for outside the country—namely, violence. Stefan Collignon's roundup of the state of affairs in Burma is concise and worth quoting here: "In the fiftieth year after the adoption of the Universal Declaration of Human Rights, Burma holds the sad record of one [of] the worst and longest-lasting dictatorships on earth. An unelected government, draconian laws, military tribunals, widespread arrests, torture, forced relocations and portering, mass refugee movements, crackdowns on political leaders, closed universities, repressed freedom of the press, expression of speech and information are the everyday reality in Burma."[1]

Although Burma is, without doubt, ruled at present by one of the world's most repressive regimes, many of us who conduct research in central Burma have often remarked to one another on how our own exposure to violence has been minimal and indirect.[2] We tend to witness little of the violence we know has been endemic during all the time we have been visiting the country. Indeed, violence is inherent in the junta's justification for rule. Its claim is that in the absence of a forceful center, the periphery would erupt into chaotic hostilities (ethnic conflict, for example) and the country's borders would be insecure against external enemies. Such was Ne Win's rationale behind his 1962 coup d'état, and many Burmese from the central region continue to quote this justification for why the junta continues to be a necessary evil. But as Saul Bellow once commented: "Everybody knows there is no fineness or accuracy of suppression; if you hold down one thing you hold down the adjoining."[3]

The reason foreign observers rarely witness violence is not, I think, because we fortuitously happen to be located away from where the regime's repression is most exercised. Rather, it seems to be because the brutality, as well as any burgeoning forms of resistance to it, often occurs beneath the surface of what Jürgen Habermas originally referred to as "the public sphere."[4] By this, he was referring to "a discursive arena that is home to citizen debate, deliberation, agreement and action."[5] At this level, the atmosphere of fear, threat, and latent brutality is most observable, provided one is alert to detecting it. In this chapter, I will consider the usefulness or lack thereof of Habermas's public sphere and its obverse in considering one form of the regime's suppression of political freedoms in Burma, as well as the spaces or spheres in which opposition to and/or accommodation of the regime take place.

I do not mention the position of the researcher relative to the suppression and violence of the regime incidentally. I believe that some of the same impulses that spur us as outside researchers to avert our gaze from politically taboo matters are shared by the Burmese people themselves, living as subjects under these conditions. As a researcher, you might be inquiring along a certain track when it suddenly seems that you are treading on uncomfortable ground. Your conversation partner begins to show apprehension or to avert his or her gaze, for fear of being under surveillance. In addition to not wanting to place your confidants in an awkward or dangerous position, you yourself do not wish to risk being expelled from the country and having your visitation rights revoked. I know this all too well, for I was barred from reentering the country for four years following a brief and innocent meeting with the late prime minister U Nu in Yangon in 1988. Calling on my own experiences as a researcher then and during more recent visits, I believe I can offer the reader some insight into the nature of secrecy, suppression, and public discourse in Burma.

In 1995, seven years after the military's brutal crackdown on prodemocracy demonstrations,[6] I returned to Yangon and to Mahasi Thathana Yeiktha, the meditation center where I had first resided as a thilashin (nun) in 1984 and 1985. This was not my first return to Burma (now as an anthropologist), but to my eyes, time seemed to weigh more heavily on the city and its people on this visit. SLORC's unremittingly oppressive imprint was everywhere in evidence. Preparations for the Year of Tourism were under way. The junta busied itself with Burma's grand opening.[7] The whitewashed facade of the city, its sterile billboards bearing state propaganda, the absence of the little shanty rows that used to line the road leading to the heart of the city, the tawdry ocher-gold paint that blanketed ancient Buddhist monuments—everywhere, the signs cried out that a different city lay somewhere beneath this bedizened, dazzlingly vulgar, disciplined display. Numerous world-class hotels and Southeast Asian–styled shopping complexes had popped up, yet only the very smallest segment of the elite could afford to patronize them. Military decree severely restricted individuals from assembling. Constant surveillance— open and secret—produced the palpable sensation of terror and suspiciousness, a contagious feeling toward which I felt no immunity. State domination over the city's public space appeared absolute.

How did one encounter the surveillance? If I was speaking with people even in private and I touched on a topic that did not seem suitable because it was in some way connected to politics, they would immediately put their fingers to their lips and point to different places in the room to suggest that we might be being bugged. I would then turn the conversation back toward an explicitly Buddhist subject. As should follow from earlier chapters, the fusion of political and religious spheres in Burma meant that you could easily traverse this divide. In any case, even if you were in a public location such as a marketplace, you would constantly look around because people would tell you: "This person is following you, he's military" or "That person over there is a spy here in the market . . . watch out! Don't do anything in front of him." In my case, a monk whom the executives at the Mahasi center considered to be a government spy was assigned to tag along with me, putatively as my helper but also my constant companion. By assigning him to me, the executive committee at the center may have been shrewdly sending a message to the Ministry of Home and Religious Affairs: "See? She's not a spy. She is here to study Buddha sāsana." Although I did not consider my companion to be directly dangerous to me, my own suspicions were reinforced by the fact that it was I who was careful not to show indiscretion in the matters discussed.

And of course, as a visiting researcher, you have an obligation to not betray the people who are sponsoring you as their guest, in whatever circumstances. Your actions will redound to them. You are careful not to accept the wrong dinner invitation or to be seen somewhere you should not be, and you get in the habit of constantly trim-tabbing your speech, speaking only of the subjects you have told the government you have come to talk about, which in my case was doctrinal Buddhism.

It is fair, then, to conclude this introduction with a focus on precisely the question of the public sphere and what is regarded as appropriate, safe discourse or forms of discourse in such circumstances. The regime has sought to secure its authority in one aspect by enforcing an oppressive silence on the public sphere. It will not tolerate free assembly or collective debate. In a 2004 news article, it was reported that Rangoon University students who had gathered to form a sports club without direct permission from the government were each served a fifteen-year prison sentence.[8] Yet if the Burmese have been silenced in their critiques of a repressive regime, where and how might they discuss these matters? How do they present an alternative position to the government when doing so is not allowed? Put more analytically for our purposes, where has public space gone? Have Burmese simply retreated to the private domain of their homes? Has a critique of the state become sublimated in some other fashion?

In this chapter, I will discuss this latter possibility in terms of a number of subjects or domains of inquiry. This analysis will address issues of power, authority, and government legitimacy in distinctly Burmese Buddhist contexts and, in these terms, the specific ways in which the military regime has gone about asserting its power. Once this framework is clear, I will turn to the forms of resistance to the regime's assertions that are discernible in two spheres of action in particular: within the renunciate positioning of monks and among (largely) women devotees who engage in meditation and participate in the mass lay meditation movement. I will argue that an alternative moral social order based on right intentions and the assertion of a right society in Buddhist terms is invoked to coerce the government to partial compliance, at the same time that the Burmese themselves accommodate or at least sustain the awful demands, in turn, of the military junta. Finally, as in the last chapter, the question of sincerity is relevant here. Are religious acts performed manipulatively? Conversely, are violations of one's religious precepts performed with alternate intentions, under force, binding to one's kamma? These are considerations raised but not necessarily resolved in the Buddhist resistance sphere that I describe in the balance of this chapter.

An Alternate Action Sphere

In her recent account of terror and oppression in Burma, Christina Fink relates how students secretly circulate banned books in an effort to "use literature to educate people about the political situation and motivate them to consider taking action. . . . Once a person had read [a book], he or she would write a short comment and the name of his or her home town in the back and pass it on to another member."⁹ In this way, students make explicit their common purpose and sense of community. In a society where it is impossible to have free and open conversation, Fink suggests, students have created a kind of public space in the interior of their private spheres. Individuals who may never have met face to face in public spaces encounter one another through serial communication in an underground realm of public life. In this stunted political environment, so to speak, communication thrives on the determination to secure an alternate space from which to communicate and exchange ideas critical of the state, in order to escape its hegemonic control. In Fink's words, "For those who had developed political ideas, knowing they had similarly-minded peers in other parts of the country was very important. They often felt isolated among their own school-mates, most of whom thought it pointless to question military control."[10]

I, too, wish to address the issue of how public space gets created in an interior sphere. This sort of pragmatic and palpable reconfiguration of public space in the interest of resisting the government is probably taking place in a number of situations, but I believe the underlying model on which this sighting builds in fact conceals from view a more profound and culturally particular process. This alternate process accomplishes some of the same ends, and its dynamics resonate more directly with a majority of Burmese Buddhists because, as a form of social action, it satisfies cosmological criteria for validity.

Fink's notion of where to look for resistance fits with where we would expect to find a nascent democracy movement in the West if similar circumstances somehow prevailed. In this case, the "public sphere" is implicitly taken to be a synonym for democratic society itself. Indeed, in this model, it is predictable that under circumstances of oppression, the vox populi would simply find an alternate microphone with which to disseminate its views. This microphone would be projected "underground," and its activists would often be students, who are the world over enthusiastic in their resistance to oppression, human rights violations, and so on. Here, I do not mean to downplay this level of resistance in Burma, nor, certainly, do I want to discourage it. However, I will argue that a more mature and, by another measure, a far greater segment of the Burmese population is involved in what can be construed as an antiregime discourse but one that is not outwardly expressed.

To make my case, I will point to one further framework implicit in Fink's account—the Habermasian assumption that the public sphere is characterized by verbal and written communication, that is, rhetoric, conversation, debate, and so on. Fink explains that "the generals understand that if people do not have concrete ideas about how to change Burma and are lacking leaders and organizations to spearhead a movement, they will remain quiescent."[11] The public space, which is analytically linked to (democratic) civil society, is supposed to be the place where citizens work out ideas known familiarly to us as public opinion and where grounds for agitation against the government are deliberated and established. The regime, for its part, acts out its role as the oppressive state by seeking to extinguish the opportunities for open discourse among its citizens. Thus, we see the characteristic political scientific framework of state versus civil society emerge as the implicit model for analysis.

Two clues point to the inadequacy of this model in Burma. First, there is the fact, often raised by commentators on Burma, that as hard as one looks for activism, what one mostly sees in the end is an apparent apathy to the awful situation.[12] The origins of this apathy are traced, in this view, to a fatalistic interpretation of the doctrine of kamma. In 1996, U Aunt Maung, the minister of home and religious affairs, explained to me, giving voice to common wisdom, that "the people have to realize that they have this relation with Ne Win because of their past actions. How can they escape their own kamma?"[13] Yet it is important to recognize that it is not *civil society* against the *state* that animates this understanding of kamma but the competition between agents vying with one another in a cosmic cycle played out over multiple lifetimes.

To take the point a bit further, we in the West have an idea about regime legitimacy that is based on "regime performance," grounded in terms of whether there is slave labor, oppression, torture, imprisonment, and the delivery of various goods to the populace. In Burma, those ideas of performance, at least from the perspective of a fatalistic assertion of kamma, are not determinative criteria for legitimate rule. A king who is brutal may nevertheless be legitimate. This idea was emphatically reiterated to me by Sao Htun Hmat Win at the Department of Religious Affairs, who explained (with not a little exasperation when I was slow to grasp the full implications of the rights of rulers) that "the rulers decide the lives of their subjects.

They are the lords of all. There are no rules against a king killing or committing homicide. The raja is owner. Kings and queens are owners of men. They can give away people to pagodas if they want. They are final authorities."

From another perspective, however, this time from the perspective of the ruled, kings are to be counted among the five enemies or perils. In her book *Freedom from Fear,* NLD leader and Nobel Peace Prize winner Aung San Suu Kyi reflects on another old Burmese version of the rights and limits of rulers by recounting the moral duties of Buddhist kings:[14]

The Buddhist view of kingship does not invest the ruler with the divine right to govern the realm as he pleases. He is expected to observe the Ten Duties of Kings, the Seven Safeguards against Decline, the Four Assistances to the People, and to be guided by numerous other codes of conduct such as the Twelve Practices of Rulers, the Six Attributes of Leaders, the Eight Virtues of Kings and the Four Ways to Overcome Peril. . . . Integrity (*ajjava*) implies incorruptibility in the discharge of public duties as well as honesty and sincerity in personal relations. There is a Burmese saying: "With rulers, truth, with (ordinary) men, vows." While a private individual may be bound only by the formal vows that he makes, *those who govern should be wholly bound by the truth in thought, word and deed.* Truth is the very essence of the teachings of the Buddha, who referred to himself as the *Tathagata* or "one who has come to the truth." The Buddhist king must therefore live and rule by truth, with is the perfect uniformity between nomenclature and nature. To deceive or to mislead the people in any way would be an occupational failing as well as a moral offence.[15]

The cultural rectitude of this notwithstanding, interpretations of virtuous kingship according to a Buddhist moral framework are not easily or directly translatable into a theory of modern democratic politics for Burma. Western criteria for regime performance and democratically informed ideas about popular sovereignty depend on other ideas about the origins of society and the proper relations obtaining between civil society and the state. What my informants often said is "With patience [*kanti*] we can endure." Is this the very soul of apathy? Or is it a window into a culturally particular way of bearing hardship that also encompasses a species of resistance that we can probe and investigate?

The second indication of the inadequacy of a state–versus–civil society model is that the long-term researcher continues to have difficulty locating the conceptual apparatus for apprehending power struggles in these terms. The students, one recognizes, are making use of foreign models that bring with them the state–civil society duality.[16] In this regard, though their participation is to be granted and endorsed, the terms of its engagement must be recognized at this point as essentially alien in cultural character.[17] Analogously, though I say this in quite tenuous terms due to the prudence with which one must address this topic, in the mid-1990s I often heard Burmese intellectuals associated with various religious, educational, and governmental institutions in Yangon complain that the ineffectiveness of the democratic movement's leader, Aung San Suu Kyi, was partly the result of the foreignness of her ideas to Burmese Buddhist sensibilities, for she lived and was educated abroad in her formative years.

In my own research in Burma, I have also found an unmitigated skepticism toward the government. However, the form this takes is paradoxically apolitical, which is precisely what has hidden it from the view of political scientists who search for answers only in the unambiguous realm of politics. Like the joke about the man who searches for a lost item under the street lamp because that is where he can see it despite the fact that that is not where he misplaced it, analysts have tended to reify the duality of civil society versus the state,[18] to the detriment of understanding the situation on the ground. What I would argue is that it is in the ubiquitous realm of Buddhism—precisely the place in which political commentary is least expected—where we must look to discern political action. Or, more precisely, we must look at how action is directed not at the political sphere as we identity it but at the cosmological sphere, the "regime of truth," to use Michel Foucault's apt phrase.

Monks, who are considered "world renouncers," are, by definition, the antithesis of politics. But in 1995, an adviser at the Religious Affairs Department explained to me how important it is that the government controls the sangha. "Monks," he said, "are like kings. Whatever they say the people will do. The government doesn't want to purge [that is, purify the religion of heterodoxy] during this period because they want support of people and monks have people's support." By this, he meant that monks stand at the head of moral communities, and should they turn their attention to the practical concerns of a suffering populace rather than just spiritual matters, they could pose a threat to the regime. This view is reinforced by the specter of the commonly referred to metahistorical oscillatory model, found originally in the texts (Digha Nikaya II and III) between world renouncer and world conqueror.[19] Whereas the king's function is to sustain and support the sangha, it is the sangha's function to admonish the ruler who does not rule as a *dhammaraja* (a king of righteousness).

In the face of this threat, the regime monitors the monks and will disrobe (and then perhaps prosecute) any monk engaged in overt or covert political activity. In the latter case, the pretext for disrobing becomes the purported violation of the vinaya, which can be less or more severely read to define the proper behavior for monks. Thus, the disrobing of monks, which itself can be readily interpreted as sublimated political action, falls under the category of sāsana purification, for which kings are granted traditional obligation and privilege. And yet—and here is my conclusion foreshadowed in a nutshell—the way in which monks and their followers may ultimately come to have political impact is by asserting a moral convention for action that contains within it criteria for regime legitimacy, as well as the communal building blocks of political power. Monks pose a threat to the regime because they can claim a higher moral ground; they are the heads of moral communities that adjudicate questions of potency and sincerity. The regime is fearful of being widely deemed insincere in its efforts to support and protect the sāsana, which is the will of the religious masses. This is true on a collective level as well as for individuals, for many members of the regime are themselves observant Buddhists who do not wish to alienate themselves from their sources of merit—the leading monks.

The principles of conversion from moral community to political power are intricate. A recounting of an empirical example of this procedure will bring us closer to understanding how religious communities, particularly those dominated by women, exert their influence. In the following example, I refer to an alternate action sphere for political behavior. These are forms other than those identified by Habermas and Fink, for the case of Burma, in which one can locate a sublimated critique of the state.

A Revered Monk and the Regime's Attempt to Capture His Potency

Pilgrimage is a common means to religious piety in Burma, as elsewhere. Bruce Kapferer's observation of pilgrimage in Sri Lanka as simultaneously a function of state expansionist interests, expressed through religious proselytization, and a deterritorialization/reterritorialization as described by Gilles Deleuze and Félix Gauttari, is highly relevant in Burma as well. With the proviso that the purpose of pilgrimages can also be a redrawing of geographic (as in sacred geographic) and political lines against the state and its controlling interests, Kapferer writes:

> In Sri Lanka, the revitalization of Buddhism as part of an anticolonialist nationalist politics also switched Buddhism into a missionizing and proselytizing mode. The conscious striving to be Buddhist (especially among the highly Westernized and urbanized bourgeoisie) is expressed in a growth in pilgrimage and the creation of new pilgrimage centers, often sites of ancient importance to Sinhalese. Pilgrimage is a dynamic of deterritorialization which, associated as

it is in Sri Lanka with state-directed religiously defined national interest, becomes a critical element in a reterritorialization and redrawing of spatial boundaries.[20]

The growth of pilgrimage is a poignant phenomenon in Burma because movement is closely restricted by the regime. As sāsana-related activities, pilgrimages are permitted. Once again, sacred journeys (sometimes abroad) help constitute the "alternative action sphere" I have been speaking of as a medium for underground resistance, as the following account demonstrates.

Widespread pilgrimage to the venerable monk Thamanya Sayadaw, alleged by many to be a fully enlightened saint (arahat), is noteworthy in several regards. For years before his death in December 2003, busloads of devotees departed daily from Yangon on a ten-hour ride to Karen State, where Thamanya Sayadaw resided atop a mountain that was ringed at the base by three ethnic Pa-O villages. They wanted to offer their respects and donations, to hear him discourse on the dhamma, and to bask in his radiant presence for a short while.

Thamanya Sayadaw's presence, moreover, is in evidence all over Yangon. His picture functions as protective amulet on the dashboards of cars and buses, around the necks of women and children, in the glass cases of the gem and jewelry dealers in the marketplaces, and among the paraphernalia and Buddha rūpās (statues) in public and private shrines. The typical response to the question "Have you been to see Thamanya Sayadaw?" is either "Of course" or "Not yet." People often recount the number of times they have undertaken the pilgrimage, adding wistfully that they hope to go again if the sayadaw (who was in fragile health in his final years) "lasts."

This example shows how people are communicating through the use and presence of the amulet that has Thamanya Sayadaw's picture on in. Because one finds it in both sacred and private places, it serves as a connection between the sacred and private realms, at the same time that it signifies a commonality of view and a safe context in which to talk. Whenever I wore my amulet of Thamanya Sayadaw (I visited the venerated monk), I found that people were willing to talk to me. There was not only a political safety implied but also a kind of magical safety.

Indeed, it does not require much prodding for a discussion of Thamanya Sayadaw to turn to political issues. His longtime refusal to go to the capital and be honored by the SLORC/SPDC government has remained a deep source of irritation to the military. In response to inquiries about why the sayadaw declined to go to Yangon, I was told by a variety of people there that the refusal was a sign that the monk did not view the government as legitimate. Thamanya Sayadaw, they said, refused to become a "government monk," decorated with the titles of an illegitimate regime. (The regime has taken to securing its own hierarchy of monks by awarding learned ones prizes for feats of scholarship, hoping to mirror the populace's own values and criteria for good monks.) Elaborate rumors circulate contrasting the circumstances and events surrounding the sayadaw's aloof reception of the junta's Secretary 1, Khin Nyunt, with that given National League for Democracy leader Aung San Suu Kyi. These accounts often include miraculous and magical details evidencing Thamanya Sayadaw's sainthood. Discussion of the monk's remarkable qualities is transposed into a discourse critical of the ruling junta while lionizing Aung San Suu Kyi. In the context of severely restricted freedoms of speech and assembly in contemporary Burma, such active and visible support of an exemplary monk allows a speaker to communicate political views while still leaving open the possibility for shifting to the safety of orthodox Buddhist rhetoric.

One might add that this is where a slippage between conversation levels takes place. Thus, a person has said in my presence, "No, he [Thamanya Sayadaw] is a very good monk, he only supports the good people, he knows this government is insincere so he won't support them." In this comment, we discern that sāsana language subsumes the political realm. However, the line about the government could as easily be left off, so that the remaining language is purely about sāsana; only by extension and in some contexts does it also incorporate a political commentary. Even when the intention is to explicitly focus on the unfairness of the regime, one can immediately code switch and say, "Oh, I'm just talking about sāsana." And in that zone, there is safety.

The fact that Thamanya Sayadaw's overt rejection of the junta reinforces perceptions of his saintliness,[21] even as his saintliness demonstrates the illegitimacy of the regime, has its roots both in political rhetorical practices of Burmese Buddhists and in understandings of what the transcendent sources of power are. Contemporary Burmese ideas about political rule still draw heavily on the rhetoric of kingship and associated notions of the role of the sangha in conferring legitimacy to the political order. Answering to this populist and indeed social structural demand, the regime supports the sangha in the role of king and chief donor to the sangha. However, it would be insufficient to think of these processes of legitimation and the military clique's engagement with the sangha as mere performative spectacles in pursuit of the appearance of legitimate political rule. Moral performative acts such as donation or pagoda building and repair, in which the government conspicuously participates,[22] are believed to create the actual transcendent causal circumstances that result in political power. Min Zin explains:

> [T]he Burmese concept of hpoun, . . . originally meant the cumulative result of past meritorious deeds, but later came to be synonymous with power. . . . The discourse of hpoun is so deeply embedded in Burmese culture that few even think to question it. Since hpoun is theoretically a "prize" earned through past good deeds, it is self-legitimating: Simply by virtue of possessing power, one has demonstrated that one has acquired considerable merit in past lives. Thus the question of moral legitimacy does not arise. As long as one remains in the ascendancy (whether socially, politically, or economically), one is presumed to possess merit. . . . In the political realm, this reliance upon the notion of hpoun is even more pronounced. No matter how morally unfit a ruler may appear to be, as long as he is able to cling to power, he can claim that his hpoun is still flourishing.[23]

Appreciating how potency translates into power and political legitimacy in Burmese Buddhist terms is integral to understanding government actions.[24] Thamanya Sayadaw's refusal to place his considerable field for merit making at the disposal of the ruling junta was understood to be a purposeful effort to prevent the military from accruing merits that might sustain its hold on power. This last interpretation is supported by a remarkable event recounted to me by a highly placed official at the Ministry of Home and Religious Affairs in 2002. The event helps put into focus the dimensions of a shared set of representations held by the state and the Buddhist populace in regard to what the sources of political legitimacy are. In May 2002, Thamanya Sayadaw, who was suffering from diabetes, slipped into a coma. In desperation, his guardian committee rushed him to a Yangon hospital, where he remained comatose for several days. While he lay unconscious, the military leaders and key members of the government came to pay their respects to the sayadaw and to make offerings in his hospital room. This high official from Religious Affairs reveled in how he had the good pāramī (moral perfection cultivated over incalculable lifetimes) to be near the great monk and how he was able to offer him dāna.

The official's boast entailed a double claim. First, his high status was justified as the consequence of prior meritorious actions for which his present incarnation in this life is the result. Privilege and status are not conceived as subtracting from another person's natural rights. Relationships of exploitation and privilege say things about prior kammic relationships. The present is always justly warranted, since each individual reaps the consequences of his or her own prior intentions and actions. Second, the director's relating of how he had offered dāna to Thamanya Sayadaw in such intimate circumstances was meant to communicate to me his privileged access to the great monk. It was understood that leveraged merit-making opportunities would ultimately translate into auspicious conditions in the future. The genuine respect that the monk garners from both government officials and their critics testifies to the force that can be exerted on the regime through religious/cosmological means. The government's surreptitious attempt to exploit the moral causal assets of Thamanya Sayadaw provides us with an interpretive tool for understanding the process by which the regime seeks to control monks, the Buddhist populace, and the many merit fields that are the leveraged locations for the production of pon (merit-based power).

A survey of its activities demonstrates that SLORC/SPDC has made a greater effort than any other postindependence government to demonstrate that the military clique is the foremost among all the laity in its support of the sangha and Buddha sāsana. Acting as the foremost donor among the laity in support of the sāsana and sangha is more than a mere metaphorical effort directed at associating the symbols of classical kingship with military rule and thereby presuming political legitimacy among the populace. State efforts to "capture potency" are as much a concern over controlling monks' merit fields as a concern over controlling the moral communities surrounding monks. Inasmuch as the government did not maintain a relationship of official patronage with Thamanya Sayadaw, its legitimacy (at best) remained in doubt among the monk's many devotees.[25]

Mass Meditation and the Double Order of Law

On one level, what has emerged thus far is a model that only slightly amends that of the public/private sphere theory of Habermas and Fink. In other words, there is a deflection or perhaps a sublimation of public political discourse to an alternate sphere and in an alternate mode. However, I wish to signal my departure from such a model on two accounts. First, I am not asserting here that there is an alleged latent or emergent civil society movement with the potential to organize and resist the state. In this context, resistance is not a monolithic, ideological act taken against the state by civil society. Individual actors are differently exposed to the state's coercive power, and they resist, escape, and accommodate these forces differently. As James Scott has shown for Malaysian peasants,[26] resistance may take the form of grumbling, foot dragging, and spreading rumors. Resistance constricts the ways in which the state can assert its power on society. Insofar as the military rulership attempts to regulate morality and transform violence into moral authority for the state, it encounters forms of resistance in the microchannels through which it extends its "networks of power that connect them to society."[27]

Second, I wish to reiterate for the Burma case what Tony Day lucidly articulates for state formation in Southeast Asia more generally—that these states are "constituted as cosmologies," or what Foucault calls truth regimes.[28] For Burma, state/society models have tended to focus too much on the state's role as the sole or primary agent sustaining and transforming the cosmological state. The sheer force and brutality of the regime's violent enactment of power, coupled with the apparent apathy and resignation to such forms of power by most of the populace, have led to an abundance of scholarship on the question of how violence is accepted or prefigured in ideas of authority and the state.[29]

Inasmuch as the regime has successfully quashed incipient civilian institutional forms with power-sharing capabilities, some scholars have argued that *only* the regime is in a position to function in the role of a centralizing state power.[30] This point of view has been criticized by scholars and democracy advocates outside the country for its alleged implicit legitimation of the military regime, based on an assumption of traditional authoritarianism and the sovereign right of nations to determine their internal affairs.[31] However, as David Steinberg argues, even in a "procedural democracy," where the barest minimum of the instruments and institutions of democracy function (for example, free elections, an independent judiciary, a vocal legislature, multiple political parties, a free press, and a vibrant civil society), "attitudes [held by] the populace and those in authority towards the concepts of power, authority and the role of the state" must be considered:

[A]ttitudes towards power and authority may be quite traditional and antithetical to the spirit of democracy. In those societies which retain certain traditional concepts of personalized power, and in which power and authority, and the concept of the role of the state and its leadership are equated with hierarchy and even with a form of virtue, then compromise, conciliation and delegation of authority become more difficult. Compromise becomes anathema because virtue and authority are equated, and to compromise means to lose virtue, and delegation of authority is a zero-sum game. The concept of a loyal opposition becomes an oxymoron, for loyalty is personal. Political parties become entourages around leadership, often void of a programme beyond their leaders' predilections, and without stability and continuity.[32]

Steinberg rightly acknowledges the critical importance that traditional concepts of power, authority, and the role of the state have for our understandings of political realities in Burma. However, a recognition that the people and the authority share these concepts only brings us part of the way to an understanding of what generates social and political realities on the ground. We must be cautious in how we apply so-called traditional cultural concepts to our explanations in order to avoid the excesses of overdeterministic cultural models that would see abiding and unchanging (primordial) identities in practices that do not conform to Western modern democratic ones. These are not immutable ideologies and concepts; though they may be enduring, they are simultaneously transforming. The mass lay meditation movement, with its emphasis on meditation truths, is one location where we can observe how such concepts are made real (that is, indisputable and self-evident). It is to the practices of the sangha, state, and New Laity that I now turn in considering practices that produce status, hierarchy, and power through the assertion of fields of consciousness that are generative of truth and virtue and the symbolic *and* actual grounds of power and legitimate political authority.[33]

Monks are both the symbolic and the tangible field for the merit production of the rulers. As the legitimate living continuity of the Buddha's sāsana, they represent ultimate truth (the dhamma) and may also legitimately evaluate the moral actions of political authority. The sangha both asserts and justifies public metavalues, and it is the empirical grounds for its warrant. Monks are, therefore, the legitimate critics of political authority. However, as world renouncers, they are also constrained by their moral code to eschew involvement in the politics of worldly life. For this reason, monks are best able to redress unjust rulers primarily through forms of public justifications warranting the truth of moral claims rather than explicit political criticism. This sort of assertion of the moral terms of public life needs to be evaluated as a form of context framing that is not explicitly political but that has political implications. The terms of moral reality are made by way of reference to intention (*seit* in Burmese; *cetanā* in Pāli). Causal explications of power and authority are made by way of a productive logic that links thought, speech, and action to event, hierarchy, and power.

Where public space is suppressed and controlled by a repressive regime, Burmese Buddhists claim control over *the private space of their intention* in pursuit of creating better future life circumstances. This is accomplished through the widespread practices of meditation. From this place, I argue, people can challenge the government's sincerity in its sāsana-supporting actions while simultaneously exerting a sort of pressure on it. The overall effect is that a seemingly very private and individualistic practice, meditation, conceived as acting on one's own psychophysical processes, becomes a fulcrum of action in the social and political world. The mass lay meditation movement has emerged as the vehicle for this action on the world both in the logic of its encounter and in the force of its sheer numbers—its millions of adherents.

As we have seen, the mass lay meditation movement is a relatively recent historical phenomenon that began as a rural millenarian movement in reaction to British colonialism in the middle to late 1800s. One of the implicit goals of the early movement was to protect the Buddha sāsana from degeneration and decay in the absence of a Buddhist king whose first responsibility as head of society was to protect and preserve the Buddha's teachings and dispensations. The goals of the state and the goals of sāsana perpetuation were so fundamentally intertwined that when the British deposed the Burmese king (including removing his throne from the country so that no usurpers might lay claim to it), monks began to teach laity in earnest how to practice meditation for enlightenment, believing that the end of the world was approaching. This much I have reviewed in earlier chapters.

In its potential guise as a social movement, the New Laity is characterized by the breadth of the socioeconomic differences among its members (from educated elites to farmers who leave the countryside by the busload during the agricultural slow season to undertake brief courses) and by the wide range in ages in the membership. The most distinguishing feature of this New Laity is that women are by far the main participants in meditation. For example, they outnumber men five to one in the Mahasi Thathana Yeiktha. Yet despite the massive entry of women into the lay meditation movement especially since the 1950s, lay meditation is not perceived as a woman's project.

The meditation movement is more than a revitalization movement, but it stops somewhere short of being a civil society movement. Civil society movements tend to be considered in terms of their goals of sharing power and resources by authoritarian rule. The meditation movement, by contrast, is not a movement in search of a particular political solution—for example, democracy.[34] The movement also does not challenge the state in the sense Scott relates in his "weapons of the weak" argument.[35] And yet, the movement has definite implications for the political environment that I have explored in this book. In the present context, I wish to approach the questions of revitalization and resistance with particular reference to the participation of women, who are far more numerous than men within the meditation movement.

The New Laity, I have been arguing, has shaped new dimensions to Buddhist practice, and it has asserted a sacred public sphere that is critical of the coercive power of the regime. It has been influential in defining the politics of sincerity and, ultimately, the terms for uncompelled political legitimacy. Also characteristic of the New Laity is its emphasis on temporary world renunciation to engage in satipaṭṭhāna vipassanā meditation and enlightenment here and now, followed by reintegration into worldly life. Reintegration is a particularly key feature for women, since men can become long-term monks, thereby embodying the category of world renouncers. Women who practice for a long time may at most become ten-precept lay nuns.[36] Most often, they practice and then go back to the householder's life. They thereby reincorporate their experiences in meditation into daily life. And there are millions of women doing this. What happens for these millions who practice meditation and then return to their normal lives is a reformulation of their attitude toward everyday suffering. What potential role does this process, this personal pilgrimage, as it were, play in women meditators' resistance to the regime, as a counterpart to what I have just discussed relative to monks? A digression into the nature of gender and potency is necessary to explore this question.

GENDER AND THE EMBODIMENT OF POWER

Burmese gender is compartmentalized into three categories: man, woman, and monk. The monk is the only social category recognized as inhabiting a penultimate reality. The penultimate reality status of this third gender is defined according to descriptions of reality drawn from the Abhiddhamma. Abhiddhamma theory emphasizes the relations between mind and matter, matter and matter, and mind and mind as components making up the universe and experience. According to doctrine, man and woman are mere concepts, just as the notion "self" is a concept. The very purpose in studying and practicing the Buddha's teachings is to see through this conventional and shared delusion and to perceive things as they are: as impermanent, unsatisfactory, and empty of essence (anicca, dukkha, and anatta). Monks are asexual beings, according to this reckoning, not only because they are "noble celibates" who renounce the world of sexual engagements but also because their materiality is irrelevant to the task of realizing enlightenment consciousness, which does not take biological sex as part of its condition. A distinctive honorific language reserved expressly for monks and entirely free of gender inflections reinforces the idea that monks are not part of worldly, conventional life.

Although being male is the primary criterion for entering the sangha, taking up the robes is a transformative act in which the individual renounces his or her gendered identity along with worldly life. *Tabyi-daw,* Hiroko Kawanami observes, is a gender-free term of self-address used when speaking to monks. *Hsaya-lay* (small teacher), used for schoolteachers as well as thilashin, is also a gender-free term emphasizing the role of the thilashin in teaching and therefore recognition of their role in the transmission of the Buddha dhamma.[37]

Occupying the social space of a world renouncer allows monks to transcend social roles and conventionally recognized identification markers that elicit social classification and role demands. One who has renounced the world, who no longer participates in the most fundamental activities of securing a livelihood for material sustenance, and who instead lives off the free-will offerings of society without attachments to family and possessions achieves a rare and privileged opportunity for dhamma cultivation and realization.

The female counterpart to a monk is a thilashin (nun), whose status in gendered terms I have discussed elsewhere.[38] Germane here is that their struggles to be socially recognized as an ungendered category of person detached from conventional realities have been greatly helped by the meditation movement, with its emphasis on penultimate realities. Whereas membership in the sangha overshadows the spiritual value of enlightenment from the point of view of the social recognition of categories of persons, popular discourses about the emptiness of phenomena and the fact that one of the first insights (nyanzin) perceived by a yogi is that all phenomena are either mind or matter (nāma/rūpā) has brought into question the rigid exclusion of thilashin as persons "inside the sāsana."

Where laity is concerned, the universalization of the penultimate practices once again has meant that not only lay-monk relations have transformed. The meditation movement has had the greatest significance for women because it has provided them with an alternative institution for practice—one that has permitted them access to the highest goals and achievements in the religion while allowing them to keep the social and economic status garnered in the householder's life. This change in ideas about women's spiritual capabilities had consequences for women's renunciation activities as well after the early 1950s, when the state began to officially sponsor women's monastic institutions.[39]

However, despite the perception that her sex does not bar her from its ultimate spiritual achievements, a woman cannot completely achieve the status of a world renouncer. Only monks are socially recognized as individuals who have transcended gender in pursuit of nibbāna, pāramī cultivation, and sāsana propagation. And only monks merit the support of the laity in the everyday renunciation of social worldly life, thereby creating in the space of their own activities the sacred and transcendent. The laity, for their part, participate in supporting and extending this space of the sacred, providing support to the Buddha sāsana through their charitable acts of dāna and by undertaking to keep morality (sīla). In this way, their merit accumulates and their pāramī incrementally ripens.

The conventional world of man and woman is transcended in the sangha—by men who have entered the order and abandoned their engendered identities as members of the lay world. That men can renounce their sex while women cannot does not fully account for the extent of traditional ideas that relate merit to the masculine principle. Melford Spiro, in a 1965 study of village life in Upper Burma, explains:

Despite the remarkable extent of sexual equality in Burmese society . . . it is nevertheless a basic premise of Burmese culture that men are *inherently* superior to women. . . . In Burma, the primary reason offered for male superiority is the belief that men possess that innate, inborn quality, known as *hpoun*. . . . [U]sually glossed as "glory," *hpoun* . . . is a psycho-spiritual quality, an ineffable essence, which invests its possessor with superior moral, spiritual, and intellectual attributes. . . . Although the spiritual superiority of males is based on their hpoun, its proof, according to the Burmese, is found in a number of Buddhist beliefs and practices. Only a male has the Buddhist initiation ceremony (shinpyu), only a male can become a monk (which leads to a vicious circle: the male's innate superiority enables him to become a monk, which in turn increases his already pronounced superiority to the female), only a male can become a saint (arahat), and most important, only a male can become a Buddha.[40]

Spiro's consideration of village folk understandings of pon in the late 1970s and the subordination of the feminine principle to that of the masculine need to be reconsidered for contemporary, especially urban, Burma. The Burmese word for monk, *pongyi,* suggests the strength of the idea that the defining substance of a monk is the spiritual principle of merit that men uniquely possess. Etymologically derived from the Pāli word *puñña,* the term *pongyi* in its conventional usage in Burmese culture locates the psychomaterial phenomena of sentient embodiment in the Burmese Buddhist cosmological theory of the thirty-two planes of existence. In this theory, the causative effect of merit and demerit is played out in the cycle of rebirths. Pon is associated with an affiliated cluster of ideas about the implications of this potency for spiritual practice. The pon concept is profitably viewed as a continuum of ideas regarding merit and pāramī production.

Women do not have pon—after all, they cannot become monks. Monks have great merit because they are monks but not because they are men first. Pon is a concept of spiritual potential, but this potential can play out in conventional ways in worldly life, too. This tautological aspect of the concept—that men having been born men have a spiritual advantage over women because they can join the sangha and that their spiritual advantage translates into an advantage of power and authority over women in the conventional world as well—demonstrates the crucial location of the linkage between power and moral authority in the Burmese system. In short, it is precisely the unique merit that men have and can renounce that is the basis of their power in the world.

The application of the merit concept to the male principle describes more than just how merits are transformed into renunciation and realization of the Buddha's teachings. Pon is also the basis of a man's power and influence more generally. The continuum of ideas about merit and potency is found in Burmese conceptions about power and its source—renunciation, especially of the mental defilements (*kilesas*). The idea of pon is conceived as a kind of special quality of purity, potential, and power conferred on a man by dint of his biological sex.

However, pon is not conceived as an immutable substance that is the same for all men. Some men may have more pon than others. Their potency may convert to power in the way that the pon of monks converts to renunciation and pāramī accumulation. Inherent in these ideas are notions of how potency converts to the renunciation of worldly life, culminating in its penultimate form in Buddhahood, or sainthood, on the one hand, and in influence and power resulting in the canonical formulation of the world-conquering king, on the other.[41] Women do not have a part in pon, and moreover, their sex is thought to be contaminating and capable of diminishing a man's pon.

The meditation movement has brought about an accommodation of new ideas about gender and enlightenment and therefore also new ideas of sāsana practice in Burma. These new emphases diverge from traditional roles in precolonial Burma, especially regarding ideas on what a woman's greatest source of merit making may be. In folk tradition, the primary means for a woman to achieve the highest merit was through the ordination of her son. The merit of his actions accrued to her, since she was his merit base. When a married man wanted to undertake temporary ordination, permission from his wife was necessary; subsequently, merit accrued to her. Women therefore accumulated merit through providing the sangha with its membership and alms to its members. Female identity was perceived to be the subordinate and supportive basis for the man's pon and the material support of the sangha.

I asked one woman, a yogi at the Mahasi Yeiktha, how she has been able to endure all the sufferings under military rule. She responded, "With kanti [patience] we can endure" (*Thee kan kwin lwet dey*). It would be theoretically facile to explain (or reduce) the mass practice of meditation to a psychological impulse for survival. However, explanations of how mental states are cultivated to withstand poverty and violent repression only distantly approximate the sense in which these experiences are meaningfully felt. The phrase *Thee kan kwin lwet dey* includes the idea that having kanti necessarily implies that one also has "dropped" or let go of the resentment one harbors against a person for his or her wrongful actions. In forbearance, there is forgiveness. Forms of consciousness are interrelated on a separate level, the level people experience when they meditate. Kanti thus becomes not just a psychological defense but also a social space that conforms to certain collective values and dispositions and that incorporates distinct means of communication. People inhabiting that space respond to the key words associated with meditation.

To reiterate the same idea in a slightly different way, it is not merely the psychological value of patience or equanimity cultivated by practitioners through vipassanā meditation that I mean to use as explanation for how vital experiences encountered in meditation become the empirical reference for the assertion of metavalues in the public domain. The appeal to a transcendent truth through the experiences of vipassanā insights becomes, in the public sphere, a form of public justification asserting the terms of a politics of sincerity. It is precisely because these assertions are not criticisms but verifications that they are capable of positively differentiating a moral arena separate from that of the state.

To discern this, it is best to start with a certain notion of interiority or privacy, which becomes the space in which one copes with the contradictions of the contemporary historical moment, and its violations against the sāsana. The only place where one can take refuge is in one's own intentions toward oneself. Once this becomes a mass movement, regulated by the systematic technique of satipaṭṭhāna vipassanā meditation and with institutional apparatuses to support its practice, the experience of shared insight itself becomes a reality—a verification procedure. It becomes a warrant about the truth of a lived reality.

It is important to differentiate the lived reality that emerges from the meditation movement, with all its latent criticism of the regime included, from an explicit antilaw reality. The model in which students, for example, oppose the regime would conform to a law-versus-antilaw scenario. To antilaw activities, the regime responds with force: increased enforcement, suppression, violence. By contrast, here I wish to introduce the notion of a double order of law, in which the moral orders invoked by separate groups overlap, accommodate, or conflict with one another according to circumstances. Two statements from my field interviews are sufficient to signal the concept in action.

One woman explained to me, "Just to live you have to break your precepts." Once one has reached the insight stage of being unable to break one's precepts,[42] this situation presents a contradiction. Yet here we have a woman who claims (by various nonovert means, including reference to the bindingness of her precepts) to be enlightened, and she tells me that just to live, you have to break your precepts. "This is no law. Sometimes we have to not tell the truth just so we can live. The government is trying to make criminals out of the whole population. So we think, 'This is not the real law.' Only the dhamma is the real law, so we just do like this [that is, break the first precept not to lie]. In our minds we know." This negation of the lie by imagining a double order of law—the conventional one that is imposed and the transcendent law of dhamma—depends on an understanding that there exists an alternative public space wherein the conventions of truth telling remain consistent. Words and intentions become perversely separated in a practical act that interiorizes the public space of moral society.

How does the distinction between internal and external, private and public as described here apply to politics? People perceive that there will be a consequence for the regime's insincere actions. The junta's good deeds are regarded by some as sorcery because there is no sincerity behind the actions. A committee member of the laywomen's association at MTY offers an interpretation:

> This government is only trying to look like they support the sangha. They say the monks have so much influence on the public. So they claim that the *dayakas* [lay supporters of monks] were doing politics. First they arrested so many monks in 1988. They searched monasteries and kicked out people and arrested monks saying they were sleeping with women. They showed bodices and suspenders of ladies to show how the monks were bad. They planted all these things. They said the monks were dealing in gems. Then they created rival factions within the sāsana. They elected all the big names, the old sayadaws, the monks who wouldn't speak politics. They created a nomination process by which the sangha elects their members but the government tries to push their own candidates by putting pressure on monks they think are on their side. Formerly, every monk was against them. This government is bluffing. They're not sincere. Why don't these monks do something?

We see here that sangha purification is not in itself considered a bad thing but that the government's intentions are deemed dubious and politically motivated. Government officials are accused of insincerity, of bluffing. The dual recognition of the blunt efficacy of sacred acts in reproducing auspicious circumstances for agents and of the fact that sacred acts may be enacted with thoroughgoing duplicity—for example, as manipulation of the dhamma through sorcery—is hinted at here. Intention and action in Burmese Buddhist reckoning are recognized as two kinds of acts productive of future ontological realities. Acts disconnected from an agent's intentions are believed to be causally efficacious despite the stress on intention as the forerunner of action. Even so, intention inflects speech and bodily acts, with the resultant kammic effect to take place in some unspecified future. And it is understood to have causal efficacy independent of actions.

The New Laity is characterized by the conviction that the technique for the objective foundations of psychic experiences can be attained through the practice of satipaṭṭhāna vipassanā meditation. The inner process of systematic insights is outwardly verified according to criteria that cannot directly impute evidence of inner states in other people. However, as is true of language, there is agreement and consent about the systematic structure of experiences and the criteria for their validation. Whether or not there is understanding in the sense of individual primary experience of sense structures, there is nevertheless participation in these assertions about inner states, vis-à-vis the military and beyond. Thus, a concern has emerged over the sincerity of intentions and the interpretation of the true meaning of outer actions as they correspond to inner states. This is the level at which public political discourse takes place. The question asked in regard to military actors is this: Are their actions connected to their inner states?

Discourses about the sincerity of intentions are therefore simultaneously about contemporary and ultimate reality. Legitimate claims to power can only be made if someone is sufficiently endowed with merits cultivated in this and previous lifetimes. And, as in a Calvinist model, election is evaluated on the basis of what is seen from the outside as sincere efforts by an individual to perform meritorious acts in support of sāsana. The "withdrawal of trust," to borrow an expression from Veena Das, in words and actions has created a profound skepticism among the population concerning the intentions of the junta, and this skepticism places the junta's legitimacy-seeking performances under scrutiny and skepticism.

Action Spheres and Moral Debate

I have referred, first, to the existence of three levels at which one can discern action spheres vis-à-vis an evaluation of the regime's activities. Socially and analytically, these action spheres lie on a continuum relative to each other. On the simplest level, one finds a shunting of debate and formation of public opinion to a kind of underground railroad–level discussion, as among students. The second level entails a kind of code switching, often not recognized as strategically enacted, in which political commentary is inserted in the context of religious discourse and institutions. The pilgrimages, amulets, and so on concerning Thamanya Sayadaw comprise an example of this second level of action sphere. Finally, one can observe the interiorly focused practice of meditation as also encompassing a form of political commentary. The preponderance of women meditators shades that category in a particular way, filtered as it is through silence, accommodation in everyday life, and the moral adaptation to the strictures of living under corrupt rule. In the case of the students, if they are caught the regime will respond quickly to root out and imprison offenders. In the case of religious practitioners, however, among whom many senior members of the military junta (and their wives) can also be found, the response can more closely be described as accommodation. Ironically, public critique rests on the very question of whether the regime is being sincere in its Buddhist practices.

The second point I want to reinforce is that any critique of the regime that we could find in the two more subtly manifested political action spheres would be situated more immediately in people's experiences of everyday life. I refer here to experience as opposed to ideology and, again, not just forms of gossip and rumor but elemental efforts directed toward remaking the moral world. The popularly held conception is that through the revitalization of meditation, an enlightened society is being produced. Meditation is a place where one has a shared experience with other meditators that invokes a mythical society serving as an exemplar for civilized and enlightened society in the future. This is one reason why a person cannot simply regard critique that takes place in the context of the religious sphere as merely a sublimated form of public debate. The moral issues at stake are more broadly conceived, embedded in epistemology and cosmology, and are applied to matters other than politics, which at times appears to be only a tertiary application. Devout women may not be looking to act politically even though their actions might have political effects.

Chapter 5

FROM RELATIONS OF POWER
TO RELATIONS OF AUTHORITY
The Dynamics of Symbolic Legitimacy

Political Claims, Practices, and Ideology

Two key questions underpinning this study are: What constitutes political legitimacy in Burma, toward which each postindependence government has aspired? And how have the sundry approaches taken by the several governments fulfilled or failed to fulfill this quest for legitimacy?

Following the 1962 coup that overthrew Burma's first postindependence and parliamentary democratic government, a succession of military regimes has asserted legitimacy on diverse grounds. Their successes in containing the upland minorities and keeping the country unified, in implementing a socialist-style redistributive system, and contemporaneously in acting as chief patron to the sangha have all functioned as claims to legitimate rule and to nation-statehood. In 1990, the regime refused to hand over power to Aung San Suu Kyi and her National League for Democracy party after a landslide election victory. Aung San Suu Kyi's resistance to the regime and claims for her own political legitimacy have been based primarily on a universalizing discourse of the emergent global society and its sensibilities about human rights, regime performance, and democratic self-determination. I regard these separate assertions for legitimacy as distinct but interrelated frameworks for thinking and action. The inconsistencies among them complicate the process of stable state making in Burma.

Although I devote the last chapter to describing the ways in which resistance to regime domination must be expressed indirectly for fear of reprisals, the root of my analysis in this final chapter is the question of how the regime continues to rule without direct and widespread confrontation to its authority. An argument claiming that rule is maintained simply through the threat of force might be reasonable for a shorter-lived regime. But the fact is, at forty-three years and counting as of this writing, the junta that rules Burma is one of the most successful of its kind in modern history—if success is measured by the relative stability of its continuity despite its dubious track record in economy and welfare, human rights and foreign relations. Increasingly, a domestic and international community of states and their citizens expect all these criteria to be met. Although disapproval and fear of the regime within Burma is widespread, there is something in the relations between the regime and its subjects that is grounded in common, accepted viewpoints and terms for rule.

Acknowledging this as a sort of axiom, I reiterate Weber's insight (as condensed by Mouthier Alagappa) that "[t]he legitimation of power relies on the conviction of the governed that their government (whether democratic, monarchic, communist, theocratic, or authoritarian) is morally right and they are duty-bound to obey it. In the absence of such conviction there can only be relations of power, not of authority, and political legitimacy will be contested."[1] Political authority, in other words, must be situated from the point of view of the governed; their belief regarding the moral rectitude in the actions of their government will determine the political legitimacy of that government. The absence of such assent will result in the exercise of "relations of power." Relations of this type are liable to be both trying and demoralizing for the governed, resulting in smaller or grander acts of resistance. A regime confronted by complete denial of its authority must, in the end, be more like an occupying force than a government, with all that is implied historically by this structure. And, as Weber continues, once a "particular claim to legitimacy is to a significant degree and according to its type treated as 'valid' . . . this fact confirms the position of the persons claiming the authority and . . . helps to determine the choice of means of its exercise."[2]

This concept, if not formulated directly in such terms, has already been in effect in much of the analysis of contemporary Burma, where the military regime is seen as having donned the garb of Buddhist kingship in order, presumably, to achieve just such moral legitimacy as Weber indicated. Practically, however, questions of strategic versus cosmologically taken-for-granted sincerity on the part of the regime are not easily resolved. Rather, this debate has tended to be partitioned into a strained dichotomy between manipulated versus sincere acts of legitimacy seeking and, ultimately, into a competition between secular and religious sources of interpretation.[3] I want to take a last step away from this debate with the consideration of two additional factors.

First, I will seek to locate some of the processes by which legitimate order is constituted not by asking whether the regime is or is not capable of manipulating the public's beliefs but by determining the sources and conditions of knowledge that may warrant or justify moral political legitimacy in Burma today. Second, I will put the notion of power itself into play.

It is material to point out, from the outset, that the military regime's rule continues in a context in which the legitimacy of the state has never been ratified, at the very least from the perspective of the ethnic minorities.[4] The seven leading minority populations make up some 30 to 35 percent of the total population. The consequence of this and similar quandaries emerges from a brief consideration of the historical background of Burma since attaining independence in 1948. On the eve of independence, seven armies were formed to fight the new central government. The principal source of the contention came from up-country ethnic minority groups who had no natural political reason to consider themselves subject to the national boundaries the British had specified; to this day, the country remains unstable along the same lines. Ideological and bureaucratic divisions, in addition to religious sectarianism within the lowland Buddhist Burman majority, destabilized the effort to establish a single state entity, even at its geographic center in Yangon. The geoterritorial boundaries of the Burmese nation-state do not correspond to a single ethnopolitical community with shared norms and values. As Yangwhe comments, "Rebellions, insurgencies, and civil unrest have figured prominently since 1948 and have more or less become a permanent political feature of Burma . . . the legitimacy of the nation-state, régime, and government in Burma is highly contested."[5]

In their efforts to create and maintain autonomous political regions in opposition to the central government, the ethnic minorities have engaged Yangon in a debate—itself in statist language—over both the terms and the boundaries of the state as originally handed down by the British colonial government. Further, the question of state borders is determined by more than internal debates and considerations. The boundaries of neighboring states pose a de facto definition of state space for Burma as well. This situation is complicated by the fact that ethnic populations spill across other state borders, and it sometimes can lead to nationalist movements that do not reflect existing country boundaries. Since the early 1950s, for example, the country's estimated one hundred thousand Nagas have been seeking, in consort with the estimated one million Nagas living across the border in India, to form an independent nation.[6]

Early documents of intent of the newfound state are a hodgepodge of socialist, Marxist, democratic, and Buddhist principles—reflective of what I will later refer to as competing and overlapping surfaces of knowledge. Seeking the most democratically representative form of government and the moral high ground, the first prime minister, U Nu, attempted to establish an explicitly Buddhist state. In 1962, this effort collapsed in a coup staged by Ne Win. Ne Win's military government reversed the Buddhist resolution entirely, adopting instead a socialist-materialist philosophy. Religion was to be excluded from the affairs of the state, which would derive its authority from successful provisioning and organizing collectivities for that purpose.

Until 1971, the Ne Win regime formulated this political philosophy as "Only when your stomach is full can you keep your sīla."[7] The statement implicates the Buddhist logic by which progressive stages of purification practices (dāna, sīla, and bhāvanā) lead to the penultimate goal of nibbāna. But in this version, a righteous and prosperous society first depended not on charitable giving (especially toward the sangha) but on the redistributive functions of the government. Claims to socialist-style redistribution were contradicted, both by the overall diminishment of economic resources and by the conspicuous accretion of the remainder in the hands of those in or close to the military. The second measure of failure came to be represented in the popular claim—taking the form of a mass revitalization movement, with discernible structural features reinforcing its interpretation as just such a claim—that the government was being remiss by relinquishing its duties to be chief patron to the sangha and protector and propagator of the faith. Thus, as I have described in chapter 1, a mass lay meditation movement with new institutional features arose among the majority Buddhist population to compensate for the role of the state or king in the classical triple order of sangha, state, and laity.

Recognizing that the new, closer alignment between the sangha and the laity represented a threat in political and economic terms, the government reversed itself and began participating in the Buddhist revitalization. Starting by availing itself of its classically endowed authority to purify the sangha—and note here that the regime's authority derives from pre- or extrastatist sources—the military government sanctioned the resolution of the sangha into nine official sects. It disrobed monks who refused to conform to this division. Laity who had taken to residing on lands they had donated to specific monks, thereby avoiding government taxation and repatriation, were forced off these properties, and the government undertook to control lay Buddhist institutions by placing military officials on their guardian committees.

As of this writing, although the military government has come to fulfill its kingly role as chief donor and supporter of the sāsana— and I will recount how succession to leadership within the regime is often marked by rituals of Buddhist coronation or the pretending to it by various means—the regime's authority is yet not secure in statist terms. The centerpiece of the state's ideological claims is embodied in its attempts to legitimize its authority in Buddhist monarchical terms.

Burmese Rulers and Pretenders to the Throne:
A Postindependence Sequence

It is reported that between 85 and 89 percent of the people of Burma are Buddhist, and the majority of these are ethnic Bama or Burmans. U Nu, Burma's first prime minister (from 1948 to 1962), sought legitimacy in terms of the classical function of Burman kings. This meant supporting the Buddha sāsana by sponsoring, protecting, and purifying it through his role as chief patron of the Sangha of the Four Quarters. Purifying involved, among other actions, removing from the sangha monks who did not adhere to the disciplinary code (vinaya). U Nu was also obliged to be foremost among the laity in providing the requisites for the sangha (lands, monasteries, robes, and food) and to propagate the teachings and convert populations he had conquered for the benefit of all beings.

As world renouncers, members of the sangha officially remain outside of politics, but they nevertheless stay involved in many aspects of worldly life. Sometimes, they do so through their direct engagement with the sources of their material sustenance. But there is also an abstract, necessary, and paradoxical linkage between monks and worldly life. This engagement stems from the fact that in Buddhist cosmology, renunciation is a source of moral authority and cosmic potency. The state draws from this source of potency to legitimize its political authority in moral and cosmic terms. Where U Nu was concerned, veneration of and donation to Buddhist institutions helped him accumulate his merit stores as a "king." (And the king, with his access to resources, is afforded much greater leverage in being able to undertake meritorious acts that eventually [by the law of kamma] return the fruits of his good deeds in this and future lives.) Undertaking meritorious actions directed toward the sangha was, therefore, a way for U Nu to balance the scale against the demerits that his role as ruler eventually required of him.

Whether the historical facts of prior eras bear this out or not is less important than the fact that U Nu perceived the sangha as constituting the main source of a king's actual worldly power. Colonialism may have interrupted this political pattern with the introduction of an administrative bureaucracy organized around the goals of extracting resources and administrating a peaceful colony. But the principles that organized the potency and hence the moral and practical authority of a king/ruler were interpretable along these lines in the postmonarchical arrangement as well.

By the time of independence in 1948, the prospect of restoring kingship as the legitimate form of government was viewed as a clear impossibility. Yet, as U Myo Myint, an eminent historian at the University of Mandalay, once commented to me, "Kingship is always at the back of Burmese politics." For U Nu, who sought to establish a society based on Buddhist moral principles (and who himself had made a vow to become a bodhisattva[8]—as was quite typical for classical Buddhist kings), national unity was to be accomplished by purifying the citizens of their moral impurities and wrong views (*miccha ditti*). Only then could Burmese society approximate the mythical state of Mahasammatha, the first king, who was unanimously elected by the mandate of the people; they recognized him to be the most morally pure and noble human being among them and therefore their rightful ruler. In fact, the word for president is *thammada,* the Burmanized form of the Buddhist Pāli Mahasammatha. It should be noted that the rise of Mahasammatha occurs when the people are no longer capable of self-governance because of a general increase in craving or greed, which, by mythical accounts, is the cause for the decline in World Ages.

The mythical ideal of the rightful ruler and the historical idea of Burmese kings also participate together in another theory of kings. This is the theory of the nature of moral decline in the World Age as part of the natural process of moral devolution and evolution that makes up the wheel of saṃsāra, or the endless cycle of death and rebirths to which all sentient beings are chained. From the Burmese Buddhist perspective, bad kings are a given. They are categorized as one of the five great evils, along with flood, fire, thieves, and enemies.[9] It is important to recognize in our consideration of native conceptions of political authority that a continuum of ideas about authoritarian rule already exists. At one end of the spectrum, the king functions merely to keep the citizenry in line with their own lay, moral conduct (especially the layperson's five precepts); at the other end of the spectrum, where a king rules unjustly and arbitrarily and without concern for the populace, he rules over and only for his own aggrandizement.

U Nu fashioned himself in the role of a cakkavatti king (a king destined for Buddhahood), but despite his aspirations and conceptualization of the nature of political authority, he nevertheless was very explicit about the fact that the age of kings (min win) had come to a close and could not be resurrected. In its place, he imagined a society structured more on the Mahasammatha model. For U Nu, society required moral purification and unification in order that the citizens might become responsible participants in *democratic* society.[10] U Nu's demand that one person from every village should practice meditation at MTY is an example of how he sought to transform the nation-state into a like-minded country where democracy could flourish on the basis of a shared set of societal goals.[11] Unity would be achieved not through conquest and conversion but by "turning the wheel of dhamma"—that is, by allowing truth (dhamma) to transform society through self-realization. In this version, U Nu's conception of democracy was not premised on the sovereign will of a people made up of independent-minded citizen individuals. Rather, democracy was the end result of having already unified and established shared norms and values—especially Buddhist universal, causative, objective, and self-evident moral values.

At the same time that U Nu looked to Buddhism as a way of unifying the country, the constraints and demands of nation-state building (communist and ethnic insurgencies, rising military power, and factionalism within his own party) led him to endorse procedural democracy. He identified three enemies of democracy in newly independent countries: (1) politicians who are elected to office but who, on finding themselves facing electoral defeat at a later point, delay or rig elections or seize power outright; (2) politicians who, recognizing they will not win votes in an election, turn to foreign governments to support them against their own people; and (3) military officers who begin to covet the power of the politicians.[12] In a speech delivered in 1954, he said, "[T]he thesis of the Marxists that the last war on earth would be fought between capitalists and the proletariat was false. Instead, . . . the last war would be between the masses who loved democracy and the despots who would reduce human beings to the level of castrated animals."[13]

Procedural democracy is silent on the question of what the particular moral goals for society should be. U Nu's efforts to educate for democracy (so that "the people . . . may take democracy to heart and defend it with their lives"[14]) blended with Burmese Buddhist notions for a virtuous (mingala) society. His incorporation of procedural democratic principles into the project of nation-state building fit with Buddhist conceptions of righteous kings. Subsequent military governments turned toward other conceptions of Burmese kingship, emphasizing instead the right to unfettered power (justified as the pursuit of national unity). It needs to be remembered that the military leaders have always claimed that they would allow an eventual return to democracy once the country had stabilized—and, presumably, once they had assured their hold on authority (and not just power). The holding of elections in 1990, therefore, can be interpreted as a fulfillment of this justification to their "temporary" rule by force. It was also a vast miscalculation by the military government regarding the degree to which the populace perceived it as legitimate.[15]

As regards U Nu's nation-state building project, I remind the reader of how the prime minister was instrumental in making part of the government's task the revitalization of sāsana after nearly 100 years of British colonial subjugation. He helped establish lay meditation centers, monks' universities, nunneries, training centers, and state-sponsored titles for the scholastic attainments of monks who memorized the classical texts. His pièce de résistance was the Sixth Buddhist Synod. At this international event, the revision or purification of the canonical (Tipitaka) texts were undertaken in order to normalize the orthodoxy of the texts across national boundaries.

Buddhism was to be revitalized not only within the boundaries of Burma but also throughout the world. Presumably, the synod would also demonstrate Burma's unique role as foremost among the nations as the location and repository for the Buddha's true teachings.

In 1962, in response to ongoing ethnic conflicts and splits in the civilian Antifascist People's Freedom League (AFPFL) government party and on the eve of U Nu's proclamation of intent to declare Burma a Buddhist state and grant the ethnic Shan's secession from the Union of Burma, Ne Win staged a bloodless coup and instituted military rule. The justification for this action was that the nation was disintegrating. Ne Win's plan was to rid the state apparatus of all Buddhist involvements, citing these as sources of corruption in the government.

During the first fifteen years of military rule, the government took an approach of noninvolvement in religious affairs. From 1962 to 1965, the government set out to secularize the polity. Religious legislation from the previous administration was removed, the Buddha Sāsana Council was dissolved, and ecclesiastical courts and state sponsorship of the Pāli Universities was curtailed. Nationalization of private and corporate ownership in sectors of the economy such as agriculture, timber, mineral production, and foreign trade in 1963 and the demonetization of large notes in 1964 eroded the economic base of the private sector. The effects of these events would be felt over the next decade in a general decline in the physical maintenance of the infrastructure of the sangha (monasteries, temples, pagodas, and so on). As political institutional sponsorship was removed, the support of Buddhism was taken up by lay organizations and individual lay devotees. Tin Maung Maung Than states:

[A]s Burmese society tried to cope with the realities of the secular socialist revolution, the post-independence trend popularizing the quest for insight knowledge appeared to reassert itself after a hiatus following the demise of U Nu's leadership. This was manifested in a resurgence of meditational practices centered around different techniques for, or doctrines on, vipassana . . . as interpreted and enunciated by prominent teachers—who were more often than not, revered members of the sangha.[16]

In 1974, a constitution was drawn up and a socialist government was put in place under the military—the Burmese Socialist Program Party. The ideology of the BSPP was a peculiar blend of Buddhism and Marxism, which the military described as the Burmese Way to Socialism. Under the BSPP, the country experienced disastrous economic decline. Whereas Burma had once been known as the rice bowl of Southeast Asia, it was now barely able to provide enough rice for its own citizens. In 1974, food shortages sparked demonstrations and strikes in Rangoon. Later that year, U Thant, the former secretary-general of the United Nations, died. When his body was returned to Burma, students and monks—this was the first time in more than a decade that monks would be politically active—rallied at U Thant's burial site. They shouted slogans such as "Down with the one-party dictatorship" and "Down with the fascist government."[17] In the wake of more demonstrations, the military declared martial law and closed universities and schools.

In apparent response to the unrest, Ne Win launched a project to purify the sangha from its impure (that is, political) elements. Invoking the duty of classical Buddhist kings, he set out to unify and purify the sangha according to orthodox practice, operating on the assumption that if he controlled the monks, he thereby also controlled the people. The recognition that sangha and laity could pose a threatening unity against the state altered Ne Win's strategic outlook. Sangha-laity arrangements had bypassed government control and permitted a different kind of economic flow through a dāna economy tied to the black market economy, as well as chains of patron-client ties that cross-laced the state bureaucracy itself, as described in chapter 3.

Ne Win began his purification with the burning of nonorthodox books. Trials were arranged for heretical monks, and those who were convicted were disrobed and sent into hard labor. I myself was in the office of the director-general for the Department of Religious

Affairs, U Aunt Maung, when he chastised a monk for having been seen at a football game. "If it happens again," he warned the monk, "you will be disrobed and thrown in prison." Identity cards were issued to all members of the sangha. Ne Win established an elaborate state sangha cóuncil mirroring the sangha organization down to the village tract, so that at every level, sangha and state would be integrated and intertwined.

Tin Maung Maung Than observes that the regime initially sought to avoid direct sponsorship of Buddhism. The approach was to create an environment of self-purification and perpetuation by the sangha and lay devotees through such indirect pressures as reinstituting honorary state titles for achievements of members of the monastic order. At the same time, it was intended to project "the power and authority of the state in such a way as to rid the sāsana of unscrupulous elements as well as dubious doctrines and to act as a deterrent against further encroachments by undesirable elements."[18]

In commemoration of the unification of the sangha, a feat that had not been accomplished since King Mindon in the 1850s, Ne Win built a pagoda, thereby establishing himself through having performed the function of classical kings.

In 1987, I observed:

Ecclesiastical courts have been re-established, monk identification papers issued, the sangha has been hierarchically organized to the village level to mirror the political body of the BSPP, the sangharaja (tha-tha-na-baing)—an institution I am told has not existed since the time of the British—has been reinstituted; government-sponsored religious exams and titles have been reinstated.

The political success and social consequences of the sangha purification movement are significant. Nine sects were legitimized and all the others abolished. Their members have been forced to join legitimate sects, renouncing any "wrong views" held previously. Ecclesiastical courts worked with a lay government–sponsored purification council. Decisions were made at least at face value by the monk courts. However, it should be noted that the Deputy Minister of the Ministry of Home and Religious Affairs, U Khin Nyunt, was also the head of Military Intelligence. It is clear that the government prefigured the outcome by means of their selection process of monks to the State Sangha Council, and through directing the points of investigation by having lay advisors to these committees. (In fact, the people I have spoken with at Mahasi feel that the "government monks" are the military's puppets and they hold little regard for them.) The court's decisions are enforced, e.g., the army has routed thousands of people living on monastery grounds in the Rangoon area because it was against the vinaya that monks and the laity should live so closely together. The government, of course, fears the close contact between the monks and laity. Several monks told me that the especially close contact between monks and the laity began during WWII when urban monasteries took in thousands of people who felt they would be protected from bombings if they were sheltered by the sangha. There grew up a very close relationship whereby lay houses came to be built on monastery grounds in exchange for the laity overseeing the worldly tasks monks could not perform for themselves. The laity in turn received advice and protection from the monks they supported. The government is forcibly emptying these places and is resettling the people in the new settlements on the outskirts of Rangoon. However, I understand that even while this continues, the people are slowly returning to the monasteries.

On April 5, 1980, the Congregation of the Sangha of All Orders for Purification, Perpetuation, and Propagation of the Sāsana was held, and the unification of the sangha was declared to have been achieved. Nine sects were officially recognized, ecclesiastical courts were established, and registration and identity papers for all monks were completed. Some of the other tasks implemented for the purification of the sāsana included

facilitating the removal of laymen from the monastic premises with the co-operation of the organs of state power; . . . investigating, prosecuting and disrobing bogus monks and monks who had committed serious viniya offences with the assistance of local authorities; . . . scrutinizing applications from monks who wished to go abroad; . . . evaluating existing government-sponsored religious examinations and, when necessary, proposing revisions of syllabi and procedures for conducting lessons and examinations; . . . drafting a comprehensive Pariyatti education scheme involving a structured, modernized sangha educational system with provisions for different levels from the elementary introductory course to the international postgraduate level culminating in the formation of State Pariyatti Sasana Tekathos or Buddhist universities at Rangoon and Mandalay; instituting training courses and multiplier courses for viniyadharas, abbots or heads of monasteries and Sangha Nayaka members.[19]

In 1984, Buddhist culture examinations were established, and over one hundred thousand youths and children participated in more than a hundred towns. Ten years later, I was told by a Religious Affairs bureaucrat that the government was still actively encouraging these "culture classes" (which, incidentally, are also held at MTY during the one-month school break) in order to morally prepare the Burmese people for the impending influx of visitors and business from the outside world with the planned opening of the country to tourism and trade in 1996.

In 1984, during my first stay in Burma, a common query I overheard questioned whether it did not, after all, seem that Ne Win had pon. As I have discussed in chapter 4, pon is a Buddhist concept describing an ineffable quality of merit, or glory. All rulers are said to possess it, and it is considered a sign of the individual's prior meritorious action come to fruit in the present. That Ne Win was still judged illegitimate on all other counts of his performance toward the nation (corruption, crippling the economy, human rights infringements, and so forth) did not alter the fact that perhaps he was the legitimate ruler because he was beginning to act like one. Sao Htun Hmat Win of the Ministry of Home and Religious Affairs and a close religious adviser to Ne Win told me:

The Burmese mentality of government is still that of the king. U Ne Win, during his 26 years, took an interest in sāsana only in the last 16 years. In the beginning, religion and state must be separate. But afterwards he realized that it is not easy to change the spiritual direction of the people. He ordained for a few months around 1975 and studied the scriptures. I was his instructor. I can tell you that he was very sincere. He learned scriptures and built the pagoda. He became the king builder, and I was in charge of the central committee. Soldier, politician . . . now U Ne Win is a religious man. You cannot bluff yourself! A Myanma [Burmese] must be like this . . . only slowly can he change.

Another telling example of Ne Win's attempt to legitimize himself in classical terms was the marriage he contracted with one of the last descendents in the line of Burmese kings, a descendent of King Thibaw. Despite the fact that the Burmese public might be willing to leave open the question of Ne Win's pon, his technical manipulations of the principle of succession in pursuit of outright kingship were ridiculed. Sao Htun Hmat Win continued:

Kingship [in Burma] is not [a matter of] verbal acts, or signs, or making mystical consecrations. It comes by blood. Your blood must be royal. But, U Ne Win is ordinary farmer blood—a peasant from Prome Village. . . . Actually speaking he cannot become a king. He can become President, Chairman, Leader . . . but not a king! No royal blood. That is what we believe. He began to realize this. U Nu and U Ne Win thought they could be universal kings, but neither could become a king. So, [U Ne Win] found a way to become a king in this country by extending his rule. He brought one royal person from England—an Anglo-Burman, Yadana Nat Mei. She was a widow with two sons from an English husband. Her husband passed away so U Ne Win had the chance to become a pretender. She was a grandchild of King Thibaw. So he had royal blood in her. He married this princess so he could become a king so Myanma people would obey him. . . . But the whole plan was a failure! The people all just laughed that he is only a peasant and he is putting on all these airs.

Ne Win's aspirations to kingship were viewed as those of a pretender to an as yet void throne. Like every contender to the throne in the classical patterns of Burmese kingship, the pretender consecrates his legitimacy by marrying the former king's queen, thereby assuring that the issuance of his line yet partakes of royal blood. Ne Win's originally secularist government had, by 1988, become thoroughly entangled in sāsana projects. Under the current regime, SLORC/SPDC, this has been all the more the case, and the regime's engagements have drawn skeptical attention from the people. As a Rangoon University professor told me, the SLORC/SPDC government "more than any other post-independence government is trying to legitimize itself through the sangha." The signs of this are everywhere. The Department of Religious Affairs has doubled in size from the time of U Nu. The state sangha coparticipate with the civil justice system in determining legal cases related to monks and monk-lay disputes. Patronage of Buddhist scholarship includes offering monks honorary titles with special state privileges (such as riding for free on trains and steamboats and, for the most venerable and learned, airplanes). A state censorship committee regulates the orthodoxy of discourses on Buddhism presented by monks traveling outside the country on dhamma proselytizing tours.

THE BUTCHER OF RANGOON: SEIN LWIN

The next landmark in modern Burmese political history occurred in 1988, when antigovernment demonstrations precipitated the fall of the Ne Win government. On July 23 of that year, Ne Win resigned from his post as BSPP chairman and designated Sein Lwin, a lieutenant from the Fourth Burma Rifles, as his handpicked successor.[20] Sein Lwin was universally hated and feared, having been responsible for carrying out the Rangoon University massacre in 1962 and for violently suppressing the demonstrations in March and June, a few months earlier. For the latter, he had earned the moniker "the Butcher of Rangoon." It is also worth remembering that Sein Lwin had been the main inspirational and organizing force for the thathana thanshin ye (the purification and unification of the sanghas movement) that took place beginning in the mid-1970s and culminating in 1980.

It was widely understood that despite his announcement that he was stepping down as BSPP chairman, Ne Win did not intend to renounce power. By selecting the public's most feared and hated military personage to succeed him, he signaled that the military's hold on power would only be tighter and that there would be zero tolerance for antigovernment demonstrations. In his resignation speech, he warned: "In continuing to maintain control, I want the entire nation, the people, to know that if in the future there are mob disturbances, if the army shoots, it hits—there is no firing in the air to scare."[21] In the days following his assumption of power, Sein Lwin had been making a very public and conspicuous display of offering dāna to the important monasteries and meditation centers in the Yangon area. He was also known to be consulting with astrologers, presumably to align his actions with auspicious times and to undertake various dark rituals. The effect these actions had (at least on the Yangon public) was sensational. People speculated that Sein Lwin was up to something that would secure his power, and there was much gossip, rumor, and intrepidation. People flocked to consult with their bedin sayas (fortune-tellers), waiting in lines outside their residences for up to four and five hours. One client explained that people wanted to know if their family members would be safe in the upcoming days and what they should do with their economic resources in the event of new government policies.[22]

I was present in the days leading up to what was planned as a peaceful popular protest against the government, to take place on August 8, 1988, a date deemed auspicious for its repeating eights— 8/8/88. Meanwhile, U Nu had been placed (I was told) under heavy surveillance.[23] U Thaw Kaung, Rangoon University's chief librarian, came, at my invitation, to the house where I was staying for a visit on August 6, only to learn immediately on arriving that the military was in the process of locking down the university, where he lived. He apologized and at once turned around to hurry home before he could be locked out. Everyone I spoke with anticipated that there would be trouble, and I was encouraged by my hosts to leave the country,[24] which I did on August 7, 1988.

A few days before the demonstrations turned to massacre, Sein Lwin had the streets in his residential neighborhood cordoned off, and he commanded that everyone was to stay indoors, with their shutters closed. At an auspicious hour, he dressed in the full regalia of a Burmese king. He took nine steps from the front of his house and awaited a sign. An unseasonable clap of thunder is said to have occurred, thereby giving the sign that he would come into power. Later, many Burmese were asking and verifying to each other that this omen had in fact taken place.

Sein Lwin was essentially prefiguring his rule and creating an advance prophecy for it. The prophetic act served as the source of a rumor to presage his incumbency. (It was contested when people said, "No I did not hear the clap of thunder.") My own source for knowing about this event was Sein Lwin's doctor, at whose house I was staying at the time and who, during this period, needed to render close medical attention to Sein Lwin because he was having heart troubles in the days leading up to August 8, 1988. I was told that in the absence of nongovernmental forms of public announcement, the BBC was forecasting and organizing the event. The repetition of eights in the date selected for the gathering (8-8-88) lent an air of auspiciousness to the occasion.

Lintner (1989) provides a full account of the 8-8-88 massacres, which ended in the estimated slaughter of over two thousand peaceful demonstrators, many of whom were university and high school students. In 1994, my Burmese friends recalled how, after firing on demonstrators, the government barricaded the downtown area and declared a curfew. With anguish, they related that families were not permitted to claim their dead, and how for days and nights trucks came and went to take the bodies away for burning.[25]

Despite all of the ritual of prophecy surrounding his coming into power, Sein Lwin was able to hold that power for only seventeen days, for he was widely despised. The unanimous hatred motivated SLORC to remove him—he wasn't stabilizing anything. On the day after his reign ended, on what would have been his eighteenth day, Sein Lwin enrolled in the Mahasi Thathana Yeiktha. He did so, at least in accordance with a Buddhist interpretation, to balance the debits in his merit store, which he had accumulated via the recent events. This was the typical custom, it is said, of Burmese kings who were sometimes required to undertake unwholesome acts on behalf of the state. They would perform meritorious acts to raise the balance of their merits for purposes of continuing their ability to have power as well as for soteriological purposes—to lessen the kammic consequences of their actions.

The "VIP room" at Mahasi Thathana Yeiktha happens to be located in the foreign men's building. I had an Australian acquaintance who was practicing at the same time as Sein Lwin. This yogi related to me how pious and mindful Sein Lwin was in his meditation. He stated that the image was etched on his mind of the way in which the recent oppressor and murderer of innocents would, in privacy and with the utmost of care, release mosquitoes from his mosquito net so as not to destroy them and invite further bad kamma.

THE TOOTH RELIC, REFURBISHING SHWEDAGON, AND WHITE ELEPHANTS: PERFORMATIVE ACTS OF LEGITIMACY

In 1996, a tooth relic of the Buddha was taken to Burma from China. In a chariot drawn by a caparisoned elephant, the relic was carried to the government's pagoda and then all over the country, giving people the opportunity to revere it and make merit. This performance recalled the obligation of a Buddhist king to provide his subjects opportunities for merit making.[26]

The refurbishing of Shwedagon, the most revered pagoda in the country, was an undertaking of elaborate proportions. It was completed in April 1999. Nearly half a ton of diamonds, rubies, sapphires, and other precious gems adorned a spire made of 0.21 tons of gold. A seventy-six-carat diamond rested at the center of the orb. Much of this precious material was newly donated, and it was set in place by the senior general of the SPDC and Secretaries 1 and 2 (as the two military regime chiefs are known), among other dignitaries. Renovation of Shwedagon represented the regime's intent to prolong the teachings of the Buddha for thousands of years. This, too, is the work of kings. When the military rulers had first announced their intention to restore the *ti* (the umbrella, or finial, that adorns the utmost top of the spire), many were apprehensive. Such work, it was thought, was the obligation and privilege of true kings alone. Should a pretender to the throne undertake such cosmically important work and not be legitimate, natural calamities would be certain to ensue.

The pagoda restoration culminated with the final hoisting of the ti, which entailed removing the ti placed by the last king (King Mindon, from the late 1800s) and replacing it with that of the new ruler. During the days following the ceremony, residents of Yangon told me that a collective hush settled on the city as people waited to see what would happen next. When no earthquake shook open the foundations of the land, rumors began to circulate that perhaps this government was legitimate after all. "And all the worse for the people of Burma!" as one person put it to me.

The work on Shwedagon had even greater ramifications than conferring on the military regime merits and domestic legitimacy. Shwedagon is held to be the property not just of Burmese Buddhists but also of all human beings. From a Burmese Buddhist standpoint, this gives a special kind of international legitimacy to the military regime. Burma is held to be the last repository of the Buddha's unaltered teachings. As Mary Douglas has explained, the alignment of the truth claims of an institution with the nature of the universe confers on the institution an ultimate seal of legitimacy.[27] Moreover, once the institution itself is regarded as valid, the particular position of those claiming authority and of the means they use to exercise that authority can be confirmed.

In another recent example of the regime seeking cosmological endorsement, the government announced in 1997, 2001, and 2002 that it had captured three white elephants in western Burma's Arakan State. For hundreds of years, white elephants have been regarded as symbols of royalty, power, and prosperity in many Southeast Asian Buddhist countries.[28] One might add that the parading of these symbols, accompanied by the lavish donation fests from poor as from rich, furthered the quest to incorporate minority populations into the Buddhist and, hence, the central state fold. The military government employs elaborate means to convert non-Buddhist minorities to Buddhism—again, an act emblematic of kingship. Conversion statistics are kept.[29] The proselytizing efforts could only be enhanced by the red carpet pageantry of the elephants, the tooth relic, and the heaps of gold plastered onto Shwedagon, which could not fail to impress the people, perhaps in the manner that the magnificent spires of medieval churches struck a kind of awe in the residents of the towns and cities of the age.

Other Ways of Knowing Legitimate Authority

The performative efficacy of the regime's symbolic actions is certainly open to interpretation. Ko Thar Nyunt Oo, a member of the All Burma Federation of Student Unions' Foreign Affairs Committee, explains: "People who still believe in the monarchy believe in white elephants. The junta tries to use the white elephant as a sign of coming prosperity for the people of Burma, but I think the white elephant just has damaged skin."[30] Rumors that one of the white elephants drowned itself by holding its trunk in a bucket of water, that one animal was really more gray than white, or that the tooth relic donation extravaganza was, in fact, concocted as a strategy to combat inflation by taking currency out of circulation are worthy of note as counterdiscourses to the regime's claims to legitimacy. Interestingly, the dissident students themselves frame their opposition in Buddhist monarchical terms. As Mya Maung observes:

Evidence of how those opposed to the military rulers also think and behave in terms of the Burmese kingdom's traditional political framework can be found in the choice of pseudonyms used by many dissident student leaders involved in the 1988 political uprising to hide their identities . . . specifically, their *noms de guerre* often incorporate the word *min* (king), which both signifies opposition to the reigning military junta and symbolically positions the students as rival kings with the potential to usurp the throne. Indeed, the use of a peacock insignia on the flag of student opposition organization, the All Burma Students' Democratic Front (ABSDF), is an explicit reference to the peacock throne of the ancient Burmese kings.[31]

Thus, we can see that the regime renders its actions in what may be referred to as epistemic claims, insofar as they are organized according to a system of knowledge familiar to both the regime and the populace; indeed, the counterdiscourses themselves acknowledge the potential validity of such claims.

The discourse of Buddhist kingship is but one way of deciphering the regime's (and its resisters') activities, however. The efforts the military expends in hardening its statist authority take place along various channels and entail, I would argue, different ways of political knowing and being.[32] To get at this notion, I must refer to the epistemic practices in government ministries, which are longer-lived than the present regime but have been staffed and commandeered to suit the regime's program of rule. These practices also sometimes mirror Buddhist values and hierarchies of relations. However, they independently reveal the prevalence of certain self-evident truths not borne of the regime's attempts to incorporate Buddhist cosmological and monarchical principles as legitimating discourses. What this means is that the practices and organization of the bureaucratic ministries (of welfare, land, religion, education, and so forth), with their long history of structured relations based on internal patron-client ties, serve to substantiate specifically Burmese moral-political conceptions of influence (awza) and power (ana),[33] independent of the military regime's co-optation of religious and monarchical (and religious monarchical) discourses. The key lies in my departure from "discourse" as the sole analytic field in which the question of legitimacy is to be determined. Epistemic practices of ministry officials can, in this case, reveal a separate domain on which to base the discussion. Let me explain by way of two examples.

There is a system of practices in the ministries that could be referred to as that of the "big elephant." Tambiah observes this as a value orientation in Thai bureaucracy: "Hierarchical status is inherently valued," he notes, and there is a pervasive "personalism, that is, reliance on the value of a limited circle of personal relations (the antithesis of relations in the legal-rational bureaucratic model)."[34] The big elephant organizes, in the dynamic configuration of patron-client obligations, a retinue of underlings who have loyalties to their superiors rather than to the goals of the bureaucracy. Thus, in the mid-1980s, when the tax minister and his subordinates together donated the tax ministry building to an allegedly enlightened monk—an act independent of the system of goals one would ordinarily associate with a civil bureaucracy—what was really being asserted was a merit hierarchy establishing relations of obligation and patronage around an individual with great personal influence. Influence converts to power on the basis of such demonstrations of personalism that are recognized as the expression of larger moral-causal (that is, kammic) realities.

It is pertinent to reiterate what we have seen in chapter 3—that incipient political groupings typically spring from donation cliques. Recognizing this fact, the regime has, since the mid-1990s, stepped up efforts to solidify the institutional salience of state bureaucratic ministries according to these same criteria. The regime has sought to associate the system of patron-client networks in the state bureaucracy with the legitimate work of kings whose task it is to cajole their subjects, if necessary, toward the goal of nibbāna. They have done so by garnishing state salary workers' pay for purposes of organizing donations from specific bureaucratic units; by constructing dhamma-preaching halls that connect the members of each ministerial unit to a place for making offerings and inviting monks to give discourses; and through the admonishment of individuals to make offerings on their birthdays, as in the traditional folk Buddhist practice.

Other practices within the bureaucracies, however, can lead to the affirmation of values contradictory to those of Buddhist faith. For example, the father of one of my acquaintances worked as a high-ranking official during the BSPP period in a ministry that controlled a provisions cooperative. As a devout Buddhist, he was reluctant to exploit his position within the ministry to improve his family's material condition. However, even as a high-level bureaucrat, his income was insufficient to support his modest standard of living. Indeed, his superiors already understood this. The calculation of his salary took advance account of what he could "skim." On one occasion, his wife went to the ministry office on a day she knew her husband would be out: she was not going to let his pious adherence to the Buddhist five precepts impoverish the household economy. She instructed his subordinate to bring this and that item from the cooperative to her home, which he did. When the official returned home to find his subordinate in the act of delivering these materials, he was outraged with both of them and had the items returned to the cooperative. His daughter commented on the affair to me: "By keeping the bureaucrats' salaries so low, the government intentionally makes criminals of them. You have to steal and take bribes to survive."

Apart from the implication for matters of administrative economy and potential political blackmail to control functionaries, this situation also demonstrates how clientship, administrative irrationality, and indifference are likely to arise and how the regime's attempts to legitimate its authority on a Buddhist substrate may be undermined within its own bureaucracies by corrupt practices it cannot or does not discourage. The widespread public association of government bureaucracies (including, by extension, the military) with corruption leads people to put stock in the sangha and in lay Buddhist associations as alternate sources of moral-political influence.

Situating Power and Authority within a Broader Cosmology

In Burma, the politics of power and influence is always asserted within or against the conditions of the sāsana. Hence, Burmese speak of two kinds of history—of kings (min win) and of sāsana (thathana win). The history of kings is made sense of only in terms of the history of the sasana and is taken to be the categories of ultimate reality, which is the dhamma. There is yet a third kind of history, maha win—the history of *ariya* (enlightened ones) not just in this world cycle but also beyond it, stretching both backward in history and forward into the future. U Nu had made self-conscious use of this category when, in the founding charter for the Buddha Sāsana Nuggaha Apwe, he proclaimed that the history of kings had come to a close but that the world now stood poised to participate in the great history, the maha win, the history of enlightened beings. U Nu saw the maha win as the history that would replace the min win. It would be a history of enlightenment, and democracy would be the legitimate form of political governance. This thread has been taken up by Aung San Suu Kyi, although she has not articulated her version of Burmese democracy in quite these terms.

I will turn to these considerations in light of the relations between a view of politics that is sāsana centered and one that is king centered. That power and politics are conceived in terms of a "type" of history is revealing, for it shows how power is never constituted outside the system within which it is acted out and made sensible. Kings cannot participate in power while neglecting the sāsana because by so acting, they will have neglected the conditions of their own power. Conditions of power are causative in two senses—first, in the sense that they are based on the dhamma as law and, second, in the sense that Burmese Buddhist society regenerates itself as spores of community that operate according to the logic of awza (influence) and ana (strength). The process of social reproduction thus always stands in potential resistance to political authority as a distinctive and separate power source.

Structurally, Burmese political authority must always be involved in political processes by which incorporation into the core is accomplished through capturing and mediating the activities of such moral communities. This is accomplished through controlling the community's sources of potency, as demonstrated in the logic of donation cliques. Classical paradigms of "conquer, pacify, convert," which also exists as a contemporary strategy of SLORC/SPDC, are integral to the formation of state arrangements. This is because they are implicated in a cosmology-making project that must be undertaken by the state in parallel to mass revitalization carried out by Burmese Buddhist civil society.

The theory of moral causality is outlined in principle in the Abhidhamma and especially in the Paṭiccasamuppāda text as the theory of dependent origination. For the ordinary person, it says, the full workings of physical and psychical causality are comprehended in theory alone. Only a Buddha is capable of fully seeing the conditions in the play of kammic cause and effect in their actual workings.

Another way in which the collective effect of the total environment is expressed is in terms of the cycle of regeneration and degeneration of morality and the physical conditions that arise as a result of it. As the collective condition of morality declines, so too does the material condition of the environment—poverty, droughts, bad kings, and so forth. The life span becomes shortened as moral degeneration continues, in a sort of snowball effect, until the World Age finally comes to an end in a cataclysm of the material elements of earth, wind, fire, and water. Within these larger environmental conditions and despite overwhelming odds, it is still possible for individuals to remain true to their sīla and thereby cultivate their pāramī and good kamma. Every Burman child studies the Jataka tales, the exemplary stories of the Buddha's lives as the embryo Buddha, by means of which the ideal that one's actions are always to be cultivated in relation to a transcendent morality is engendered. This morality is located at the place of one's own personal actions and mental intentions as they arise in every moment.

These understandings of moral causality must be included in any account of power and political legitimacy in Buddhist Burma. Moreover, it is imperative that the ideology of especially Ashokan Buddhist kingship be distinguished from a general theory of moral causality. This is necessary in order to provide a better account of the creative and open-ended process in which a particular understanding of the world is constituted. As reviewed in chapter 2, ideology and all representational forms of knowledge production are communicative forms of knowledge that point or refer to more immediate practical understandings that are kinesthetically embodied as the living moment of intention arising in each moment of being. The experience of these is not profitably reduced to ideological schemata, language, signs, or an imprinting or selection between "models of and models for."

It is with this distinction in mind that I return to the Burmese Buddhist theory of power in order to suggest that the response to so-called bad kings and arbitrary, coercive, and violent power is to take refuge in the dhamma. One may take refuge through the purification of one's owns actions: "Be an island unto yourself," the Buddha urges. Alternatively, one may take refuge in the "space of dhamma"—by associating with noble friends (*kalyanamitta*), by participating in the wholesome reflection of taking refuge in the Triple Gem, or by remaining near the radiating and potent embodiments of dhamma (relics, pagodas, Buddha images, monasteries, sima, robes, monks, and so on). In this way, the sangha and the laity have a natural affiliation and bond that ultimately may be threatening to a ruler seeking to subject his population. The sangha always holds the moral high ground, and the king must justify his power and rule in terms of the sangha or a sect within it if he is to maintain control over the population. Therefore, sangha, state, and laity can best be viewed as a ternary order in which each has some power in keeping the others in check by invoking purification as the outside condition of ultimate moral force.

The king's will to power is always constrained not by a social contract between the state and civil society but by a moral causal law that sustains that power according to two principles: the continued production of meritorious actions for purposes of sustaining the king's merit stores (in other words, present actions and mental intentions creating the continuation of power) and the kammic relation between the *ana-baing* (the owner of power) and those under his ultimate sovereignty. This is the *kammaraja,* that is, the resultant effect of prior kammic actions taking expression in the relations between oppressor and oppressed in the present.[35] Buddhas alone have cultivated the powers to discern the conditions and time span for particular acts of kamma to come to fruition. The Burmese Buddhists' general recognition of those processes that defy the evident logic of immediate kammic repercussion from unwholesome actions (the violent acts of bad rulers, for example) is situated in terms of a framework of time and event that will unfold in the future. The bad things that happen to innocent people in the present life are viewed as the rightful inheritance of that individual. But a fatalistic determinism is not part of these ideas of kamma. For a particular act of kamma to come to fruition, other factors must also be present. Since kamma is infinite and inexhaustible, the conditions for specific resultants is dependent on the rest of the conditions as a whole. History becomes a repetitive cycle of decay and regeneration based on a moral action and reaction on the collective level.[36]

In the pragmatic world, the individual confronts an "environment of the demeritorious," which demands undertaking unwholesome activities as countermeasures to these conditions. This domain is the dimension in which kingly action and duty are viewed to be active. An insightful diagnostic of this logic is described in the relations between U Nu and Ne Win just prior to Ne Win's 1962 coup d'état. U Nu had decided to pass a bill forbidding the slaughter of cows throughout the country. He offered Ne Win the opportunity to sign the bill, so that he might be the recipient of the merits for this compassionate act. Ne Win refused, taking the higher moral ground by stating that *he* was willing to take on demerits on behalf of the nation. Ne Win's sacrifice—to be the kammic receptacle for demeritorious actions on behalf of the people—later constituted one of the driving logics for his moral claims to legitimate political authority. Through his military might, he would unite the country to the

benefit of its citizens. U Nu, by contrast, was looked on as an inef-
fective ruler who was unwilling to make personal ethical sacrifices
on behalf of the country. A monk who had participated in the Sixth
Buddhist Synod told me with real disdain that U Nu was merely interested in using the sangha and the state as a gigantic merit field
within which he could attend to his own future life supports and
fulfillment of his bodhisattva vow.

Once again we can perceive the implications for a double order of
law at work. U Nu asserted political legitimacy on the basis of his
personal ethics (sīla) as in the example of maintaining the precept
not to kill through forbidding the slaughter of cattle in the country.
This is the practice of dhammarajas (kings whose sovereignty is based
on moral law). Ne Win, by contrast, invoked the logic of a kammaraja (king whose sovereignty is based on prior merit accumula-
tions resulting in power). Ne Win's willingness to undertake demeritorious actions for meritorious end goals (for example, permitting
cattle as a food source) shaped the logic for his rule. In Pāli textual
sources, as well as in public discourse, the logic that a sovereign must
undertake unwholesome actions (violently securing the borders of
the state, punishing criminals, and securing animal food sources, for
example) is a self-evident, if inauspicious necessity. It is precisely because members of the citizenry are not ethically self-regulating (per
the original society in the Mahasammatha myth) that the sovereign
must assert the forceful rule of law. Ne Win traded on this logic by
inverting U Nu's superior ethic of personal dhamma morality and
subordinating it to a claim for the preeminence of the people's present material welfare.

Where do laity fit into this schema? Laity situate their goals within
a system of morally ranked, intentional operations in the mind as
manifested in speech and action. The New Laity of the postindependence period established the outside condition from which the
hierarchical framework would be oriented. Their practices came to
be circumscribed within a system of meanings and values that they
ultimately controlled through meditation and through preoccupations over sāsana purity and perpetuation. The meditation movement

is directed toward the revitalization of the total sāsana world, in which the priority is to define what the broadest dimensions and horizons of the cosmological frame are. The state is directed toward constituting a unity by creating the structures of a domination that relies on conquest and repression, even while it courts world opinion on the level of regime performance, as I will discuss shortly. Both have a place in the wider historical, metahistorical, and cosmological ideologies of the Burmese Buddha world. In the twentieth century, the mass lay meditation movement has become a resistance and a parallel construction of economy, spheres of potency, and influence that stand against the state in its militaristic unity.

Multiple Frameworks and Sources of Knowledge

The push to rapid shifts of democracy everywhere, aided by foreign support of insurgency groups or financial or other threats and encouragement to hold democratic elections, is a conceit that ignores the long-held historical and cosmological conditions that domestic regimes in every country must obey in order to achieve legitimacy in the eyes of their constituencies. In a place such as Burma, where there is no palpable historical separation of church and state, in European terminology, one is not surprised to learn that each postindependence government's effort to establish grounds for its own legitimacy has been constrained by this fact. The bold confidence with which several of the governments I have mentioned set out to found a new political society based on modern principles has therefore also become commingled with Buddhist cosmology. To demonstrate this briefly, I will cite a few lines from the Burmese Socialist Program Party's *System of Correlation of Man and His Environment* to show how, even in the attempt to create the nation-state in secularist and modern terms, Buddhist phenomenological assumptions still remain part and parcel of a view of what the self-evident constitution of reality is. This Marxist Buddhist syncretism fascinatingly reveals the relationship between a Western modern pragmatism (in this instance, Marxist, though the capitalist paradigm has been addressed elsewhere and at different times) and a Buddhist view of moral causation:

- We believe in the maxim that wholesome morality is possible only when the stomach is full.

- The programme of the socialist economy is to establish a new peaceful and prosperous society by filling the stomach of every one and raising his moral standards.

- Just as it is true that wholesome morality is possible only on a full stomach so is it true that only when men of excellent morals are in the leadership the programme of filling stomachs (in other words the socialist programme) can be carried through.

- In the study of the nature of man we find that man has inherent in himself inclinations towards such unwholesome volitions as insatiable greed [lobha].

- These unwholesome volitions cannot be killed by mere fulfillment of the needs of the material body. [Note how the Buddhist theory of the causes and conditions for suffering and their extinction (the Four Noble Truths and the Eightfold Path) are suggested here.]

- In marching towards socialist economy it is imperative that we first reorientate all erroneous views of our people. [This statement echoes the idea of removing wrong views, *miccha ditti*, in vipassanā meditation in order to overcome delusion and achieve enlightenment.]

- Under the socialist system the waning and lessening of these unwholesome volitions may be possible only to a certain extent. [In other words, sāsana work is not the task of the government.]

- Even in a socialist society it is possible that men, tempted by lust and greed, enraged by hate and violence, blinded by pride and conceit, and overwhelmed with self-aggrandizement, will rear their heads as and when opportunities are favourable. This can cause the ruin of a socialist society. [That is, the laity must look after their own purification in order to be moral citizens and create a just and auspicious society.]

Elaboration of the ways in which the regime's attempts to shore up its legitimacy are contradicted or independently supported by entrenched practices within bureaucracies or elsewhere is not beside the point I wish to make. A more specifically located study, as within a single bureaucracy, might point to a range of epistemic practices that show how the regime's aims are supported or contradicted by such systems of practice. However, insofar as I began with the assertion that the regime's attempts to legitimate its authority are coextensive with its aim to harden the conditions of statist authority, I should like, in these final pages, to consider the efforts the regime expends to constitute epistemic claims and practices relative to frameworks other than Buddhist cosmology, kingship, or, for that matter, the question of its supposed sincerity in these pursuits, to which I have devoted so much attention.

Of first note is the socialist-materialist framework, which serves as a practical justification and organizational model for a variety of infrastructure projects, such as the building of roads and bridges and the development of a tourist industry. That the nationalization of property and the recruitment of work groups end up becoming indistinguishable from the abrupt arrogation of household assets and forced labor speaks both to the regime's disregard for human rights and the bureaucratic failure of the socialist model. Nevertheless, these projects reveal the regime's intention, vis-à-vis civil society, to shore up its legitimacy also in terms of what is referred to in the political science literature as regime performance.

Regime performance as an openly comparative criterion leads us to the realization that the legitimacy of authority in terms of statehood is conferred not solely by domestic criteria—else we should be tempted to hypothesize that Burma's statehood will be secured when the last of the minorities are either subdued or converted to Buddhism—but in conjunction with the affirmation of the international community. A few years ago, when the regime changed the English name of the country from Burma to Myanmar (Myanmar being a more inclusive appellation and thereby an incorporation claim of the still contesting minorities), this was a move directed to both domestic and international audiences in order to legitimate statehood. The unthinking adoption of what was, in reality, a renewed assertion to statehood by the *New York Times* and the United Nations, among others, conferred a wedge of legitimacy in a way that the military government had been unable to achieve by other means. Openly, it boasted in the newspapers of how the international community recognized its legitimacy as a state and as a regime.

International evaluations of a regime's record on economic development, human rights, democratic self-determination, and so forth—the criteria of regime performance—have become the fulcrum for challenging the sovereignty of regimes in specific places such as Burma, which are thereon dubbed rogue states. Aung San Suu Kyi's platform rests largely on its promise to fulfill these criteria better than the present regime. She is the icon for a democratic free country, and her legitimacy has already been "granted" by the international community of democratic nations by rights of her party's landslide election victory in 1990. The daughter of the martyred father of the modern Burmese nation-state, Aung San Suu Kyi is the living continuity of earlier struggles for freedom. And yet, in Burma, she still faces the challenge of satisfying domestic criteria for authority. Partly in response to this perception, she has undertaken meditation, which lies at the heart of Burmese Buddhist soteriology. Whereas the military leaders have sought to demonstrate their rightful claim to rule in terms of the role of ancient kings as chief patrons and supporters of the Buddha world, Aung San Suu Kyi's claim is based on a more abstract foundation. She is the meditator as witness.[37]

In conclusion, by substantiating the entity of the state, the regime would be able to reduce its requirement for periodic shows of force that only serve to destabilize specific administrations and invite a moralizing backlash from the international community. The regime leaders' attempts to achieve legitimacy and establish the unity implied by the category of statehood—concurrently averting the international community's denunciation of rogue statehood—are, however, characterized by vacillation among multiple and inconsistent frameworks for thinking and action. This vacillation is driven by the requirements of the different constituencies, and it is set in the intertwined soteriological categories of understanding and bureaucratic practices that circumscribe the possibilities for reform: Buddhist kingship, the minorities, international regime performance, crosscutting patron-client loyalties within administrative bureaucracies, and so forth, not to mention differences of opinion among the military rulers themselves.

In analytical terms, these various categories of understanding and action represent what might be described as *surfaces of knowledge,* wherein the interface between experience and meaning—both primary-individual and secondary-social forms of knowledge—is imbricated but not coextensive with any other domain. By using the term *surface of knowledge,* I am trying to get at the varied yet tangible epistemic modalities that produce self-reflexivity and social reflexivity (that is, the way in which a system or holism of some kind is known by a community of knowers). The military regime's attempt to impose a single surface of knowledge for purposes of ruling more effectively amounts to an effort to eliminate opposition and difference. Its attempts to transform relations of power to relations of authority demand efficiency in the creation of hegemonic ideologies, techniques, and practices capable of subverting and replacing antecedent systems and their meanings. Yet the stripping away of the autonomy among the parts of society, such as by controlling access to labor, financial institutions, and the press, demands that the regime operate everywhere on the only single surface of knowledge production and reproduction that can contain all of these surfaces—that is, through force.

The pressures for legitimacy against the background of these multiple audiences (the minorities, the National League for Democracy, the Association of Southeast Asian Nations [ASEAN], the international community) have meant that the quest for legitimacy by successive governments in Burma has entailed the use of multiple rationales. The dominant theme, however, as also characterizes the demeanor of the present military junta, has been the careful attempt to assure that no institutional forms arise that could serve as extragovernmental vehicles for airing and redressing grievances. This is, of course, especially true vis-à-vis the ethnic minorities. However, it reflects as well an ongoing negotiation with the majority Buddhist Burman population.

Mired in these instabilities, the regime indulges in the counterproductive impulse to crush all institutions with the potential to share in power. Finding sufficient support domestically, as well as among some foreign analysts, for its belief that only a domineering entity—one that can quickly implement relations of power—is capable of safeguarding the country from skidding into belligerent disunity, the regime finds a kind of de facto sanction to rule.

EPILOGUE

In keeping with conventional ethnography, I have studied a collective phenomenon from the ground up in this volume. But the ground in this case has not been a small collectivity of individuals who then are shown or implied to feed upward into a greater social group. Instead, my starting point has been what looks from the outside like a private religious practice: meditation. Although it is true that the aggregate of meditators amounts to a number large enough to constitute a movement by any measure, my use of the term *mass lay meditation movement* to describe this phenomenon is nonetheless directed less at the aggregate dimension than at the consensus implied when so many people—over a million individuals with attainments toward enlightenment, by the count of the Mahasi center—share a philosophical outlook of a specifiable nature. This outlook is conditioned by systematic practice of vipassanā meditation. The consensus is achieved not by means of debate or other familiar forms of public discourse available in a democratic environment but through religious and contemplative channels. The consensus is best investigated in the context of moral communities, donation cliques, and other lay institutions whose explicit purposes have little apparent connection to anything outside the organization of religious life and learning in Burma.

But the mass pursuit of enlightenment has consequences for and upon the constitution of political realities in Burma, and it is these consequences that have occupied me in this book. My use of the expression *political realities* is not incidental. The intended procedure and discernible outcome of intense meditation is the production of "right views," amounting to a reconstitution of the everyday perceptions of its practitioners. On one level—that which is closest to people's individual intention—what is being refigured is one's commitment to engaging with purity and other soteriological realities. At the same time, the terms and conditions for granting legitimacy to the regime are also being meted out.

I have argued that the mass lay meditation movement is a key dynamic in the dialectic between what political scientists have conventionally described as the state and civil society. But the meditation movement does not represent a typical civil society movement or even an underground resistance awaiting its moment to enter on the political stage. In comparison with other political activist movements, it is too much a religious and even philosophical fulfillment of a historical trajectory, which is seen to encompass other historical moments of "bad kings," and it is not thereby diluted purely to political elements. Yet I do not advocate the notion that the meditation movement is principally a religious revitalization movement, such as those studied by anthropologists in other places. Instead, I have tried to demonstrate that the movement has functioned, vis-à-vis the regime, in a continuous manner, to build a particular vision of culture that is meant to encompass individualism, the state, and society. The focus is soteriological and concretely social, but there is little of the unselfconscious search to be lost in otherworldly realities so as to escape this one. It is not, by any reasonable measure, a millenarian movement. The most conventional politicoreligious language I would care to apply to the meditation movement would be that it can be seen as a means to accommodate the harsh political realities of contemporary times; its most consistent bearing toward the regime may be characterized as yielding in order to overcome. But one-sentence summations often obscure as much as they clarify.

I would interrupt my recapitulation and final summary here with a comment or two on how my approach—dictated, as I see it, by the state of affairs I researched—contrasts with some of the common trends in political anthropology. In the following paragraph or two, I do not intend to offer a review of the discipline but only a final orienting key to where I have seen my own work falling relative to general trends in anthropology. All social scientists conduct their reasoning against an imagined backboard of reigning theories and wisdoms in their field.

In presenting parts of my work at conferences or department colloquiums, I have found that many anthropologists (at least in the United States) are, at present, uncomfortable with the suggestion of holisms when discussing culture. Indeed, the term *culture* has itself come under continuous fire over the past decade or two precisely because it implies a kind of diffuse, hard-to-grasp holism, an encompassing of public symbols and interpretations of experience that in real life are highly variable from subcommunity to subcommunity and even from person to person. Moreover, the word *culture* and its synonyms (*cosmology,* for instance) seem to point in the direction of consensus, lack of actor cognizance, and thus the weak agency of individuals. Michel Foucault's notion of discourse, ironically, which seems to have been accepted as a replacement for culture in some circles, is likewise diffuse and encompassing. But because it is redolent of the ethos of power and admits the constant presence of counterviews, it rarely comes under critical scrutiny.[1] What one is said to find in real life, according to this crowd, is conflict, contestation, fragmentation, hived off interest groups, resistance, instrumental interpretation or manipulation of public symbols, and power plays characterized by high degrees of creative awareness. It is said that differences among subpopulations—typically differentiated according to gender, ethnicity, age, and other identity categories—are more significant than any theoretical holism that can possibly unite an entire population.

After I presented part of what became chapter 4 in this book, one prominent anthropologist commented to me, with a grimace, that what was missing in my presentation was "the jagged edges" that must characterize life in so violent a place as Burma. I do not exactly disagree with this formulation, but I have been unable to attach myself to the notion that social life consists only or mainly of jagged edges or that jagged edges can even exist if not relative to some collectively imagined center, unless that center is truly in the midst of destabilization on the scale of war or revolution. History, at any rate, is rarely so irrelevant. Individual identity and its desideratum to rights and fairness, even when discussing so powerful and universal a divider as gender, have seemed to me to be a Western import, even though they are steeped in the everyday Burmese struggle for political reform.[2] What I and others (Tambiah 1970; Reynolds 1982; Collins 1982; Masefield 1983; Gethin 1997) have been calling Burmese Buddhist cosmology exists to a high degree of refinement and exerts what can unapologetically be called structural force in the places I have studied and have traveled to in the country. Its effects are as we have seen them everywhere in religion and culture: encompassment, totalization, and the constitution of reality.

Thus, the meditation movement itself acts as a culture-making mechanism that exerts a convincing, organizing force on the splintering character of contemporary politics in Burma, including even the effort to tame the ethnic periphery of the country through religious conversion. Because the original justification for the military junta was to unite all the warring regions of the country under a single nation-state government, the support of the meditation movement by the successors to that first junta is logically linked to the belief that conversion to Buddhism is a conversion to national legitimacy—part of what the regime has called Myanmafication. The regime keeps conversion statistics as evidence of its progress toward national unity. It should not surprise us that if Foucauldian contestation is observed, it takes place within the shared space of Buddhist criteria. The question ordinary people want to ask when they see the government engaged in these and other proper Buddhist activities is: Are they being sincere?

Yes, this skepticism is, on one level, tantamount to the wish that the junta would once and for all step down. But it would be a mistake to view this attitude as an absolute negation of all the regime's activities, in the manner that democratic principles are said to oppose totalitarianism.[3] In the interpretive space allowed by the application of sincerity as a criterion for legitimacy, the regime can capitalize on the partial truth of its righteousness in the role of king and chief patron of the sangha, so as to dampen the spirit of revolution in the country. I will say a bit more about this later. Here, I wish to suggest not that religion is the manipulable opiate of the masses or that Buddhist principles and Buddhist institutional arrangements act as a failed vox populi on the regime but rather that they act as a force majeure on both the state and the civil society. The totalizing force of Buddhist cosmology acts as cogently on the frail democracy movement in Burma as on the military junta. Were democracy to gain ascendancy in Burma, as one hopes it would, its configuration would be no less influenced by Burmese Buddhist cosmology and institutional arrangements than that of any of the other postwar variations on national governance.

The reason for this sustained obedience of Burmese postindependence politics to cosmological constructions must remain at the level of hypothesis. There are several key variables and indexes that might be raised in an explanation, including the unknowable beliefs of key players (harking back to the sincerity of the regime leaders), the influence of syncretic religious formations between esoteric Buddhism and folk religions, and the vagaries of networks of obligations flowing between powerholders, such as in the context of patron-client relations. One possible overarching explanation for the powerful influence of Buddhism on politics in Burma is that we are witnessing in the country a protracted state-formation process, in which holisms, founding myths, and the like are not abandoned by political rulers but are actively sought out. All over Southeast Asia and elsewhere, the appeal to nativistic elements has been a regular feature of state formation, and it was so observed about Burma many decades ago. Because independence was attained roughly sixty years ago, it does not occur to observers of contemporary Burma that the process might still be ongoing. State formation is complete in some sense when legitimacy or the right to rule is established. In Burma, this process has been repeatedly stalled; every regime since (and including) U Nu's first government following independence has had to wrestle with the question of legitimacy. The terms for that legitimacy, as I have often repeated, cannot come from the exercise of force alone. In Burma, even the most militant despots have been compelled to seek reconciliation with Buddhist principles.

Another historical source of the authority of Buddhist cosmological principles derives from the means by which these principles are enacted in practice in the present era, as against prior ones. Vipassanā meditation, which lies at the heart of mass enlightenment, is no mere ritual. Rather, as I have tried to convey in chapter 2, vipassanā is an epistemology-making engine, an existential premise that has repeatedly undercut competing worldviews that might underwrite the moral-political organization of society. Socialism, democracy, military dictatorship, and Marxism, to name a few of the foreign political ideologies that have been entertained as a means of organizing the polity, were each discovered to assume certain characteristics of nature, society, and human beings that conflict or, at best, imbricate with Buddhist principles as they are currently interpreted.

The meditation movement as institution represents the realization of the systematization and acceptance of techniques of meditation meant to create the necessary epistemic shift that will lead to a right-mindedness. The outcome is a society-led movement that seeks to transform consciousness and individual morality and, in the process, create an enlightened citizenry and a just society in keeping with Buddhist moral principles. Yet even as vipassanā meditation takes this organizational and ultimately political contour in Burma, its technical and philosophical premise stands independent of any particular political formation or even possibly of Buddhist content itself. The successful exportation of vipassanā across cultural and national boundaries, as a technique for mental examination with no requirement for it to be understood as a Buddhist practice per se (as, for example, when employed as a technique for pain management in U.S. hospices), supports my claim that in order to fathom its impact in Burmese society, its phenomenological characteristics need to be understood on their own grounds. This was one of my purposes in chapter 2.

The principal orientation of vipassanā meditation is not other-worldly (for example, devās or reincarnation); rather, it concerns this world—*In This Very Life* is the title of a key explanatory text by U Pandita, one of the New Laity's key teachers and Aug San Suu

Kyi's personal monk. How do we know this world? How do we remove the conditions of suffering in this life? Sense experience is the sole source for knowledge that can transform. The pariyatti/paṭipatti (text learning versus meditation) distinction of course already existed in the Abhidhamma and in monks' practices. What changed was the institutional formalization of these two domains into spheres of activities that reconfigured prior arrangements among the laity, the sangha, and the state. Knowledge gained through concepts, books, thinking, and rational analysis are secondary forms of knowledge. These forms of knowing are not experienced directly and therefore do not epistemically reconstruct being.

What does meditation confirm for people? For one, meditation is used as the evidence for the veracity of texts, as *verification* for the teachings. The mass pursuit of enlightenment was prophesied, and so the sequence—the revised sequence (to borrow an expression from the late John Kenneth Galbraith)—is accepted. In this sense, we are witnessing a full-fledged revitalization movement that harkens back to known metahistorical patterns, all the way back through the Ashokan line of kings and on back to the discursive teaching pattern during the apostolic period of the Buddha. The reenactment of the sangayana, in the Sixth Synod during U Nu's premiership, is the clarion call to this societywide self-interpretation of modern experience.

The pariyatti/paṭipatti distinction that emerged in the postsynod era, dominated by what is widely called the Mahasi sāsana (Mahasi was the chief questioner at the synod and codifier of the texts on meditation), represents an institutionally new development that comes out of this philosophical division. The Ministry of Home and Religious Affairs itself accepts this distinction over the earlier sectarian pattern; its offices are divided according to pariyatti and paṭipatti activities. This reflects both the administrative requirement to keep up with societal realities and the government's own efforts to purify the sangha, which, in this case, means to reduce rivalries within it and thereby control it. The word *purification* is a functional synonym for *verification;* the rightness of the texts is verified through meditation, and they are thereby purified. The relation between these concepts becomes important when we consider that in the context of the ternary order—sangha, state, and laity—the laity also has the role of purifying, of asserting the right to verify the activities of both the sangha and the state. Morality and its orientation to truth, to what Geertz referred to in his famous 1973 essay on religion as "the really real," is the underpinning for all forms of legitimacy—monkly legitimacy, political legitimacy, and so on. It is in this sense that I argue that the regime is constrained by the populace because the moral conditions of particular philosophical forms of truth making must be adhered to in order for the people to grant a regime some measure of authority.

The process of verifying through insight knowledge arrived at by meditation resembles universal forms of religious knowing. It is useless if it is not self-evident and self-reinforcing. What begins as a set of religious criteria for the worthiness of a person—does he have pon?—ends, in the ternary system, as a mechanism for the formation of moral communities around monks (donation cliques, for instance) and criteria applied beyond these to the alignment of government power with truth. Power must be verified as being in line with the dhamma.

The directional force of the mass lay meditation movement is grounded in its institutionalization. This institutionalization in the lay monastery and its activities derives from and brings about several specific circumstances. In chapter 1, I described the historical process by which the ternary order of sangha, state, and laity was refigured following colonialism. From this point of view, U Nu, Ne Win, and, finally, SLORC conformed to the role of kings: as purifiers of the sangha and its most prominent material supporters. To ignore the underlying monarchical allegory of postwar Burmese politics is to miss an opportunity to satisfyingly interpret many baffling events and actions, as I have described. It is also to ignore the proclamations and reflections of members of the ruling class themselves, who very much see themselves as participants in this min win history of kings.

Why did the lay meditation movement reach its zenith during the years when Ne Win removed state patronage of Buddhist institutions? It is possible that the movement that had begun with U Nu had simply been growing according to its own internal pulsations, independent of the political realities that replaced U Nu with the socialist military regime of Ne Win. Alternatively, the removal of sangha and sāsana patronage by the state created a vacuum within which key roles for the support of spectacular monks and sāsana projects suddenly became available to more ordinary citizens, who leaped at the opportunity to be associated with the support of prestigious monks. During this time, Mahasi Sayadaw was at the height of his powers, and the laity flocked to the center to practice for enlightenment. The thrill of participating in the mass lay project of enlightenment had never before been so conceived in institutional terms. The center grew around Mahasi in the way that the texts describe laity coming around the Buddha. People vied with one another to have their offerings accepted by him, and new forms of participation emerged: schoolchildren on vacation, night yogis who returned to their offices during the day, retirees, and nuns all immersed themselves in a rigorous schedule of sitting and walking meditation, punctuated by monkly meal offerings at which the laity thronged around the eating tables to observe the project of sāsana revitalization happening before their very eyes.

The transformation of the lay ethic to being one in pursuit of the penultimate soteriological goal has not resulted in the monasticization of the laity. Instead, the social production for the *conditions* for achieving enlightenment have been rationalized by the creation of lay-owned and lay-centered institutions. Laity are now concerned with the penultimate practice. What are the consequences of this orientation? I have spoken of the enlightened citizenry phenomenon and the morality implied for the collectivity through such practice. I have also spoken of laypersons achieving the "insurance policy" vis-à-vis future lives. Finally, I must refer to the act of spurring the sangha to its own purification. After the dissolution of the kingship, the laity could not enforce the purification of the sangha as a king would; there was no central authority from which to approach such a project. Sectarian rivalries were exploited for political purposes and control over populations. This was antithetical to the project of keeping monks from involvement in worldly affairs. Through meditation, laity could assert a purification of view that even the majority of monks did not have. From this perspective, they could demand purification in viniya and pariyatti from the monks. The New Laity's project of mass epistemic reconstruction created a new position within society that could decide about the purity of the monks and their practices. This mimics the king's right to adjudicate the purity of the sangha, which was permitted to him on the basis of his role as a Dhammaraja—one who ruled with dhamma and was the chief among all laity in the support of the Sangha of the Four Quarters.

This dynamic, in the name of perpetuating sāsana society and institutions, has led to the growth of three kinds of movements. The first is around the sangha, and here I refer to the often spontaneous emergence of a society of lay supporters around a monk (sometimes also a nun). The next is the growth of lay-controlled meditation centers with branch organizations throughout Burma and beyond its borders. This is the backbone of the movement. Finally, the state develops, shapes, and supports the official Sangha of the Four Quarters through titles, through state sponsorship of monks, and through creating official sectarian divisions and sangha courts and seeing that the monks adhere to their code of conduct.

In chapter 3, I began to investigate what sort of social actor the meditation movement is. That is, in the fulfillment of meditation as an everyday routine and an institutional arrangement, how can we also see the powers of recruitment and material support of the movement and how does this in turn shape the emergence of moral communities that can exert force in the political arena? In Burma, as other researchers in the region have found, I could see how patron-client networks form the basis for the production of power. One of the most powerful patron-clientships emerges from donation cliques for monks and monasteries.

Patron-client ties help "structure the flow of resources, exchange, and power relations and their legitimation in society,"[4] and they regulate the organization and flow of resources between social actors. In Burma, the flow of resources moving into the sangha institution produces two sorts of patron-client relations. First are those obtaining between social actors in which economic and power relations are established and legitimized; second are those between members of the sangha and the laity. This second nexus produces, in a far more diffuse manner, both soteriological and more proximate power relations.

When Ne Win attempted to redefine the public good in terms of socialist ideas in the 1960s—for example, providing for the material welfare of citizens—the military was no longer officially engaged in the flow of resources into sāsana institutions. For more than a decade, patron-client ties proliferated at the monk-donor nexus, resulting in networks that penetrated the state bureaucracy, the nationalized corporations, the universities, and the small businesses that operate in the formal and black markets. Often, subordinates rely on these networks for status within the military or state bureaucracy. It is not the official bureaucratic office title alone that evokes authority, as we tend to expect in modern rationalized bureaucracies. Rather, it is the personal power of the individual holding that office that evokes authority. Personal power and the ability to activate a network of subordinates or to competitively engage other powerful individuals result in the ability to carry out one's office.

In Burma, the personal power and the ability to activate networks is described by the notion of pon, which, "[U]sually glossed as 'glory,' . . . is a psycho-spiritual quality, an ineffable essence, which invests its possessor with superior moral, spiritual, and intellectual attributes."[5] The ability a minister may have, for instance, to offer up official state buildings in the name of sāsana is a demonstration of pon. It is not his individual action as such that allows him to undertake such an action; instead, his ability to engage a powerful chain of networks for which he is the chief patron enables him to undertake the collective activity of state bureaucrats. In this way, the authority of military leaders is less dependent on popular consent or some such other democratic notion than on their ability to marshal the involvement and input of their underlings. As long as the objective of their actions surrounds the patronage of sāsana, their hold on subordinates through patron-clientalism, with crosscutting loyalties and dependencies into the sangha itself, is secure. Hence, as chief donors to the sangha, the military rulers secure a de facto legitimacy that might otherwise never be voluntarily granted. By virtue of the fact that the act of giving dāna uniquely interfaces the transcendent and the worldly—the spiritual and the practical—doing so implies the cultivation of right-mindedness in a similar way to meditation itself. This confluence further complicates the question of sincerity when directed at evaluating the Buddhist actions of a tyrannical regime.

One may complain in the United States, for example, of secrecy or a suppression of access to intelligence, but there is no denying that a public sphere exists, in which the question of legitimacy may be weighed. In the absence of a comparable open public sphere in Burma, as I suggested in chapter 4, dissent must be moved underground. On one level, as Christina Fink has sought to illustrate, this becomes a case study in the cultural politics of resistance and legitimacy of rule.[6] The tools James Scott has bequeathed the discipline—weapons of the weak, hidden transcripts, and the like (1985, 1990)—are immediately useful in mapping out places to begin the search for resistance to the regime.

For my purposes, however, the term *resistance* itself becomes diluted in the specific expression that this engagement takes in the Burmese context. We have seen how the religious cosmology in Burma already is heir to a sophisticated language for considering political issues such as legitimacy and its relationship to the soteriology of nibbāna. Moreover, because of the nature of religious practice in general, this religiopolitical philosophy has fair purchase in people's attitudes and behaviors. What form of political orientation, resistance or otherwise, does Burmese Buddhism suggest? This is an open question. I have offered one avenue of interpretation, most explicitly in chapter 4, in terms of reading the possibility for pilgrimages, amulets, and other devotions to function as a means of concealed public discourse.

I have, in sum, attempted to define an alternate register on which the debate for political legitimacy in Burma has played out in each successive regime since independence. This has led me to elaborate not the politics of state but the political implications for a strong (majority) Burmese Buddhist cosmological understanding of the relations between power, purity, hierarchy, potency, personhood, history, and transcendence as a totalizing epistemic condition that is both primary and individual and secondary and representative. The self-evidence of the constitution of reality is not a political assumption first, as surely as the mass lay meditation movement is not first and foremost a political movement in resistance to the state. Being itself is defined by the practice of meditation, and vipassanā insights lay a claim for the terms for moral legitimacy that cannot be resisted by the government, which has instead been forced to bend its political ambitions in conformity with Buddhist notions of unity and purity. If there is one assured application of the term *sincerity* to speak of in all this, it is to the effect that there is no Weberian disenchantment in evidence; Buddhism has not become a rationalization for some kind of worldliness.

In chapter 5 as elsewhere, I have spent much time looking at the intellectual origins of the nation-state, taking the early reforms in the postindependence period as the beginning point for what occurred and continues to occur in the political arena. There was an epistemic crisis following colonialism. The early revolutionaries counted many urban intellectuals among their numbers, men and women who had been imbued with British education and philosophy and who could therefore consider the Western philosophical and utopian systems alongside nativist understandings. As they saw it, revitalization was not just about revitalizing identity. Instead, they wished to confront head on the broad assertions of what constitutes truth and meaning in ways that were universalizing and not just particular to Burma. U Nu and his compatriots ultimately looked to Buddhist philosophical premises for an empirical understanding of morality.

The method by which foreign philosophies were adapted or rejected resembles the way in which Buddhism absorbs or rejects folk religious elements, such as *nat* (spirit) worship, in order to purify and distinguish itself. U Nu himself believed in nats but declared them to be superfluous to Buddhism. I believe he brought this same methodology to considering alternate political forms that might make up the modern nation-state. The result was a government dedicated to the promotion of sāsana as the basis for a nation-state, founded on both the ancient "democratic" Mahasammatha myth and the sponsorship of meditation as a path to personal moralities.

U Nu's career continues to be relevant here not only because he was the head of government from 1948 to 1962 during that crucial first period following independence but also because he was located at that historical junction when Marxism, science, and Christianity had all encroached on the native landscape, marginalizing Burmese practices (nats, weiksas, and Buddhism were all denigrated by British rationalism). U Nu's impulse was to create an example, a demonstration that Buddhism is just as rigorous as science and that its brand of empiricism is just as vigorous and its morality just as grounded as those of any competing Western model. Mahasi Sayadaw provided U Nu with the confidence that vipassanā meditation could be seen in the triple verifying light: as a systematized and rigorous practice for examining the mind; as a basis for a personal morality; and lastly, as a fulfillment of the prophesy that at the midpoint of the Gotama Buddha's sāsana, there would be a mass enlightenment. Mass meditation flourished with U Nu's backing, and it became, recognizably (if practically crippled by the general impoverishment of the country under incompetent, tyrannical rule) what he envisioned for it: not just a personal but also civic and cosmological reconstruction. When we speak today of "multiple modernities,"[7] this is precisely the appropriate instance to apply it to.

I have aimed in these pages to expose some of the historical cultural mechanisms that have circumscribed the actions taken by each of the postindependence regimes in its effort to secure political legitimacy. It is my hope that the backdrop will also help inform future studies into the incipient democracy movement in Burma. As the independence question recedes from prominence and members of a younger generation, more connected to external discourse and perhaps less tolerant of tyrannical abuse, rise to express their hopes for the future, we will no doubt see a new synthesis of Buddhist truths and political experience.

NOTES

Introduction

1. See Weber 1978, 212; see also Yahnghwe 1995 and Jordt 2003.
2. See, e.g., Fink 2001; Callahan 2003; Taylor 1987, 1996, 2001; Steinberg 2001a, 2001b; and Lintner 1989, 1994.
3. I thank F. K. Lehman for suggesting this term in reference to the mass meditation phenomenon.
4. See, e.g., Mendelson 1975; Houtman 1999; Mya Maung 1999; Schober 1997; and Smith 1965.
5. Such uncertainty led to cautious evaluations of the political scenery in Burma, as evident in the tenuous titles of post-1962 articles in the *Asian Survey:* "Burma in 1976: The Beginnings of Change?" (Martin 1976); "Burma in 1980: An Uncertain Balance Sheet" (Silverstein 1981); "Burma in 1987: Change in the Air?" (Hasman 1987); "Burma in 1999: A Slim Hope" (Seekins 2000).
6. See Wolf 1982.
7. See Aung San Suu Kyi 1991, 175.
8. See Houtman 1999, 2005.
9. See Veyne 1988, 59, in Sahlins 2004, 105.
10. See Schober 1997, 2005.
11. See, e.g., Pye 1962.
12. In a review of Josef Silverstein's 1977 book, *Burma: Military Rule and the Politics of Stagnation,* Aung Thwin (1979) further criticizes the bias implicit in economic development theories that view modernization as the sole criterion for evaluating regime performance and political legitimacy. He argues that Silverstein's approach belies "value-laden responses in our own 'conceptual systems.' . . . The period of constitutional democracy was merely a twenty-year 'interregnum' in Burma's long history, yet it serves the author as the point of reference to judge the legitimacy of the military government. 'Democratic principles' such as freedom of speech, press, assembly, and even religion—despite Buddhism's tolerance—are the criteria used to determine legitimate rule" (554). A preferable approach is offered by Aung Thwin, who would have us evaluate indigenous ideas and

institutional arrangements in terms of the priorities meaningful to Burmese society.

13. See Taylor 1987, and Steinberg 2001a, 2001b.

14. See Scott 1990.

Chapter 1

1. Scott, also known as Shway Yoe, was a Scotsman who wrote about Burma at the turn of the nineteenth century.

2. Inasmuch as the sangha is "an aggregation of individual ascetics rather than an organized church community" (Cady 1958, 58; cf. Harvey 1925, 326, and Mendelson 1975, 58), kyaungs vary in size and purpose. The smallest kyaung may have only a single monk in residence. Larger complexes (kyaungtaiks) expand through branch organizations connected to a central monastery and monk lineage and tend to be centers for scriptural (pariyatti) learning.

3. Vipassanā meditation, according to the canonical scriptures, was the penultimate practice in a series of progressively related ethical and meditational practices that collectively make up the Noble Eightfold Path.

4. Although other traditional Buddhist activities also take place at the Yeiktha, vipassanā meditation practice is the absolute priority, and the arrangements of space and time there reflect this.

5. See Spiro 1970; Tambiah 1985; and Tiyavanich 1997.

6. On full- and half-moon days, the pious should observe the following three additional precepts: not to eat after midday, not to sleep in a lofty bed, and to abstain from music and other entertainments. The ninth precept enjoins the devotee not to handle money, and the tenth is to practice mettā meditation.

7. A full description of the samatha meditations can be found in Buddhagosa's commentary, Visuddhimagga: The Path of Purification (1976), which is regarded as an orthodox commentarial source by Burmese Buddhists. Vipassanā practice was also enumerated among practices undertaken by laity in the past. For example, King Mindon and his wives were said to have practiced vipassanā and to have encouraged vipassanā practice among the laity (Myo Myint 1987). However, vipassanā appears to have been less common than samatha. Most significantly for the present study, the systematic description of the process by which insight knowledge (nyanzin) is said to lead to nibbāna and the pedagogy developed to lead the yogi successfully through each insight stage became popular and widespread under the Mahasi Sayadaw.

8. See U Silananda (2002) and U Pandita (1993) for full explications of the Noble Eightfold Path.

9. This does not mean that they are the only legitimate teachers of meditation. In Burma, a rich tradition of lay teachers has developed, consisting of both men and women with substantial followings. The best-known example is U Ba Khin, who was one of the founding members of the Buddha Sāsana Nuggaha Apwe, a member of U Nu's government, and a yogi who trained under Mahasi Sayadaw.

10. See Mendelson 1975; and Tambiah 1978.

11. See Myo Myint 1987.

12. See Tambiah 1978.

13. Comparably, Louis Dumont (1970) points out the rich creative source the world renouncer was to sociopolitical ideas in Indian society. This dialectical relationship between the world and the antiworld is the source for social reform and development and for revitalizing the society from the outside in.

14. Mingun Sayadaw appears in the 1985 *Guinness World Book of Records* for having memorized sixteen thousand pages of canonical texts in 1954.

15. *Pariyatti, paṭipatti,* and *paṭivedha* are Pāli terms used by both monks and educated laity. I found that laity often confused the words *pariyatti* and *paṭipatti* in conversation, which I attribute to the relatively recent introduction of these words into common parlance.

16. Interview, U Ko Lay 1996.

17. Ledi Sayadaw's vision came on the eve of the British annexation of Lower Burma in 1852.

18. See Mendelson 1975; Sarkisyanz 1965; Smith 1965; and Tambiah 1978.

19. See Taylor's foreword to Khin Yi 1988, ix.

20. Aung San (Aung San Suu Kyi's father and the hero of the independence fighters), first prime minister U Nu, and later junta leader General Ne Win were all members of the Dobama Asiayone (the We Burmans Association), the central organization of the early nationalist period of the 1930s. These young nationalists were commonly known as the Thakins for their practice of affixing the title Thakin (meaning "lord" or "master") to their names "as a means of developing their consciousness of being their own masters and of the superiority of the Burmans as a race" (Khin Yi 1988, 3).

21. That is, Western, modern, Marxist, materialist, and so on. This sort of "backward-looking revolution," to use S. N. Eisenstadt's notion describing the Meiji Restoration in Japan (1988), in which nationalist leaders sought nativist sources for ideological platforms of new states, was common to other Southeast Asian independence movements.

22. Clifford Geertz (1973, 287) observed, "This tradition of 'Burmaniza-tion' . . . traces back to the very beginnings of the nationalism movement in the Buddhist student clubs at the turn of the century; and by the thirties the Thakins were calling for an independent nation in which Burmese would be the national language, Burman dress would be the national cos-tume, and the classical role of the (predominantly Burman) Buddhist monk-hood as teacher, guide and counselor to the secular government would be restored."

23. The most dramatic of the weiksa millenarian cults was the Saya San revolt (1930), in which the peasant Saya San attempted to overthrow the British with the help of magical amulets and protective tattoos. Saya San was, in essence, a pretender to the throne, and the goal was the restora-tion of kingship. Earlier, the British had some effectiveness in bringing the frequency of such millenarian-inspired revolts to an end by removing the throne from Mandalay—the Burmese Buddhist center of the universe—to India.

24. See Tambiah (1976, 9–18) for a fuller exposition on the Mahasam-matha myth and the Buddhist version for the origins of society and kingship.

25. See Tambiah 1978.

26. See Khin Yi 1988.

27. See Sahlins 2004, 251.

28. See Mahasi charter. U Nu's unpublished "Primer for Vipassanā Practices: A Psychological and Cultural Interpretation of Burma" (1988) is also relevant.

29. See Smith 1965, and Mendelson 1975.

30. Mendelson (1975) relates how the international effort was really not as successful as portrayed by the Burmese and that many of the local rival-ries between the sanghas of other nationalities interfered with their mean-ingful participation. It was, in the end, a Burmese affair.

31. See Sarkisyanz 1965.

32. See Jordt 2001 for a more detailed discussion of MTY institutional arrangements.

33. This number is, of course, much smaller than the total number of people who have spent some time meditating or being engaged in other sāsana-related work at the center.

34. Attempts by the government to convert non-Burman minorities to Buddhism will be discussed in chapter 5.

35. A nayaka sayadaw explained: "In the village they have no time for meditation . . . In a year they get only one time for a retreat—ten-day or twenty-day retreat. Otherwise, they are just doing dāna and sīla and on

the Sabbath day they go to the kyaung as a yogi to take precepts and meditate."

36. As suggested earlier, this practice was once the mainstay of monks and not laypeople, principally, and the form of meditation was not vipassanā but samatha.

37. See Cady 1958, and Mendelson 1975.

38. I was informed by an individual in the lay administrative committee at Mahasi that lay rivalries between the wives of U Nu and U Kyaw Nyein during the Sangayana were the exacerbating condition that caused the split in the AFPFL in the 1950s.

39. U Zitilla is fortunate, for he has loyal kinspeople and followers who respect his wishes and use the moneys of the center in ways he determines. This is not always the case between monks and laity, which is why monks tend to prefer kinspeople to act as their kappia or serve in their kopaka apwe to oversee their resources. A renowned monk I knew had a kappia who followed him from his home village to Yangon. The young man was penniless and served the sayadaw faithfully for many years. Some years later, I visited this monk and again met the kappia. He had become fabulously rich off the monk's resources and owned a building and a car. He was dressed smartly, and a heavy gold chain hung from his neck. When I asked other old yogis at the center about it, they said that the sayadaw just tolerated it, although sometimes he scolded the kappia. "As long as he doesn't take too much, Sayadaw will tolerate," said one yogi. An adviser to the Department of Religious Affairs explained that most of the vinicchaya (sangha court) cases concerned the misappropriation of funds and resources by lay trustees, especially for poggalika property. These cases were difficult to resolve on behalf of the monk, since he is barred from owning property in the first instance.

A full-fledged bhikkhu [Pāli, meaning "monk"] cannot hold cash in hand or deal with monetary problems. If monastery, or gardens, parks, forests, or agrarian lands the sayadaw can deal and administer. But Pātimokkha [monks' rules] does not permit dealing with silver. So one of the co-owners may be a nun—she can do commerce, merchandise.... She can sell and buy. So on behalf of the monk she has the right to save money, jewelry and treasures. The pothudaw [religious layman] or kappia may also take care of a sayadaw's affairs. If he is sincere there is no problem. But, he may misuse, overuse or exploit these resources. From time to time a pothudaw has spent the resources or a thilashin has escaped with the money. Sometimes the kappia takes [everything].

But, they have equal rights to the funds as equal owners. Kappia cases arise frequently in the court cases. But sometimes monks don't want to say anything because they become embarrassed.

40. See Mendelson 1975.

41. Orthodox monks object to using the term *gaing* to mean "sect" because it invokes this political consideration. Instead, they emphasize that in common parlance, *gaing* should be understood in the sense of "divisions," from the Pāli *gana,* meaning a "chapter of monks" and signaling the way in which the sangha functions in its monadic form. When I used the term in speaking with learned monks, they would invariably reiterate these distinctions for me and often instructed me to employ the term *niḳay* (in Pāli, *niḳaya,* meaning "an assemblage or group of monks") instead.

42. See Mendelson 1975, 124.

43. U Pandita so disliked being under the control of the Nuggaha and its plans for him that he eventually left MTY to establish his own center.

44. See Juliane Schober 2003 and Lehman 2003, 1987b for a discussion of sacred geography in Burma.

45. See Houtman 1999.

46. In the 1990s, the Nuggaha undertook a number of memorializing projects at the center. One of these was the construction of a small glass pavilion housing a life-sized wax figure of Sir U Thwin. U Nu's substantial role in conceiving the center, inviting Mahasi, and promoting meditation through the state has been entirely ignored. The Nuggaha has continued to make efforts to distance itself from the late prime minister and his government since military rule was established. Part of the reason why Nuggaha members have had to be so explicit is that following the 1962 coup, many of those in U Nu's government and cabinet retired to the Yeiktha, making if a positive hotbed of U Nu supporters and government officials. U Hla Kyaing served as a high-level administrator in Kachin State during the Nu period.

47. See Tin Maung Maung Than 1988.

48. Perhaps even more telling, its orthodoxy has been verified from outside the country as well. Burma has developed a reputation in the Theravadan South and Southeast Asia region for being a stronghold for the true teachings of the Buddha, unadulterated by the modernization processes that "open societies" have undergone since World War II. It is not uncommon to hear of monks who go to Burma to study the texts and take the examinations to receive scholarly titles or to practice meditation. In the 1990s, hundreds of Korean monks and nuns went to MTY for vipassanā practice. Foreign meditators from Nepal, Europe, the United States, and Australia are also frequent visitors to MTY and other meditation centers.

Chapter 2

1. See Tambiah 1985.
2. See Lévi-Strauss 1963, 281.
3. See Durkheim 1912.
4. See Kapferer 1997, 13.
5. "Both universality and the world lie at the core of individuality and the subject, and this will never be understood as long as the world is made into an object. It is understood immediately if the world is the field of our experience, and if we are nothing but a view of the world, for in that case it is seen that the most intimate vibration of our psycho-physical being already announces the world" (Merleau-Ponty 1962, 406).
6. On one occasion, though, Sahlins attributes the thought to Ruth Benedict; see Sahlins 1985.
7. See Hirschkind 2001, 624.
8. See Kapferer 1997, 2 (emphasis in original).
9. Subject for another study, this may be why meditation has translated so well to other cultural contexts, in which Buddhist principles are not affirmed.
10. Techniques promoted by other famous meditation sayadaws contemporary with Mahasi (for example, Sun Lun Sayadaw and Mogok Sayadaw) emphasize observation of the in-out of the breath at the tip of the nose. Laity's support of one or the other technique of these sayadaws on this distinguishing point have been the cause for bitter rivalry and contention, less between the sayadaws themselves than among their disciples. Textual proof for the agreement of the "rise and fall" method with the canonical texts and commentaries is assiduously provided in Mahasi's subcommentary, in which he describes an exposition of sources relevant to vipassanā meditation practice. Nowhere in the actual words of the Buddha (as found in the canonical texts) is it stated that one should specifically undertake observation of the rise and fall of the abdomen. Mahasi's subcommentary therefore undertakes to establish the consistency and coherence for observing the psychophysical process at the location of the abdomen as it rises and falls with the breath.
11. Thus, in *Practical Insight Meditation: Basic and Progressive Stages* (1980), Mahasi quotes excerpts from the Mahasatipaṭṭhāna Sutta to demonstrate consonance between the Buddha's exhortation to "reflect upon this very body, however it is placed or disposed, with respect to its fundamentals (i.e. the four elements). . . . In consonance with these teachings of the Buddha, it has been stated in colloquial language thus: 'rising' while the abdomen is rising; 'falling' while the abdomen is falling; 'bending' while

the limbs are bending; 'stretching' while the limbs are stretching; 'wandering' while the mind is wandering; 'thinking, reflecting or knowing' while one is so engaged; 'feeling stiff, hot or in pain' while one feels so; 'walking, standing, or sitting or lying' while one is so placed, etc." (Mahasi 1980, 46–47).

12. Another point of controversy in the Mahasi method regarded whether one had first to be established in concentration through practicing samatha meditation (Buddhaghosa lists forty meditation subjects) before proceeding to vipassanā (insight) meditation. Mahasi averred that vipassanā meditation could proceed without prior jhana development (jhanas are ecstatic states of consciousness developed through profound concentration). In other words, he believed that through focus on the rise and fall (*anapanasati*), sufficient concentration could be developed so that the yogi could turn to vipassanā. It remains a source of dispute among monks today. Pa-Auk Sayadaw, one of Mahasi's disciples, asserts an entirely literal approach to the Path of Purification, arguing that each of the forty meditations must first be mastered, including reobservation of one's prior life experiences going back to seven lifetimes, before one can undertake vipassanā. His meditation center has drawn much attention, although it is admitted that few if any students have been competent at mastering the full range of these meditative techniques, despite claims made for Pa-Auk Sayadaw himself and for a thilashin practicing there. During my last visit in 1995, Pa-Auk Sayadaw's five books describing his methods and techniques were still awaiting approval for publication from the Government Scrutiny Board on religious writings. Though he has devotees on that board who are anxious to pass his books, his implicit claims of accomplishment in so many types of practice (samatha and vipassanā) run the fine line of sounding like boasts or declarations of attainment. Were this determined to be the case, Pa-Auk Sayadaw could be considered to have breached the vinaya rules, and he would be required (by classical reckoning) to disrobe.

13. This quote is from the introduction of the "Meditation Teacher's Diary (or) Records." The manual is an unpublished text compiled by two monks (Saya Kyan and Saya Kywet) under the supervision of Mahasi Sayadaw. The manual is not publicly available and is transmitted from teacher to student for pedagogical purposes.

14. I have cited excerpts from the manual that are not considered sensitive. My purpose is to describe the pedagogy employed by the Mahasi meditation teachers.

15. See U Pandita 1993, 269. It is in reference to what is by now a commonplace understanding of how thinking and conceptualizing gets in

the way of practice that one of the nayaka sayadaws explained to me that monks tend not to be good yogis because they have studied the Abhidhamma and are therefore always "anticipating": "They are only thinking." Male yogis, by contrast, are better meditators than monks. However, because they do not readily accept the admonitions and instructions of the monks and instead are always questioning the monks skeptically, they also have obstacles to overcome in their practice. The best yogis are women, they say, because women yogis "obey" the sayadaw's instructions without skepticism.

16. A sixth hindrance, ignorance, is listed in the Samuccayasangaha section of the Abhidhamma, but because it refers to the major obstacle of the arising of wisdom and not to the hindrances obstructing the conditions for developing that wisdom through the cultivation of mental factors in preparation for the development of wisdom, it is not discussed as part of the practicum of vipassanā development.

17. See U Aggacitta 1988 for an account of yogi experiences in healing chronic and critical illnesses.

18. The Puggalapanatti deals with the psychological aptitudes and characteristics of human types, with reference to the strengths and weaknesses they have for attaining enlightenment.

19. The Mahasammatha myth and the Ashokan kingship paradigm are mythical and metahistorical charters for these conceptions.

20. Sarkisyanz (1965, 5, 6), quoting R. Gard, *Buddhism and Political Authority*.

21. Perhaps the most common misconception about the differences between Mahayana and Theravada Buddhism has been the idea that in Theravada Buddhism, the personal striving of individual monks to attain enlightenment constitutes a kind of "personal selfishness" that is absent in the Mahayana tradition, with its bodhisattva emphasis on saving all sentient beings before taking one's own *parinibbāna* (final entry into nibbanā). In fact, one cannot make complete sense of the stress placed on individual striving for nibbāna without also accounting for the total context of ideas about what constitutes an individual as an impersonal process of mind and matter; what causal conditions produce the possibility for pāramī production (and therefore the potential of an individual to achieve enlightenment); and what suffering is in a theory in which ideas about purification stress a hierarchy of mental dispositions taken up toward the lifeworld in which wholesome mental states, just like unwholesome ones, have the ability to keep one chained to the wheel of saṃsāra, the cycle of rebirths.

22. This is Ferguson and Mendelson's formulation, in their work entitled "Masters of the Buddhist Occult: The Burmese Weikzas" (1981).

23. Western analysts (see, for example, Silverstein 1977), persist in focusing on Buddhism's expressly antiworld and antipolitical impulses and thereby miss completely the way in which politics, economy, and society are circumscribed by Buddhism as a totalizing system that does not simply participate in legitimizing the political in terms of the religious but also defines the very terms and conditions of power and legitimate political rule at the outset.

24. This pattern is echoed in history. Lehman (1987a) observes this as an ancient pattern, not only among the monks with their sectarian rivalries but also for kings. For example, King Dhammaceddi in the seventeenth century established the Buddhist state by encapsulating animist "founders cults" under the umbrella of Buddhism in his founding of the "cult of the 37 nats."

Chapter 3

1. Freedom House, "Country Report: Burma," http://freedomhouse.org (accessed March 10, 2003).

2. In 1997, the military government changed its name after consultation with a Washington-based public relations firm. The acronym SLORC, the State Law and Order Restoration Council, was replaced with the acronym SPDC, the State Peace and Development Council. The public relations firm advised that "Slorc" had a menacing sound to it. The same regime under General Than Shwe retains power today.

3. Min Zin 1999.

4. See Godelier 1986, 1999.

5. See Godelier 1999, 11.

6. See Godelier 1999, 3.

7. My "aerial" perspective derives from the sites of my research, which included government ministries and key monastic institutions in Yangon. For an alternate interpretive position regarding the state's sponsorship of Buddhist events, see Schober 1997 and Houtman 1999. Houtman's is the most comprehensive account to date of how the military regime has structured discourses of regime legitimacy in terms of Buddhist cosmological ideas about the realms of existence. For that matter, from the earlier, pre-1962 generation of researchers, Mendelson (1975), Smith (1965), Nash (1963), and Spiro (1970) have contributed to understandings of the application of Buddhist conceptions to Burmese politics and power. See also Jordt 2001, 2003.

8. See Mingun Sayadaw, Buddhavamsa, vol. 2, pt. 1, 1990.

9. See Tambiah 1978.

10. I borrow this expression from McNamara (1996), who uses it to emphasize the intentional aspect of charity in Catholicism.

11. For a range of discussions of this topic, see Sizemore and Swearer 1990.

12. Monks at the Yeiktha said that laity in the urban areas are greatly interested in learning what the role of volition is in the performance of dāna. This includes the importance of such factors as how to mentally prepare oneself before an act of dāna so that temporary purity of mind is attained and therefore the cultivation of a pure intention to donate freely and with feelings completely removed from thoughts of the meritorious return of the gift. Laity are motivated to practice dāna because such practices will result in better future life circumstances. Here, donation is not an act intended for purposes of generating new life and pleasures (Mingun Sayadaw, Buddhavamsa, vol. 2, pt.1, 1990, 7). Instead, it is directed at cultivating unprompted volitional acts of generosity for fulfillment of the dāna pāramī and arahat-ship with no further rebirths.

13. Compare with Parry 1989.

14. Spiro (1970) has noted this is a common feature of Buddhist practice, and he attempts to present it as a contradiction that essentially goes unrecognized by Buddhist actors.

15. *Mangala* is Pāli; *mingala* is the more commonly used Burmese term.

16. See Houtman 1999, 128–33.

17. Personal communication.

18. The official government rate of exchange in 1994 was 6 kyats to the dollar, whereas black market rates were roughly 100 kyats to the dollar.

19. A recent addition to the Yeiktha's sources of income are wedding banquets. Previously, it was traditional at the time of a wedding only to pay respects to a monk, offer him food and gifts, and conduct the water-pouring ceremony to transfer merits. When the hotels in Yangon started raising their catering prices to unreasonable levels, Yangonites took to offering elaborate banquets to the monks at Mahasi and to a small number of guests, who would share in the merit making and then take their meal after the monks had finished. This practice has become so popular that weddings with guest lists of up to four or five hundred people have become common. The Nuggaha has built a separate, covered eating area to accommodate wedding guests, who are served separately at the same time that the monks take their meal. Monks at MTY have reproached the Nuggaha for encouraging the celebration of such secular events at the center. The Nuggaha officials have held firm, saying that they must accept dāna as it comes. All this began after 1991, and since then, other lay centers have

adopted the practice. The accommodation of such social events marks an institution not only as a respected merit-making center but also as a place where high society meets.

Mahasi Thathana Yeiktha is perhaps the best-equipped center to accommodate the new hybrid wedding banquet/*suhn chwe* (monks' rice dāna). Nevertheless, other institutions have realized the economic and social advantages of drawing wealthy, high-status donors into their institutional orbit in the hope of securing donors loyal to their institutions. In response to these imitators, one of the committee members of the Women's Welfare Association commented how she and her family had been compelled to attend an event held by one of the main donors of the Jivitidana (Monks) Hospital. They felt obligated to attend because participation in a donation clique is as much about sharing in the merits of another woman's dāna (and therein also demonstrating the breadth of her network of social and business relations) as it is about performing dāna and including others in one's own merit making. In the case of the Jivitidana Hospital, Daw ——— explained, "We didn't really want to go because it is a hospital, and you can become sick. But, still we had to go or they would say, 'Those rich Mahasi people are very proud.'"

20. The government gives titles to donors, in the same fashion that monks may be titled. Mahasi Thathana Yeiktha is generally considered a bastion of U Nu cronies, and individuals associated with the Ne Win and the SLORC government are not associated with the Yeiktha. On one occasion, a Mahasi devotee successfully invited one of Burma's government-titled donors to an ahlu (donation ceremony). There was much fuss and excitement over this. If she could be "hooked" into the Mahasi donation network, there would be a great advantage in terms of financial resources and access to government connections for cheaper goods. The woman attended but did not become affiliated. For her, there was no advantage to doing so because the merit field at Mahasi was already saturated and access to the merit pool as a "close" donor with everything implied by that (meditating there, for example) would be difficult to achieve.

21. See Mi Mi Khaing 1984.

22. See Spiro 1970, 259, 264.

23. See Spiro 1970, 279.

24. See Tambiah 1985; Spiro 1970; and Keyes 1995.

25. See Tambiah 1976.

26. See Lehman 1987a.

27. Alternatively, one might profitably introduce here the notion of "performative efficacy," as discussed by Tambiah (1985, 89).

28. See Bourdieu 1977.

29. Shan Herald Agency for News, "Gen. Khin Nyunt 'No Buddhist,' Say Shans," http:www.shanland.org/politics/2003/gen_khin_nyunt.htm/?searchterm=%22Shans%20returning%20from%20panghsang%22.

30. See Rabinow 1984.

31. See Eiss and Wolf 1994, 4.

32. For a consideration of this practice during King Mindon's time, see Myo Myint 1987.

33. Personal communication with Juliane Schober, January 2000.

34. In 1990, democratic elections were held in Burma under the auspices of the military government; they followed two years of political instability that had begun with mass demonstrations calling for an end to twenty-six years of repressive military rule under the dictatorship of Ne Win. Aung San Suu Kyi, the Nobel Peace Prize recipient, rose to the top of a democratic movement that swept the country, leading to the elections. Contrary to SLORC's expectations, Aung San Suu Kyi's democratic party overwhelmingly carried the majority of the governmental seats. A crackdown ensued, and since then, the military has worked ruthlessly to crush the incipient democratic movement—killing, imprisoning, and torturing dissidents.

35. The state's response to this situation—and during the 1990s, the monastery grounds were overrun with lay residents who took refuge near the sangha—was to declare that the sangha lands needed to be cleared of laity so that the monastic order could maintain its distance from the laity to assure its own purity. The campaign to clear these lands in Yangon was part of a broader campaign to move thousands of families to the outskirts of the city, in the effort to control the population in the capital. These efforts were combined with other tactics intended to undermine the moral legitimacy of the sangha. For example, the government had monastery grounds searched for evidence that monks were breaking the rules of the order.

36. See Mendelson 1975; Sarkisyanz 1965; and Smith 1965.

37. In a personal communication, Skidmore proposed an additional consideration regarding the escalator, as follows: "The elevator is a key symbol of the totalitarian-capitalism synthesis that we see in Sino-Burmese department stores (where democracy is equated with the freedom to consume) precisely because it inserts the modern into the most important Burmese Buddhist space and because of the prolific media profiling the state has exerted upon it. Equally important, however, is its significance as a key symbol of the deep ambiguity and even confusion felt by Burmese Buddhists about the Golden facade project and the regime's engagement with Buddhism in general. The elevator at the Shwedagon is a visible manifestation of the deep complicity required by individuals under authoritarianism and

the inability of separating out domains such as the populace, the military regime, the Sangha, and the laity." For a further elaboration of his ideas about nation-state relations in Burma, see Skidmore 2004.

38. In 2001, I asked a religious affairs minister about this account. With real indignation, he explained that this was a collective effort that many officials had participated in. He was outraged at the thought that one individual had taken responsibility for the whole project.

39. For further elaboration of this theme, see Jordt 2001.

40. I acknowledge Maurice Godelier for pointing out the importance of this observation to my thesis.

41. One level up toward an objectivist social interpretation, we must observe dāna to be the circulatory engine of resources within the sacred economy—i.e., it is directed toward the sustenance of the sāsana (teachings) and its worldly institution, the sangha. Because the sangha is a worldly institution with substantial power in the political realm—both in its "rights of refusal" and in its being a flashpoint for public beliefs and sentiment—we must add that at this level, too, dāna is likewise operative in social causalities.

42. See Weber 1978, 212; see also Yahnghwe 1995 and Jordt 2003.

43. In the classical monarchical arrangement prior to British colonialism, a ternary order made up of sangha, state, and laity functioned in unison to support the Buddha sāsana. The king demonstrated his right to rule by being the chief donor among the laity in provisioning the sangha and erecting pagodas, monasteries, and other Buddhist edifices, as well as attending to other public works of merit. Within the Buddhist theory of moral causation that linked the king's actions to cosmic, social, and natural events, the well-being of the state and the people was understood to be dependent on the personal morality of the king.

44. Other sāsana-supporting activities of the present regime include the establishment of a new paṭipatti, or meditation, ministry and participation in missionary work, particularly in the hill tribes area.

45. See Herzfeld 1997a for a discussion of the way in which the Greek state controls judgment over how to interpret the internal states of actors.

46. See Godelier 1986, 208.

Chapter 4

1. Collingnon is quoted in Taylor 2001, 70.

2. Experience of the tatmadaw (army) is configured differently for the minorities living in the frontiers areas than it has been for the majority

Burman Buddhist population living in the central regions. Callahan (2003, 16) traces the origins for these geographically and functionally distinct approaches toward the majority Burmans and the minority ethnic groups to the colonial period, when "bureaucratic and security mechanisms politicized violence along territorial and racial lines, creating 'two Burmas' in the administrative and security arms of the state." She observes that this situation may account for the fact that "most Burmese living in the central regions considered the villains of the repressive, pre-1988 socialist state to be not the army but the police, whose corruption and heavy-handedness made them the target of widespread disgust" (223).

3. See Bellow 1953, 3.

4. "The bourgeois public sphere may be conceived above all as the sphere of private people come together as a public; they soon claimed the public sphere regulated from above against the public authorities themselves, to engage them in a debate over the general rules governing relations in the basically privatized but publicly relevant sphere of commodity exchange and social labor" (Habermas 1991, 27).

5. See Villa 1992, 712.

6. See Lintner 1989.

7. Closed since 1963, when Ne Win replaced U Nu's fledgling parliamentary democracy with a military dictatorship and a military-run BSPP government, the new military junta sought to draw fresh resources to a country badly in need of economic rescue. Aung San Suu Kyi's call to the international community to boycott Burma as a tourist destination has largely been successful in deterring tourism. The boycott has not, however, resulted in the intended goal of bringing down the military regime. The military officials have only tightened their own grip on power and resources. In 2002, many Yangonites I spoke with said that for them, democracy issues had been completely eclipsed by bread-and-butter issues.

8. See "Newsbrief," *Irrawaddy* 12, no. 9 (2004): n.p.

9. See Fink 2001, 185.

10. See Fink 2001, 185.

11. See Fink 2001, 189.

12. See, e.g., Min Zin 2003.

13. Ne Win was Burma's first military dictator, in power from 1962 to 1988, but he was thought by many Burmese and Western analysts to be an éminence grise to later dictators until his death in 2003.

14. See Aung San Suu Kyi 1991, 170. This version of kingship—of the kammaraja (king of merit—a king whose morality is the basis for his sustained power)—is one conception of kingship among several types found in Burmese Buddhist theories.

15. See Aung San Suu Kyi 1991, 170–71 (emphasis added).

16. Students and revolutionaries have experimented with various imported ideologies (parliamentary democracy, communism, socialism) since the early nationalist movements of the 1930s.

17. I am not suggesting that these culturological features are unchanging and essential. Clearly, the adoption of foreign ideas, as well as the creation and emergence of new forms of agency and ideology, is part and parcel of the process by which state building and its response by nonstate actors occur. Tony Day (2002, 288) articulates this lucidly: "But cosmologies and truth regimes are not monolithic. They are constructed out of arguments, conflicts, and hybridizing networks of practices, texts, and ideas that offer more than one mode of participation and escape. . . . In fact, they are nothing more than networks of human relationships, practices, and concepts, repertoires that are very old and well rehearsed, but nonetheless susceptible to change." See Jordt 2003 for a discussion of how multiple models of legitimacy making coexist in contemporary Burma.

18. David Steinberg (2001b) reiterates this paradigm by arguing that there is no civil society in Burma—the result of the military's success in purging all institutions with power-sharing capabilities. In this view, the possibility for Burma to become a viable state would require a strong civil society out of which might come the institutions and civilian talent required for democratic self-representation and rule.

19. See Tambiah 1976.

20. See Kapferer 1997, 217.

21. I am not, of course, making a causal argument reducing popular recognition of Thamanya Sayadaw's saintliness to a political barometer for antiregime sentiment. Thamanya Sayadaw participates in many more embedded contexts of religious practice.

22. For more detailed accounts of how the military regime participates in religious activities, see Jordt 2003 and Schober 1997, 2005.

23. See Min Zin 2001.

24. See Houtman 1999; Jordt 2003; Nash 1963; Mi Mi Khaing 1984; and Spiro 1970 for discussions of pon.

25. The military regime's efforts to gain the support of the Buddhist population by making claims about its moral actions and standing in Buddhist terms is recognized by the populace to be manipulative in a variety of ways I will consider in the discussion that follows. However, it should not go unrecognized by the reader that, from the point of view of the ordinary Burmese Buddhist citizen, the fact that duplicity is involved does not necessarily imply that the junta's actions will not have auspicious, transcendent efficacy. The military's efforts to extract magical efficacy from sacred acts is

reviled and feared by the public. The law of dhamma is understood to be a universal law, and manipulation of that law for private gain is not outside the realm of possible effective actions. The general populace recognizes that such practices are in direct pursuit of power. Moreover, rulers have attempted to balance their merit stores in order to secure their hold on power, which is an active concept drawn from classical Buddhist kingship. In these instances, interpretations of the military's moral actions are described as acts of sorcery and not sincere actions on behalf of the sāsana.

26. See Scott 1985.

27. See Day 2003, 36.

28. See Day 2003, 36.

29. See Callahan 2003; Day 2002; Taylor 1987, 1996, 2001; Steinberg 2001b; Silverstein 1977, 1981; Houtman 1999; Smith 1965; Rüland 2001; Collignon 2001; and others.

30. See Taylor 1987, 1996 and Steinberg 2001b, for example.

31. E.g., Yawnghwe 1995, 175. This has been the basis for a major split in political approaches to the stagnation of political processes in Burma. On the one hand, there are those who advocate that regime performance is a criterion of legitimacy that can be judged from outside the sovereign borders of a state according to universal criteria, such as human rights, freedom of speech, and democratic elections. On the other hand, there are those who hold that practical realities make it necessary to negotiate and reconcile with the military regime if there is to be any forward momentum in the political stalemate that has followed after the military regime refused to hand over power to a civilian government that was duly elected in 1990.

32. See Steinberg 2001b, 58.

33. See Kapferer 1997, 267.

34. I would note, though, that the possibility for democratic interpretation of the earliest mythical political institutions has been interpreted by Aung San Suu Kyi as incipient democratic forms.

35. See Scott 1985.

36. See Jordt 1988.

37. See Kawanami 2001, 30–33. Kawanami, who conducted her research among thilashin in Sagaing (the largest community of women renunicates in Burma), elaborates on the question of the status of thilashin in Burma by observing that the language used toward them demarcates their place in the sāsana order and functions to keep them "outside the sāsana." My own observations at the Mahasi Thathana Yeiktha meditation center indicate that the application of honorific language usually reserved for monks has begun to be employed for thilashin as well, which has contributed to the ambiguity of their sacred status. The blurring of social categories of purity, which

honorific language is intended to delimit, has made the question of whether thilashin are "inside" or "outside" the sāsana increasingly ambiguous. A thilashin's paramattha (ultimate reality) characteristics are far more likely to be emphasized in the context of a meditation center where practitioners are engaged in the perception and epistemic construction of reality from the point of view of anatta. Alternatively, when conventional roles—formal embodiment in robes and precept holding—are considered, there is a more ready reflex to assign women to a spiritual hierarchy that places them squarely outside the sāsana and not among its embodiments. See also Houtman 1990.

38. See Jordt 1988, 2004.

39. During the Ne Win military regime's purification movement of the late 1970s and early 1980s, thilashin also became a target for purification. The state definition of the acceptable boundaries of thilashin behavior—nuns who begged in the marketplace, for instance, were disrobed on the grounds that they were tarnishing the purity of the whole thilashin order—and the fact that thilashin institutions were viewed as parallel to those of monks meant that the dual monastic order was reinforced in principle. Through the government's efforts to control nuns' institutions by recognizing their parallel aspect vis-à-vis monks' institutions, the nuns' activities became enhanced. This has strengthened thilashin claims of parity with the sangha. Albeit aiming to contain thilashin within the fold of their legal scrutiny, all the government since independence have helped support this direction of thilashin's practices. Solidification of the idea of a vocational nun has therefore fastened on other features of thilashin's role as renunciates that would distinguish them from laity and put them in monastic structures parallel to those of monks.

40. See Spiro 1977, 261.

41. See Tambiah 1976 for an analysis of this paradigm's relevance to Buddhist kingship in Southeast Asia.

42. The yogi's experience of insights leads in an inevitable progression from one insight to the next, eventually culminating in enlightenment consciousness. The sotāpanna or "stream winner" has uprooted gross mental defilements. As a consequence, the yogi is presumed to be no longer capable of breaking his or her five precepts.

Chapter 5

1. See Alagappa 1995, 2. This notion purportedly dates back to Vico; see Herzfeld 1997b.

2. See Weber 1978, 212–13.

3. See, e.g., Schober 1997, and Taylor 1987.

4. Weber's starting point in considering the question of political authority is partly flawed for our purposes in this regard, as he already assumes the existence of a people subject to civil law, of a community, and of a contract with some existing state authority. Bartelson (2001, 3) demonstrates how we are currently incapable of imagining political order in the absence of the state and argues that the inattention to origins can distract us from political dynamics.

5. See Yangwhe 1995, 174.

6. See Diran 1997, 230.

7. In 1984, I was told by a doctor in Yangon that this phrase had been adopted by the military regime from public discourse, where it had originally been used mockingly in response to the military government's admonitions to the people to attend to their sīla for the good of the country. (This was during a period in which, in addition to ethnic and communist insurgencies, *dacoits* [armed gangs of robbers], and other common criminals abounded.) The response had been, "Only when your stomach is full can you keep your sīla," meaning that the harsh conditions of the political economy criminalized the people, who otherwise could not survive. It was thus with irony that many of my older acquaintances related how the regime had turned this into a goal for society and the primary function of the state.

8. Personal communication with U Nu, 1988.

9. The Ogatha is the standard devotional recitation that precedes any Buddhist gathering or private devotion in front of the household altar. It is both a protective recitation and a resolve to remain steadfast on the path leading to nibbāna. By taking refuge in the Buddha, Dhamma, and Sangha, the practitioner invokes protection from the five evils, the hell realms, and the eight calamities (being mute, being deaf, stammering, being blind, being mad, being crippled, lacking concentration, or being feebleminded). The devotee also resolves to be free of the four lacks of virtue (failing to maintain the precepts, spending money foolishly, failing to do one's duty, and failing to realize the Four Noble Truths) and to avoid evil and seek nibbāna. See Nash 1963, 287.

10. "In promoting the ideal of democracy, two things were essential; first, to identify the natural enemies of democracy; and, second, to educate the leaders as well as the masses in the value of moral cleanliness, selfrestraint, the spirit of compromise, and willingness to accept the verdict of the people as expressed at the polls, and to imbue them with such a spirit that they would be willing to die in defence of democracy" (Nu 1975, 220).

11. SLORC/SPDC has also used this qualification to justify not handing power over to the elected civilian government after the 1990 elections. The claim made is that because the country has not yet been unified in likeminded ideals about the goals for society, the people are not yet properly educated to participate in a democracy. They might vote for the wrong thing, not knowing what is best.

12. See Nu 1975, 220–21.

13. See Nu 1975, 224.

14. See Nu 1975, 223.

15. It is probably also a tribute to U Nu and his parliamentary democratic government that the ideals of procedural democracy were fostered to the degree that they were, thereby creating a legacy that has never really left the political scenery and the politics of legitimation in Burma. In tracing a loose genealogy of democracy politics in Burma, it should also be noted that students have always been at the forefront of these movements since the early nationalist period of the 1930s.

16. See Tin Maung Maung Than 1988.

17. See Lintner 1994, 364.

18. See Tin Maung Maung Than 1988, 36–37.

19. See Tin Maung Maung Than 1988, 45.

20. See Lintner 1989, 1994.

21. See Lintner 1994, 276.

22. In 1995, I gathered some statistics from the Bureau of Land Affairs and discovered that from 1989 to 1990, there were 379,663 acres of sāsana lands (this includes all religious categories: sanghika, poggalika, ganika, and sāsanika). From 1993 to 1994, the number of acres of sāsana lands leaped to 523,006! Sāsana landholdings were clearly growing. It is certain that under the SLORC regime, people were trying to secure their resources in places the government could not get at them. This situation has simultaneously invited closer lay-sangha relations. Lehman states that this has been a "traditional system of money laundering since the 11th century in Burma" (personal communication).

23. I mentioned in the preface my meeting at MTY with U Nu, at the conclusion of which he announced his intention to go directly to Insein Prison to visit former brigadier general U Aung Gyi. U Aung Gyi was under arrest for writing a series of open letters to Ne Win criticizing his government and calling for reforms. (Aung Gyi's letters were widely credited by people I spoke with in Yangon as having sparked Ne Win's resignation, but actually, they marked the culmination of widespread discontent and antigovernment protests that had been building since the demonetization of the kyat the year before, as well as the violent suppression and killings of

antigovernment individuals [especially student protestors] a few months earlier.) Two weeks after my meeting, U Nu (by then in his eighties) reentered politics, establishing the League for Democracy and Peace in an effort to fill the vacuum of political leadership and supply the direction that the mass popular uprising lacked. As it would turn out, Aung San Suu Kyi emerged as the dominant voice leading the country against the military regime. In the days and weeks following the military crackdown, numerous political notables attempted to galvanize the public against the regime (see Lintner 1994 for a full account). A young Yangon woman explained that in the days following the government crackdown and killings, people talked about whom they would align with and decided whom they were going to support to lead the movement against the government. In her household, the young adult children wanted to side with Aung San Suu Kyi, whereas her parents wanted to side with U Nu. Perhaps, as happened in other households, the family felt the need to arrive at a consensus over whom they would support; they engaged in long discussions until the father finally succumbed to his children's wishes to back Aung San Suu Kyi over the older U Nu, who, the children argued, had had his day.

24. Military intelligence visited my host to make a hostile inquiry about my stay at his home. It was fortuitous that my host's son-in-law, a physician, was attending Sein Lwin during the days leading up to his assumption of leadership. Nevertheless, my host family (though very gracious) was anxious that I not stay at their home, especially after I had been in contact with U Nu.

25. Following the August 8, 1988, demonstrations and killings, the United Nations, India, the United States, and Japan all called for economic sanctions against the government. But China, Thailand, Singapore, and ASEAN immediately recognized the new Sein Lwin government.

26. See Juliane Schober 1997a for a full account of this event.

27. See Douglas 1986.

28. White umbrellas are also considered symbols of kingly authority; military rulers will also trot out the royal umbrellas for special occasions.

29. Official government conversion statistics for the frontiers area are collected by the Department for the Promotion and Propagation of Sāsana. Colonel San Lwin, the director of the department, explained that the army gets the information from monks and is able to quickly transfer the results to Yangon. For the months of September through December 1994, total conversions came to 17,299. This number was broken down in the following way: Nat, 13,876; Christian, 3,411; and Islam, 12.

30. Ko Cho, "Second White Elephant Found," *Irrawaddy* 10, no. 5 (2002): n.p.

31. See Mya Maung 1999, 267

32. See Jordt and Applbaum 2003.

33. See Gustaaf Houtman's *Mental Culture in Burmese Crisis Politics* (1999) for an insightful consideration of Burmese Buddhist conceptions of power, influence, and authority. Houtman aligns the politics of Aung San Suu Kyi with the awza concept of influence stemming from mental purification, and he identifies the military regime with the ana concept of forceful power. He argues that the regime fears Suu Kyi's charisma will be identified with "traditional ideas of awza" and that, as a consequence, the regime's "current cultural and religious revival . . . is orchestrat[ed] as an attempt to manufacture awza under a future electoral polity in which they hope to secure a dominant position. . . . [The regime] can only pretend to express 'the peoples' desires'" (1991, 161). Houtman is right in asserting that "mental culture" plays a central role in Burmese politics, although I remain unconvinced that we may interpret all of the behaviors of the military as strategic and therefore disconnected to the system of knowing and being in which it participates daily.

34. See Tambiah 1976, 490.

35. In analytical terms, this cosmological political idea relies on an essential dichotomy situating power as causal and resultant. The power of colonialists, as with other bad kings, is seen to be established on past causal results with continuing latent supports. And because power is always situated in a mutually shared and constituted field, the subjugation of the Burmese was also viewed as a causal resultant effect from prior collectively shared acts.

36. This same logic applies to other planes of existence where the collectively shared kamma manifests as environment and action. For example, it is explained that in the hell realms, it is nearly impossible to perform a meritorious act because of the total environment within which one collectively participates. Likewise, for heavenly devā realms, the purity of one's moral actions is collectively shared and acted on.

37. This subject is comprehensively treated in Houtman's *Mental Culture in Burmese Crisis Politics* (1999).

Epilogue

1. See Sahlins 1999; Jordt and Applbaum 2003.

2. For some of my reflections on the role of gender in the constitution of Burmese Buddhist society, see Jordt 1988, 2005.

3. The 2005 elections in Iraq and Gaza have helped temper this simplistic dualism.

4. See Eisenstadt 1984.

5. See Spiro 1965, 261.

6. See Fink 2001.

7. See Hefner 1998.

GLOSSARY

In the definitions below, (B) indicates Burmese, and (P) indicates Pāli, the scriptural and liturgical language used in Theravada Buddhism. In loan words from Pāli, Burmese rules of euphony change /s/ to /th/.

Abhidhamma (P)—one of the three portions, or baskets, of the Tipitaka texts dealing with the complex theory of Buddhist metaphysics and psychology

adeitan (B)—[(P) *adittana*] resolve to move toward a goal

adittana (P)—[(B) *adeitan*] resolve to move toward a goal

ahlu (B)—offering

ana (B)—power

anāgāmī (P)—[(B) *anagam*] the third stage of enlightenment; a person who has realized this stage of enlightenment

anattā (B, P)—absence of self or personhood

anicca (P)—[(B) *aneisa*] impermanence, flux, change

arahat (B)—[(P) *arahatta*] the final stage of enlightenment; a person who has realized this stage of enlightenment; fully enlightened saint

awza (B)—influence

bhāvanā (P)—mental development; meditation

bhikkhu (P)—monk

bhikkhunī (P)—nun

bojjhanga (P)—seven factors of enlightenment

Buddha Sāsana Nuggaha Apwe (BSNA)—lay guardian association or trustees at MTY

BSPP—Burmese Socialist Program Party

cakkavatti (P)—a world-conquering king

cetanā (P)—[(B) *seit*] volition, intention or will; refers to the quality of mind which is productive of kamma

cetiya (P)—[(B) *chedi*] a stupa

daga (B)—male donor and supporter of monks and the sāsana

dagama (B)—female donor and supporter of monks and the sāsana

dāna (P, B)—charity; giving

devā (P)—[(B) *dewa*] celestial being

dhamma (B, P)—truth; teaching; righteousness; doctrine; nature; all things and states, conditioned and unconditioned

dhammayone (B)—discourse hall

diṭṭhi (P)—belief; speculative opinion

dosa (P)—[(B) *dotha*] hatred or anger

dukkha (B, P)—suffering; conflict; unsatisfactoriness

gaing (B)—sect

gana (P)—sect

ganika (P)—category of property belonging to a monastic sect

Hititi (B)—a voluntary organization providing free meals to indigent yogis at MTY

hpoun (alternate spellings *hpon, hpoun, pon*) (B)—[(P) *punna*, meaning "merit quality"] merit-based power; glory; the cumulative result of past meritorious deeds

jhānas (P, B)—meditative absorption state

kalyānamitta (P)—wise and noble spiritual friends

kamma (P)—[from Sanskrit *karma*] wholesome or unwholesome action

kammaṭṭhāna (P)—[(B) *kammathan*, meaning meditation] lit. "working ground" of meditation

kanti (P, B)—forbearance; patience

kappia (P, B)—lay attendant

karuna (P)—compassion

kopaka apwe (B)—guardian associations

koyin (B)—male novitiates

kuti (B, P)—hut

kyaung (B)—monastery

kyaungtaiks (B)—large monastic complexes especially for scriptural study

lobha (P)—greed

lokuttara (P)—supermundane realities that are not subject to arising and passing away

magga (P)—path or way

Mahasammatha (P)—mythical first king in origin myth

Mahasi Thathana Yeiktha (MTY) [universal spelling, Mahasi Sāsana Yeiktha]—lay meditation center

mangala (P)—[(B) *mingala*] auspiciousness; prosperity; blessing

mettā (P)—loving-kindness

mingala (B)—[(P) *mangala*] auspiciousness; prosperity; blessing

moha (P)—delusion; ignorance

muditā (P)—sympathetic joy

nāma-rūpā (B, P)—mind-and-body; mentality and corporeality

ñāṇa (P)—wisdom

nayaka sayadaw (B)—senior monk teacher

nekkhama (P)—renunciation

nibbāna (P)—extinction of greed, hatred, and delusion and deliverance from all future rebirths; enlightenment

nivaraṇa (P)—five hindrances that are obstacles to the mind (sense desire, *kāmacchanda;* ill-will, *vyāpāda;* sloth and torpor, *thīna-middha;* restlessness and worry, *uddhacca-kukkucca;* skeptical doubt, *vicikicchā*

Nuggaha (B)—short for Buddha Sāsana Nuggaha Apwe

nyanzin (B)—stages/progress of insight

ovadacariya sayadaw (B)—a monk who is a chief preceptor (*ovadacariya*) and meditation master (*sayadaw*)

Pacceka Buddha (P)—a Buddha who attains enlightenment without any assistance and who cannot enlighten others, silent Buddha

Pāli (P)—liturgical language of the Tipitaka, the Theravada Buddhist scriptures

paññā (P)—insight; wisdom

paramattha (P)—truth in the ultimate sense

pāramī (P, B)—the ten perfections leading to enlightenment (giving, *dāna;* morality, *sīla;* renunciation, *nekkhamma;* wisdom, *paññā;* energy, *viriya;* patience, *kanti;* truthfulness, *sacca;* resolve, *adhiṭṭhāna;* loving-kindness, *mettā;* equanimity, *upekkhā*

pariyatti (P)—scriptural study; theoretical knowledge of the teachings

paṭiccasamuppāda (P)—the doctrine of dependent origination

Pātimokkha (P)—monks' rules of conduct; disciplinary code

paṭipatti (P)—pursuance of the teachings through practice, as distinguished from theoretical knowledge of the wordings of the teachings

paṭivedha (P)—realization of the truth of dhamma

pindabat (B)—alms rounds

poggalika (P)—category of property belonging to an individual monk

pon (also *hpoun, hpon*) (B)—[(P) *punna,* meaning "merit quality"] merit-based power; glory; the cumulative result of past meritorious deeds

pongyi (B)—lit. great glory; a monk

pongyi daga/dagama (B)—a monk's male/female supporter

pongyi kyaung (B)—monk's monastery

puthujjana (P)—worldling; unenlightened person

saddhā (P)—[(B) *thaddha*] faith rooted in understanding; confidence

sakadāgāmī (P)—[(B) *thakadagam*] the second stage of enlightenment; a person who has realized this stage of enlightenment samādhi (P)—concentration attained in higher meditation

samatha (P)—concentration (or concentration meditation)

samatha-bhāvanā (P)—tranquility meditation; mental development cultivated through concentration

sammuti (P)—conventional definition of reality as compared to *paramattha*, the absolute true state of nature

samphappalapa (P)—frivolous speech; speech not benefiting wholesome mental development

saṃsāra (P)—rounds of rebirth

sangayana (P)—Sixth Buddhist Synod held in the 1950s and promoted by the U Nu government

Sangha of the Four Quarters—all monks within the order irrespective of their sectarian differences

saṅghādisesa (P)—a serious offense by a monk that requires a formal meeting of the sangha

sanghika (P)—category of property belonging to the whole of the Buddhist sangha

sankāruppekhā ñāṇa (P)—equanimity knowledge regarding the formations of existence

sāsana (P)—the dispensation of the Buddha; the teachings of the Buddha

sāsanika (P)—category of property belonging to the sāsana and therefore universally available to all

sati (P)—[(B) *thati*] mindfulness

satipaṭṭhāna (P)—lit., "mindfulness closely established on the object of attention"

satipaṭṭhāna vipassanā (P)—mindfulness (*satipaṭṭhāna*) + insight (*vipassanā*) meditation

sayadaw (B)—a senior monk and meditation master

seit (B)—[(P) *cetanā*] volition; intention

sīla (P)—morality

sima (P)—ordination site

sotāpanna (P)—[(B) *thotapan*] the first stage of enlightenment; a person who has realized this stage of enlightenment

suhn (B)—honorific term referring to rice eaten by monks

suhn chwe (B)—(honorific) monks' repast

thathana thanshin ye (B)—purification of the sangha

tatmadaw (B)—military

Thudhamma (B)—the largest sect of monks in contemporary Burma

Tipitaka (P)—lit., *ti*, "three," + *pitaka*, "baskets," the Pāli canon; the collection of primary Pāli language texts which form the doctrinal foundation of Theravada Buddhism

upekkhā (P)—equanimity

vipassanā (P)—insight (or insight meditation); also, "seeing things as they really are"

vipassanā-bhāvanā (P)—insight meditation; mental development cultivated through insight leading to wisdom (*paññā*)

vinaya (P)—behavioral code of monks consisting of 227 rules of conduct

vinicchaya (B)—monastic legal case

viriya (P)—effort; energy

waso (P)—Buddhist Lent

weiksa (B)—wizard

wunzao (B)—"working" monks within the sangha organization of MTY attending to the various administrative and upkeep tasks at the center

wutu (P, B)—monks' money used only for requisites

yeiktha (B)—(abbreviation for Mahasi Thathana Yeiktha, Mahasi Sāsana Yeiktha, MTY) a cool, forest refuge

yogi (P, B)—meditator

REFERENCES

Aggacitta, U. 1988. *Yogi Experiences of Healing Chronic and Critical Illnesses.* Pamphlet.

Alagappa, Muthiah. 1995. *Political Legitimacy in Southeast Asia: The Quest for Moral Authority.* Stanford, CA: Stanford University Press.

Appadurai, Arjun. 1991. "Global Ethnoscapes: Notes and Queries for a Transnational Anthropology." In *Recapturing Anthropology: Working in the Present,* ed. Richard G. Fox, 191–210. Santa Fe, NM: School of American Research Press.

Aung San Suu Kyi. 1991. *Freedom from Fear and Other Writings.* Ed. Michael Aris. New York: Viking.

Aung Thwin, Michael. 1979. *Burma: Military Rule and the Politics of Stagnation* (review article). *Pacific Affairs* 52(3): 553–55.

———. 1998. *Myth and History in the Historiography of Early Burma: Paradigms, Primary Sources, and Prejudices.* Athens: Ohio University Center for International Studies.

———. 2001–2002. "Parochial Universalism, Democracy, Jihad, and the Orientalist Image of Burma: The New Evangelism." *Pacific Affairs* 74(4): 483–506.

Bellow, Saul. 1953. *The Adventures of Augie March.* New York: Penguin.

Bourdieu, Pierre. 1977. *Outline of a Theory of Practice.* Cambridge: Cambridge University Press.

Buddhaghosa, Bhadantācariya. 1999. *The Path of Purification: Visuddhimagga.* Trans. Bhikkhu Ñāṇamoli. Seattle, WA: BPS Pariyatti Editions.

Burma Socialist Programme Party. 1964. *The System of Correlation of Man and His Environment: The Philosophy of the Burma Socialist Programme Party.* Rangoon, Burma: Sarpay Beikman Press.

Cady, John Frank. 1958. *A History of Modern Burma.* Ithaca, NY: Cornell University Press.

Callahan, Mary P. 2003. *Making Enemies: War and Statebuilding in Burma.* Ithaca, NY: Cornell University Press.

Collignon, Stefan. 2001. "Human Rights and the Economy in Burma." In *Burma: Political Economy under Military Rule,* ed. Robert H. Taylor, 70–108. London: Hurst.

Collins, Steven. 1982. *Selfless Persons: Imagery and Thought in Theravada Buddhism*. Cambridge: Cambridge University Press.

Day, Tony. 2002. *Fluid Iron: State Formation in Southeast Asia*. Honolulu: University of Hawaii Press.

Digha Nikaya II: Long Discourses of the Buddha. 1984. Rangoon: Burma Pitaka Association.

Digha Nikaya III: Long Discourses of the Buddha. 1985. Rangoon: Burma Pitaka Association.

Ding, X. L. 1994. "Institutional Amphibiousness and the Transition from Communism." *British Journal of Political Science* 24(3): 293–318.

Diran, Richard K. 1997. *The Vanishing Tribes of Burma*. New York: Weidenfeld Nicolson Illustrated.

Douglas, Mary. 1986. *How Institutions Think*. Syracuse, NY: Syracuse University Press.

Durkheim, Emile. 1912. *The Elementary Forms of Religious Life*. Trans. Karen E. Fields. New York: Free Press, 1995 (orig. pub. 1912).

Eisenstadt, S. N., and Luis Roniger. 1984. *Patrons, Clients and Friends: Interpersonal Relations and the Structure of Trust in Society*. Cambridge: Cambridge University Press.

Eiss, Paul, and Thomas C. Wolfe. 1994. "Deconstruct to Reconstruct: An Interview with Maurice Godelier." *Journal of the International Institute* 1(4): 4–7.

Englehart, Neil A. 2000. "Rights and Culture in the Asian Values Argument: The Rise and Fall of Confucian Ethics in Singapore." *Human Rights Quarterly* 22(2): 548–68.

Ferguson, John, and Michael E. Mendelson. 1981. "Masters of the Buddhist Occult: The Burmese Weikzas." *Contributions to Asian Studies* 16:62–81.

Fink, Christina. 2001. *Living Silence: Burma under Military Rule*. London: Zed Books.

Geertz, Clifford. 1973. *Thick Description: Toward an Interpretive Theory of Culture*. New York: Basic Books.

"Gen. Khin Nyunt 'No Buddhist,' Say Shans." 2003. http://www.shanland .org/politics/2003/gen_khin_nyunt.htm/?searchterm=%22Shans% 20returning%20from%20panghsang%22 (accessed 2004).

Gethin, Rupert. 1997. "Cosmology and Meditation: From the Aggañña-Sutta to the Mahāyāna." *History of Religions* 36(3): 183–217.

Godelier, Maurice. 1986. *The Mental and the Material: Thought, Economy and Society*. London: Verso Press.

———. 1999. *The Enigma of the Gift*. Chicago: University of Chicago Press.

A Guide to the Mangala Sutta. 1991. Rangoon: Ministry of Religious Affairs.

Habermas, Jürgen. 1991. *The Structural Transformation of the Public Sphere.* Cambridge, MA: MIT Press.

Harvey, G. E. 1925. *History of Burma: From the Earliest Times to 10 March 1824, the Beginning of the English Conquest.* New York: Octagon Books (repr. 1967).

Haseman, John B. 1988. "Burma in 1987: Change in the Air?" In "A Survey of Asia in 1987: Part II," special issue, *Asian Survey* 28(2): 223–28.

Hefner, Robert W. 1998. "Multiple Modernities: Christianity, Islam, and Hinduism in a Globalizing Age." *Annual Review of Anthropology* 27:83–104.

Herzfeld, Michael. 1997a. *Portrait of Greek Imagination: An Ethnographic Biography of Andreas Nenedakis.* Chicago: University of Chicago Press.

———. 1997b. *Cultural Intimacy: Social Poetics in the Nation-State.* New York: Routledge.

Hirschkind, Charles. 2001. "The Ethics of Listening: Cassette-Sermon Audition in Contemporary Egypt." *American Ethnologist* 28(3): 623–49.

Houtman, Gustaaf. 1990. "Traditions of Buddhist Practice in Burma." PhD diss., School of Oriental and African Studies, University of London.

———. 1999. *Mental Culture in Burmese Crisis Politics: Aung San Suu Kyi and the National League for Democracy.* Institute for the Study of Languages and Cultures of Asia and Africa, Monograph Series no. 33. Tokyo: University of Foreign Studies.

———. 2005. "Sacralizing or Demonizing Democracy? Aung San Suu Kyi's 'Personality Cult.'" In *Burma at the Turn of the 21st Century,* ed. Monique Skidmore, 133–53. Honolulu: University of Hawaii Press.

Jordt, Ingrid. 1988. "Bhikkhuni, Thilashin, Mae-chii: Women Who Renounce the World in Burma." *Crossroads* 4(1): 31–39.

———. 2001. "Mass Lay Meditation and State-Society Relations in Post-independence Burma." PhD diss., Harvard University.

———. 2003. "From Relations of Power to Relations of Authority: Epistemic Claims, Practices and Ideology." *Social Analysis: The International Journal of Cultural and Social Practice* 47(1): 65–76.

Jordt, Ingrid, and Kalman Applbaum, eds. 2003. "Introduction: Knowledge and Verification." *Social Analysis: The International Journal of Cultural and Social Practice* 47(1): 1–9.

Kapferer, Bruce. 1997. *The Feast of the Sorcerer: Practices of Consciousness and Power.* Chicago: University of Chicago Press.

Kawanami, Hiroko. 2000. "Patterns of Renunciation: The Changing World of Burmese Nuns." In *Women's Buddhism, Buddhism's Women: Tradition, Revision, Renewal,* ed. Ellison Banks Findly, 159–71. Somerville, MA: Wisdom Publication.

Keyes, Charles. 1995. *The Golden Peninsula: Culture and Adaptation in Mainland Southeast Asia*. Honolulu: University of Hawaii Press.

Khin Yi. 1988. *The Dobama Movement in Burma (1930–1938)*. Cornell University Press, Southeast Asia Program.

Ko Cho. 2000. "Second White Elephant Found." *Irrawaddy* 10(5): n.p.

Kyaw Htut, U, and U Mya Tin. 1994. *A Guide to the Mangala Sutta*. Rangoon: Department for the Promotion and Propagation of the Sasana.

Ledi Sayadaw. 1965. *The Manuals of Buddhism*. Rangoon: Union Buddha Sāsana Council, 1965.

Lehman, F. K. (Chit Hlaing). 1987a. "Burmese Religion." In *The Encyclopedia of Religion,* ed. M. Eliade, 2:574–80. New York: Macmillan.

———. 1987b. "Monasteries, Palaces and Ambiguities: Burmese Sacred and Secular Space." *Contributions to Indian Sociology* 21(1): 169–86.

Lévi-Strauss, Claude. 1963. *The Structural Study of Myth*. Suffolk, UK: Basic Books.

Lintner, Bertil. 1989. *Outrage: Burma's Struggle for Democracy*. Hong Kong: Review Publishing.

———. 1994. *Burma in Revolt: Opium and Insurgency since 1948*. Boulder, CO: Westview Press.

Mahasi Sayadaw. "Manual of Insight for Paṭipatti Teachers." Comp. Saya Kyan and Saya Kywet under the supervision of Mahasi Sayadaw. Unpublished.

———. 1979. *The Progress of Insight: A Treatise on Satipaṭṭhāna Meditation*. Rangoon: Buddha Sāsana Nuggaha Organization.

———. 1980. *Practical Insight Meditation: Basic and Progressive Stages*. Kandy, Sri Lanka: Buddhist Publication Society.

Mahasi Yeiktha Charter and Constitution. 1954. Rangoon: Buddha Sāsana Nuggaha Apwe.

Martin, Edwin W. 1977. "Burma in 1976: The Beginnings of Change?" *Asian Survey* 17(2): 155–59.

Masefield, Peter. 1983. "Mind/Cosmos Maps in the Pali Nikayas." In *Buddhist and Western Psychology,* ed. N. Katz, 69–93. Boulder, CO: Prajna Press.

McNamara, Jo Ann Kay. 1996. *Sisters in Arms: Catholic Nuns through Two Millennia*. Cambridge, MA: Harvard University Press.

Mendelson, E. Michael. 1975. *Sangha and State in Burma: A Study of Monastic Sectarianism and Leadership*. Ithaca, NY: Cornell University Press.

Merleau-Ponty, M. 1966. *Phenomenology of Perception*. Trans. and ed. Colin Smith. London: Routledge.

Mi Mi Khaing. 1984. *The World of Burmese Women*. London: Zed Press.

Mingun Sayadaw and Bhaddanta Vicittasarabhivamsa. 1990–96. *The Buddhavamsa* (The Great Chronicle of Buddhas). Trans. U Ko Lay and

U Tin Lwin. Vols. 1–4, State Buddha Sāsana Council version. Yangon, Burma: Ti Ni Publishing Centre.

Min Zin. 2001. "The Power of Hpoun." *Irrawaddy* 9(9): n.p.

———. 2003 "Engaging Buddhism for Social Change," *Irrawaddy* 11(2): n.p.

Mya Maung. 1997. "Burma's Economic Performance under Military Rule: An Assessment." *Asian Survey* 37(6): 503–24.

Myo Myint. 1987. "The Politics of Survival in Burma: The Politics of Statecraft in the Reign of King Mindon (1853–1878)." PhD diss., Cornell University.

Nash, Manning. 1963. *The Golden Road to Modernity: Village Life in Contemporary Burma.* Chicago: University of Chicago Press.

———. 1963. "Burmese Buddhism in Everyday Life." *American Anthropologist* (n.s.) 65(2): 285–95.

Ne Win. *Address of General Ne Win: Chairman of the Central Organising Committee—Burma Socialist Programme Party.* 1966. Rangoon: Sarpay Beikman Press.

"Newsbrief." 1999. *Irrawaddy* 7(4): n.p.

Nu, U. 1975. *Saturday's Son.* New Haven, CT: Yale University Press.

———. 1988. "A Primer for Vipassanā Practices: A Psychological and Cultural Interpretation of Burma." Unpublished.

Pandita, Sayadaw U. 1993. *In This Very Life: The Liberation Teachings of the Buddha.* 2nd ed. Boston: Wisdom Publications.

Parry, Jonathan. 1989. "On the Moral Perils of Exchange." In *Money and the Morality of Exchange,* ed. J. Parry and M. Bloch, 64–93. Cambridge: Cambridge University Press.

Pe Thin, trans. 1982. *Paṭiccasammupāda.* Rangoon: Buddha Sāsana Nuggaha Organization.

Pye, Lucien. 1962. *Politics, Personality, and Nation Building.* New Haven, CT: Yale University Press.

Quine, W. V. 1969. *Ontological Relativity and Other Essays.* New York: Columbia University Press.

Rabinow, Paul. 1984. *The Foucault Reader.* New York: Pantheon Books.

Reynolds, Frank. 1998. "Buddhism Betrayed? Reflections on Recent Developments in Thailand and Burma." Lecture, Harvard University, Cambridge, MA.

Reynolds, Frank, and Mani B. Reynolds, trans. 1982. *Three Worlds According to King Ruang: A Thai Buddhist Cosmology.* Berkeley Buddhist Studies Series 4. Berkeley: University of California, Group in Buddhist Studies, Center for South and Southeast Asian Studies, and Institute of Buddhist Studies.

Rüland, Jürgen. 2001. "Burma Ten Years after the Uprising: The Regional Dimension." In *Burma: Political Economy under Military Rule,* ed. Robert H. Taylor, 137–58. London: Hurst.

Sahlins, Marshall. 1985. *Islands of History.* Chicago: University of Chicago Press.

―――. 1999. "Two or Three Things That I Know about Culture." *Journal of the Royal Anthropological Institute* 5(3): 399–421.

―――. 2004. *Apologies to Thucydides: Understanding History as Culture and Vice Versa.* Chicago: University of Chicago Press.

Sarkisyanz, Manuel. 1965. *Buddhist Backgrounds of the Burmese Revolution.* The Hague: Martinus Nijhoff.

Schober, Juliane. 1997. "Buddhist Just Rule and Burmese National Culture: State Patronage of the Chinese Tooth Relic in Myanmar." *History of Religions* 36(3): 218–43.

―――. 2004. "Mapping the Sacred in Theravada Buddhist Southeast Asia." In *Sacred Places and Modern Landscapes—Sacred Geography and Social-Religious Transformations in South and Southeast Asia,* ed. Ronald Bull, 1–19. Program for Southeast Asian Studies Monograph Series. Tempe: Arizona State University.

―――. 2005. "Buddhist Visions of Moral Authority and Civil Society: The Search for the Post-colonial State in Burma," In *Burma at the Turn of the 21st Century,* ed. Monique Skidmore, 113–33. Honolulu: University of Hawaii Press.

Scott, James C. 1985. *Weapons of the Weak: Everyday Forms of Peasant Resistance.* New Haven, CT: Yale University Press.

―――. 1990. *Domination and the Arts of Resistance: Hidden Transcripts.* New Haven, CT: Yale University Press.

―――. 1998. *Seeing Like a State: How Certain Schemes to Improve the Human Condition Have Failed.* New Haven, CT: Yale University Press.

Seekins, Donald. 2000. "Burma in 1999: A Slim Hope." *Asian Survey* 11(1): 16–24.

Shway Yoe. 1882. *The Burman: His Life and Notions.* New York: Norton Library, 1963 (orig. pub. 1882).

Silananda, Sayadaw U. 2002. *Four Foundations of Mindfulness.* Boston, MA: Wisdom Books.

Silverstein, Josef. 1977. *Military Rule and the Politics of Stagnation.* Ithaca, NY: Cornell University Press.

―――. 1981. "Burma in 1980: An Uncertain Balance Sheet." *Asian Survey* 21(2): 212–22.

Sizemore, Russell, and Donald Swearer, eds. 1990. *Ethics, Wealth and Salvation: A Study in Buddhist Ethics.* Columbia: University of South Carolina Press.

Skidmore, Monique. 2004. *Karaoke Fascism: Burma and the Politics of Fear.* Philadelphia, PA: University of Pennsylvania Press.

Smith, Donald Eugene. 1965. *Religion and Politics in Burma.* Princeton, NJ: Princeton University Press.

Spiro, Melford. 1970. *Buddhism and Society: A Great Tradition and Its Burmese Vicissitudes.* New York: Harper and Row.

Steinberg, David I. 2001a. *Burma: The State of Myanmar.* Washington, DC: Georgetown University Press.

————. 2001b. "The Burmese Conundrum: Approaching Reformation of the Political Economy." In *Burma: Political Economy under Military Rule,* ed. Robert H. Taylor, 41–69. London: Hurst.

Tambiah, Stanley J. 1978. *World Conqueror and World Renouncer: A Study of Buddhism and Polity in Thailand against a Historical Background.* Cambridge: Cambridge University Press.

————. 1985a. *The Buddhist Saints of the Forest and the Cult of Amulets.* Cambridge: Cambridge University Press.

————. 1985b. *Culture, Thought, and Social Action.* Cambridge, MA: Harvard University Press.

Taylor, Robert. 1987. *The State in Burma.* London: Hurst.

————. 1988. Foreword to Khin Yi, *The Dobama Movement in Burma (1930–1938).* Ithaca, NY: Cornell University Press, Southeast Asia Program.

————. 1996. "Elections in Burma/Myanmar: For Whom and Why?" In *The Politics of Election in Southeast Asia,* ed. Robert Taylor, 164–83. New York: Cambridge University Press.

————, ed. 2001. *Burma: Political Economy under Military Rule.* London: Hurst.

Tin Maung Maung Than. 1988. "The Sangha and Sasana in Socialist Burma." *Sojourn: Social Issues in Southeast Asia* 3(1): 26–61.

Tiyavanich, Kamala. 1997. *Forest Recollections: Wandering Monks in Twentieth-Century Thailand.* Honolulu: University of Hawaii Press.

Villa, Dana R. 1992. "Postmodernism and the Public Sphere." *American Political Science Review* 86(3): 712–21.

Weber, Max. 1978. *Economy and Society: An Outline of Interpretative Sociology.* Ed. Guenther Roth and Claus Mittich. Berkeley: University of California Press.

Wolf, Eric. 1982. *Europe and the People without History.* Berkeley: University of California Press.

Yawnghwe, Chao-Tzang. 1995. "Burma: The Depoliticization of the Political." In *Political Legitimacy in Southeast Asia: The Quest for Moral Authority,* ed. Muthiah Alagappa, 170–92. Stanford, CA: Stanford University Press.

INDEX

The letter *n* following a page number refers to a note on that page.

interiority and, 58–59
knowing and, 86–88, 229n21
knowledge and, 13
methodological considerations, 56–60
orthodoxy of, 52–54, 65
practice of, 15–16, 56–57, 222n3
purification and, 25–26
rise and fall and, 65–66, 227n10, 227n11
scriptural study and, 54–55
teachers of, 18, 223n9
as theory of knowing, 61–67
three universal characteristics and, 63
World Age and, 25
See also Mahasi method; mass lay meditation movement
Visuddhimagga, 65

Weber, Max, 1, 136, 171, 239n4

weiksa cults, 24–25, 224n23
white elephants, 190
women
Mahasi Thathana Yeiktha (MTY) and, 35–37
mass lay meditation movement and, 158, 160–61
thilashin, 160–61, 237n37, 238n39
See also gender, embodiment of power and; male superiority; pon (hpoun)
Women's Welfare Association, 79, 83, 108, 116

Yadana Nat Mei, 184–85
Yangwhe, 173
Young Men's Buddhist Association (YMBA), 24

Zitilla, U, 46, 225n35